Adventure Tourism and Outdoor Activities Management

A 21st Century Toolkit

Adventure Tourism and Outdoor Activities Management

A 21st Century Toolkit

Ian S. Jenkins

Assistant Professor, School of Engineering and Natural Sciences, University of Iceland

CABI is a trading name of CAB International

CABI
Nosworthy Way
Wallingford
Oxfordshire OX10 8DE
UK

CABI
745 Atlantic Avenue
8th Floor
Boston, MA 02111
USA

Tel: +44 (0)1491 832111
Fax: +44 (0)1491 833508
E-mail: info@cabi.org
Website: www.cabi.org

Tel: +1 (617)682-9015
E-mail: cabi-nao@cabi.org

A catalogue record for this book is available from the British Library, London, UK.

Library of Congress Cataloging-in-Publication Data

Names: Jenkins, Ian (Ian S.), author.
Title: Adventure tourism and outdoor activities management : a 21st century
    toolkit / Ian S Jenkins.
Description: Wallingford, Oxfordshire, UK ; Boston, MA : CABI, 2019. |
    Includes bibliographical references and index.
Identifiers: LCCN 2018061265 (print) | LCCN 2018061539 (ebook) | ISBN
    9781786390882 (ePub) | ISBN 9781786390875 (ePDF) | ISBN 9781786390868
    (pbk.)
Subjects: LCSH: Adventure travel. | Adventure travel--Case studies.
Classification: LCC G516 (ebook) | LCC G516 .J46 2019 (print) | DDC
    910.4--dc23
LC record available at https://lccn.loc.gov/2018061265

ISBN-13: 9781786390868 (pbk.)
        9781786390875 (PDF)
        9781786390882 (ePub)

Commissioning editor: Claire Parfitt
Editorial assistant: Tabitha Jay
Production editor: Ali Thompson

Typeset by SPi, Pondicherry, India
Printed and bound in the UK by Severn, Gloucester

Contents

Preface

The idea of adventure has changed immensely and is currently used as a marketing tool to sell a vast array of commercial products, often focusing on iconic adventure activities such as surfing and mountaineering. In many respects this sums up the current adventure market, which has expanded beyond all recognition, blurring the clear meaning of adventure tourism.

My interest in adventure tourism began in the early 1990s, with a Wales Tourist Board sponsored research project evaluating safety and risk in adventure tourism. Initially I was not particularly interested in adventure tourism but quite quickly realized the paucity of data and lack of coordination within the industry. Furthermore, the research identified how varied the quality of the product was and the great number of different types of companies and organizations that were managing activities. The research project further demonstrated that there were excellent future employment and management opportunities for students within adventure companies. Consequently we (the University of Wales) started to offer Adventure Tourism courses, which from the beginning proved very popular.

However, it soon became evident that published literature on this topic was scarce and reflective of a new subject in academia. These factors were the inspiration for this book, as well as the fact that I could not find a course text that covered all the subject areas that we taught. I also moved to live and work, firstly in Switzerland and then in Iceland – experiences that enhanced my understanding of adventure tourism, especially with all the adventure sports that were offered at these tourist destinations. Indeed, Iceland is a perfect exemplar of the adventure tourism product and its current popularity.

This book is therefore a reflection of my experiences over the past 20 years of working with adventure students, adventure companies and undertaking adventure research, as well as my enjoyment of surfing and snowboarding. The text is written from a personal gaze and perspective upon the adventure industry, which has grown from being a niche product into what may soon be considered a 'sector of tourism' found in all four corners of the globe.

I thought it worthwhile to include case studies illustrating the theoretical aspects of adventure tourism and to whet the appetite of potential students (hopefully illustrating that academics do have some practical insight on managing and working in the adventure tourism industry). The personal stories are from some of my former students who have made it in adventure tourism, together with contributions from colleagues I have had the pleasure of working with. I hope you enjoy the book!

The Author

Dr Ian S. Jenkins began his career at the University of Wales, Trinity Saint David. Currently he is a visiting Professor and was previously an Associate Professor at the University of Iceland. Prior to this he was Research Director at Glion Institute of Higher Education, Switzerland. He has spent the past two decades researching, teaching and managing adventure tourism degrees and has run a number of research units related to aspects of adventure tourism, sustainability and safety.

PART I

1 Adventure Tourism

Climb if you will, but remember that courage and strength are nought without prudence, and that a momentary negligence may destroy the happiness of a lifetime. Do nothing in haste; look well to each step; and from the beginning think what may be the end.

Edward Whymper, *Scrambles Amongst the Alps*

Learning Objectives

At the end of this chapter the reader will be able to:

- differentiate the key skills required to be an effective adventure tourism operator; and
- appraise the different aspects of adventure tourism and its associated definitions.

Chapter Overview

Adventure is a key element in the human psyche even if this is only exploring the locale or participating in a novel journey or new activity. Humans need adventure to compensate for boredom, a state that ensures atrophy of the human condition and spirit. It is therefore unsurprising that the adventure tourism market is buoyant and growing and since the 1950s has developed exponentially.

This book was conceived as a reader for many aspects of adventure tourism management. The author has taught and delivered adventure tourism courses for some considerable time and felt that there was a need for a new book covering a more universal view of adventure tourism today, whilst also trying to explore the more practical and useful elements that this market faces, including future challenges. Adventure is risk and risk is the essence of living: without risk we are dead. Adventure, then, can be considered to be the lifeblood of psychological/physical challenges which most people need to live a fulfilled life.

What is Adventure Tourism?

Adventure has a long history in human endeavour, perhaps from the first footsteps of human exploration out of Africa several hundred thousand years ago. Yet the foundations of the current market and current experiences were set in the late 1940s, based upon a new optimism that followed the end of the Second World War. Many of the present practices of adventure in the UK were to be found in organizations such as the Outward Bound Movement and the Duke of Edinburgh Awards Scheme. The conquering of Everest in 1953 was perhaps the pinnacle of this period of adventure, bringing a new dawn and excitement to the adventure tourism movement.

The 1950s and the mass tourism markets of the 1960s expanded the horizons for adventure tourism offering new types of activities. The 1980s and 1990s saw further exponential growth of adventure centres and educational field centres, all connected to adventure activities. The market was changing too, with a far more eclectic and splintered focus. This can be seen within the paradigm of postmodernist developments, creating a clear change in the expectations and activities of tourists. Much of this has been helped by advancing technology and new equipment, together with a change in holiday expectations. There has been a transformation of the mass tourism market and a clear change with tourists wanting to experience something extra. Many holiday packages now include some aspect of adventure or an activity to add excitement to the routine of mundane beach activities. Initial taster sessions supported by holiday snaps of paragliding, surfing or some other unusual activity have driven the demand for adventure activities while on holiday.

It is also evident that some destinations have recognized the demand for specific types of activities and have specialized in order to offer new experiences, difficult to find elsewhere.

New Zealand and its South Island are well known for adventure tourism and destinations such as Dunedin and Queenstown have a global adventure tourism reach. Perhaps the single activity that most famously represents New Zealand adventure tourism is that of bungee jumping, though this, too, has become passé. Bungee jumping was first developed in the UK, one of the first jumps being made off Clifton Suspension Bridge, Bristol in 1979 (BBC, 2014), emulating a ritual of Vanuatu Islanders of the South Pacific who jumped off scaffolds with vines attached to their legs.

The growth of adventure tourism has meant that many extreme activities have now become more mainstream. For example, surfing, which was once the preserve of individuals on the margins of society, has now become somewhat 'vanilla' and most people visiting a seaside with surfing beaches will have attempted it. But is this adventure and what exactly is meant by adventure tourism?

It is suggested that many holidays are in many respects an 'adventure' and that adventure is not necessarily an activity but a 'state of mind and attitude'. Certainly it is posited that to many people the phrase 'adventure tourism' probably produces an image of individuals struggling against nature and the elements, whilst engaging in an activity that would involve 'risk and hazard', which could result in fatality or serious injury. This image is now somewhat dated and the current adventure market encompasses far softer and slower forms of adventure

It is evident that adventure tourism has a wide reach and to define it and pigeonhole it within a narrow frame is not appropriate or helpful given the current adventure tourism market. As with most definitions, the years of tourism development have changed the original delineation, incorporating new perspectives.

Definitions

The definition of adventure tourism taken for this book relates to 'any activity or journey that creates a sense of risk and thrill for the person participating in an activity which may have a degree of risk of injury'. This can encompass extreme sports and activities such as diving, skydiving, surfing and mountaineering through to journeys that expose the traveller to varying degrees of risk, but would exclude theme parks (though this might be contested). Adventure tourism should involve an activity that provides the participant with a degree of 'perceived risk' outside of

their normal place of residence, including aspects of slow tourism.

Adventure tourism can include activities that also carry low levels of exposure to risk, taking place at tourist destinations. For example, driving large 4×4 vehicles over rough and rugged terrain could be seen as an adventure but with minimal personal risk (Fig. 1.1), as the tourist is protected from the elements. Certainly, in Iceland these types of tours are being offered and are connected with the notion of adventure tourism. Iceland has some of the largest off-road vehicles and these are often used on glaciers and rough terrain that other vehicles would find impossible to traverse. This type of adventure can be seen simply as the experience of travelling from point A to point B over terrain that is different from normal metalled roads carrying some potential risk. The Icelandic landscape can be extreme and extreme conditions such as high winds, quicksands, crevasses and volcanic dust storms are regular occurrences. However, this type of adventure requires low levels of physical activity, which is something of a paradox given a common assumption of adventure tourism that physical activity is usually related to an adventure. Although vehicle accidents are a risk, riding in a vehicle provides relative protection from the elements and an 'illusion of safety'.

The breadth of adventure tourism is large and presents challenges for a definitive definition (Fig. 1.2). For example, 'slow' tourism can be a part of adventure tourism. Once again this does not necessarily involve high levels of risk: 'glacier walking' might be seen as an activity that has a perception of high risk, but the reality of injury and death is low when walks are guided. Likewise, river rafting, if correctly supervised, carries a low risk of injury and death. These types of activities might be defined as 'soft' adventure tourism.

The terms 'Hard' and 'Soft' adventure are frequently used within the adventure market, although obtaining a conclusive definition is ambiguous, as both terms are somewhat intuitive rather than absolute. The perception of 'Hard' adventure is that it involves a high risk of injury or death. This partly explains why its market (caving, climbing, heli-skiing, kite surfing, paragliding) is considered small and limited, restricted to high risk adventurers, who make up a small proportion of the total adventure market. However, there are clear aberrations within the categorization of adventure sports and ATTA note that surfing, snowboarding/skiing and rafting are considered to be 'Soft'

Fig. 1.1. Icelandic glacier tourist bus (Guðmundur Björnsson, Iceland).

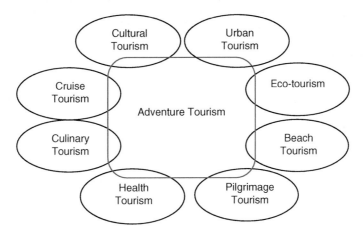

Fig. 1.2. Adventure tourism and impinging segments.

adventure; intuitively, however one would consider these activities to be more associated with extreme adventure (ATTA & GWU 2013). This clearly suggests that there is a degree of subjectivity when categorizing 'Hard' and 'Soft' adventure. The specifics of the sport and the destination can also be a means by which to define them. e.g. surfing Mavericks California (high risk and high skill levels) compared to beaches in Cornwall (lower risk and skill levels).

Conversely, activities that consumers assume to be low risk are in fact high risk. Horse riding is not necessarily seen as being dangerous, yet statistics reveal that death and serious injury is a relatively high risk for many horse riders (BBC, 2009).

Adventure does not have to be linked to high-risk activities. It can be viewed in many psychological contexts and, depending upon the adventurer's personality, can be very different for each individual. This means that 'adventure' is a perceptual frame and it is not the nature of the activity that is necessarily important, but rather the destination, the activity and nature of the perceived risk that are critical when defining adventure tourism. As will be shown in this book, adventure tourism sports are constantly evolving, pushing the 'experiential' boundaries and changing definitions of adventure tourism. As with many definitions related to tourism, they are temporal and affected by advances in technology and society.

Low Activity Input

As noted above, adventure tourism usually evokes the perception of an activity with high risk levels, but the industry encompasses a broad array of risky activities, including sports that the general public would not readily categorize as an adventure; currently, the growth of slow tourism is an example of this. However, this too can be a part of adventure tourism, especially if the journey is undertaken in wilderness and locations that are extreme and isolated.

Adventure journeys by vehicles are another example of low-risk soft adventure, though it will depend upon the chosen route, as some offer perilous tracks and high fatalities. Some routes in developing countries will have roads or tracks requiring a high skill level in order to avoid tragedy. For example:

> The path from La Paz to Coroico, Bolivia, is a treacherous one. The North Yungas Road weaves precariously through the Amazon rainforest at a height of over 15,000 feet ... has earned the nickname 'The Death Road.' While 200 to 300 drivers used to die here annually, North Yungas Road has now become more of a destination for adventurous mountain bikers than a vehicular thoroughfare.
> (Condé Nast Traveler, 2016).

Also there have been adaptations of off-road adventures. Classic examples of this include quad bikes, off-road bikes and scramblers which have become the menace of many national parks and rural areas. These vehicles provide easy access to many different areas of wilderness that would otherwise be difficult to see. Certainly, television programmes such as the *Long Way Round* (Telegraph, 2004) which showed celebrities circumnavigating the world on a motorbike and other similar programmes have helped to stimulate the imagination of potential adventure tourists. In addition, the growth of 4×4 expeditions must be included in the growing sector of adventure tourism. These activities appear to blur the margins between soft or hard adventure tourism.

Safari trips might also be considered as a form of soft adventure, containing elements of danger, but on a low activity scale. Customers are more or less chaperoned and accommodated in protective environments and in many cases these so-called adventures are no more dangerous than a visit to the local safari park. Indeed it is difficult to see the difference between these products and adventure day trips. As Grainger (2016) notes on safaris: '[t]his is not a park; it's a wilderness that happens to have a sprinkling of rather comfortable camps and expert guides to bring comfort and knowledge to the experience'.

Consideration should also be given to fast boat rafting, such as New Zealand jet boating (100% Pure New Zealand, 2016), which, although exhilarating, can be regarded as having a low and static activity level as all the skill and control of the boat has nothing to do with the customer. Is this hard or soft adventure? To what extent is this experience different from that of a theme park, such as Disney, and rides such as Space Mountain? These rides thrill but can they be classified as an adventure? By evaluating the category of soft adventure it seems evident that speed has little to do with it as customers themselves are static; rather, it is the technology and equipment that provide the essence of this adventure product. These examples show a blurring of definitions and categorization of adventure tourism. As with many attempts at defining phenomena, there are exceptions and boundaries tend to be blurred and relative.

New and Novel Adventure Tourism Developments

Likewise, there is a growth of new types of adventure activities, developed by pushing the boundaries of more classic activities. For example, base jumping has evolved to the high-risk activity of wingsuit base jumping. One could also consider the development of coasteering or canyoning, activities that have emerged from an adaption of activities such as rafting and bouldering. Indeed the idea that many adventure tourism activities are new could be challenged, as many can be viewed as simply adaptations of previously popular activities. Perhaps what is new is the need for urban dwellers to experience adventure, escaping from the often cosseted and protected environs of city life. Death is certainly not something that many of us regularly encounter, which is reflective of changes over the past century, both in the workplace and in medical advancement, reducing the risk of death from injury and disease.

A review of individuals who pursue 'extreme adventure' reveals a desire for challenges that most of us would baulk at. Yet the delineation of what is now considered as extreme adventure seems to have changed. Ascents of Everest are very popular and, it could be suggested, passé; companies who advertise these trips have grown exponentially, as has occurred with other aspects of the adventure tourism market. Many extreme challenges have been conquered, which has resulted in a gradation and splintering of adventure tourism that often follows in the footsteps of extreme adventurers. Many modern feats imitate the explorers of old (for example, crossing the world's oceans in small crafts either by sail or hand power; tourist ascents of Everest, etc.), suggesting the question: from an explorer's point of view, what is there left to conquer?

Add to this an expanding adventure tourism product pressured by the burgeoning charity market and growing demand for new experiences, many erstwhile adventure tourism destinations such as the Alps and Himalayas have lost their appeal to the adrenaline junkies, the influencers of extreme adventure tourism. Many new charity challenges are linked to forms of adventure, providing customers with an adventure experience, but which in many circumstances is just activity tourism. Adventure can also be linked to sporting activities such as marathon running and we now have explorers and celebrities running marathons in different destinations, within a set time, again blurring the idea of adventure at certain tourism destinations (Marathon des Sables, 2017).

Adventure tourism is seen as a significant product for old and new tourist destinations, in particular locations that would have been inaccessible 20–30 years ago. Iceland is an exemplar of this where adventure tourism is a significant product in the tourism package (PKF, 2013). What was once the preserve of the explorer or extreme mountaineer has now become 'vulnerable' to adventure tourists, rather than adventurers. The Arctic and Antarctic have an array of products and packages allowing the adventure tourist to reach destinations that at one time were pristine and untouched by human influence. This raises ethical issues in terms of the impact of humans on the environment, a subject that will be explored later in the book. The same can be said about mountains becoming rubbish tips of adventure tourism waste with estimates of tons of waste left on certain mountains (Safi, 2017; Lokaantar, 2017).

It is clear that adventure tourism developments have shown an amelioration and adaption of older activities resulting in new products and the emergence of composite activities using a combination of different skills and equipment. Wingsuit base jumping and kite surfing are good examples of this. Both are adaptations of other sports developed into new adventure activities.

Adventure Tourism: the Past 40 Years

Over the past 40 years, the adventure tourism market has changed and evolved. This is reflective of the extensive array and number of tourism companies specializing in adventure, including selective companies offering single activities such as surfing, rafting and safaris. As a result, the cost of equipment has not necessarily become more expensive but perhaps relatively less expensive, due to increasing participation.

Furthermore, societal changes have affected the market. The 1960s and 1970s saw a revolution in the jobs market with a move towards the service sector, resulting in most developed countries experiencing 50% or more employment in this sector. Such a change meant more sedentary employment, fostering an increase in demand for leisure activities providing the opposite to a safe office environment, i.e. outdoor and sports activities. It is suggested that this may well have fuelled the growth in the adventure tourism industry.

Moreover, there has also been a change to the way that the countryside, particularly national parks, have been used by tourists. There has been a move to recognize them as living organisms in which people live and work. In particular the provision of tourism services seems to have been mirrored by an increase in adventure tourism companies providing products within national parks. Many use rural resources, which in some cases have become so popular that it has been necessary to introduce controls on companies using particular locales.

Growth in the adventure and outdoor market has meant the need for more employees with skills to provide the services that customers want. There is and has been a demand for educational qualifications to supply this growing demand in employment, provided by colleges and universities. Universities would not offer these qualifications unless there was a clear demand for them by prospective students who see opportunities in adventure tourism. Moreover, many students have experienced adventure tourism through the school curriculum that was introduced in the 1960s and still continues today in the UK, giving further gravitas to the current adventure tourism industry.

The technological improvements of the past 40 years have further increased accessibility to the adventure tourism industry. The internet has made the availability of information and marketing much easier. Likewise, improvements in equipment, such as wetsuits and clothing, have encouraged usage throughout the year. It is common for many surfers to continue surfing in the winter months with a move to discovering more 'extreme locations', such as the Arctic, where new surf spots have been found in less crowded waters. Iceland again is a good example of such developments, where the waters are much less crowded when compared with highly popular 'breaks' such as the West Coast of France and Cornwall.

Communication improvements have also helped to disseminate adventure tourism (AT) and outdoor activities (ODA) products at exciting and new destinations, capitalizing upon this growing market. Within developing countries increasing levels of GDP (gross domestic product) are creating both internal demand and the potential for these tourists to become future global adventurers. There seems to be a move within post-industrial societies towards more and more AT, mirroring the loss of physical activities found in a more sedentary workforce. In many cases AT also seems to provide activities that replace the boredom of often mundane work (low risk and repetitive) found in many service jobs. Certainly risk exposure is not a common feature of developed societies and perhaps this is another driving factor of the AT industry – its ability to

replicate excitement and the sensation of rush or sensation seeking (Lepp and Gibson, 2007), missing from many aspects of a postmodernist society. People who have faced near-death occurrences often refer to feelings of elation and aspects of feeling alive, attributes that AT can replicate given the appropriate activity and destination.

Another feature of the expanding AT and ODA markets is the effect of changing air transport. Low-cost carriers (LCCs) have transformed intermediate travel within regions, making many destinations more accessible and affordable than ever before. Undoubtedly, destinations like Iceland have benefited from this new type of transport. It is a good example of easy air transport access to large population centres in Europe and the USA, as it is ideally situated between Europe and America, thus benefiting from new tourist demands. Indeed, an examination of some of Iceland's main products will show that AT is an important part of its tourism industry (ATTA, GWU and VWC, 2011; PKF, 2013).

Additionally, the media has assisted in increasing the profile of AT through specific programmes, with a plethora of programmes over the past 10 years specifically dealing with aspects of adventure, including wilderness survival, new types of adventure sports and the history of explorers and adventurers. This has been aided further by celebrities participating in adventure or entertainment programmes located in extreme wilderness destinations. For example, celebrities such as Ray Mears and Bear Grylls have given impetus to adventure and survival, further stimulating the public's imagination for adventure.

Solo adventurers have also been able to communicate with the outside world during their voyages, allowing the viewer a clear insight and taste of adventure tourism, whetting the appetite for adventure – perhaps not to such an extreme degree, but certainly encouraging travel to new destinations not previously considered.

Health and fitness campaigns have also enthused potential adventure tourists, stimulating interest in activities that might lead to more adventure. To illustrate this, the development of different styles of cycling and new types of bikes, together with the growth of mountain bike (MTB) riding, new circuits and cycle routes, has fostered more outdoor usage and fashioned links to adventure tourism products.

Sports races now tend to be more and more located in extreme destinations such as the Sahara Desert (Fig. 1.3). For example, the Marathon des

Fig. 1.3. The Sahara Desert. Source: Wikimedia Commons, credit to author Fiontain.

Sables, which started in 1984 and has run every year since, is an example of these products (Run Ultra, 2016). It is held in the Moroccan Desert with the distance being equivalent to five half-marathons, with the top competitors finishing either side of 24 hours of starting the race (Run Ultra, 2016).

From a UK perspective, the outdoor education sector of the 1970s and 1980s helped to increase the demand for adventure tourism products and to a large extent this was exemplified by the introduction of the AALA (Adventure Activities Licensing Scheme) after the tragic Lyme Bay accident of 1993 (Stevens and Jenkins, 1993). This change in the law reflected a growing adventure tourism sector where some companies seemed to pay scant regard to safety and formal training of instructors. There were companies in the market that were extremely competent, but the validity and reliability of the different associations who vetted the companies were criticized for their lack of consistency of accreditation.

Introduction of AALA caused much controversy within the UK adventure tourism industry but illustrated the importance of AT and ODA not only for domestic tourism, but also for international tourists. The main impetus for assuring the public of quality and safety came from the Wales Tourist Board, now VisitWales, who recognized the potential of the market and the need to standardize centres and improve quality and safety. Certainly, the introduction of this legislation – Activity Centres (Young Persons' Safety) Act 1995 – stabilized the UK industry and gave standardization to the product even though it was solely directed at the educational market.

The Extreme Adventure Channel and YouTube have also energized demand for adventure sports. Some of the activities taken by these top athletes have pushed the limits of risk and adventure to the edge. Snowboarding off mountain peaks, on near vertical drops, together with amazing athletic features of free climbing or free soloing exhibited by Reinhold Messner (Smith, 2016) were the new frontiers of adventure. Even now new boundaries are being stretched such as El Capitan in Yosemite, USA, where in 2016 Alex Honnold conquered the climb without ropes (Synnott, 2018). Extreme adventure tourism has demonstrated that humans are still capable of pushing the limits to the extreme. It is posited that these examples of extreme adventure tourism performances must have had a significant influence on general consumers and the tourism market.

Lastly, over the past 10 years, social media has extended the reach of adventure tourism to many more people. Short films, mobile phones and social media sites provide ready access to adventure and travel and many of these sites are used by adventure tourism companies, encouraging customers to post reviews, narratives, photos and films. The immediacy of the sites encourages further motivation for customers to experience different types of adventure tourism.

Issues Currently Facing the Adventure Industry

Training and skills

As discussed earlier, it is evident that a growing adventure tourism market also needs skilled employees to manage and run the industry. The past two decades have witnessed an increase in the number of universities offering courses related to adventure tourism. In 2017 there were 18 UK higher education providers of courses relating to adventure (UCAS, 2017). University courses are usually reflective of demand and relate in many cases to employment opportunities (this is not always the case, depending upon the subject studied; for example, English graduates are not necessarily sector specific). The courses in the UK offer a wide range of adventure tourism areas with many focusing on outdoor education.

There is also a clear differentiation between a degree and those offering vocational skills that are designed to help instructors or guides. A degree in adventure tourism is no guarantee of becoming an instructor or guide and therefore many of the courses offered in higher education provide additional vocational skills, which can be gained prior to graduation. Work placements or vocational training are frequently part of many courses.

Some courses are highly specialized; for example, the UK's University of Plymouth was one of the first to pioneer a surf science degree. This was extremely innovative and clearly capitalized upon the geographical location of the university and its accessibility to some of the best surfing beaches in the UK. However, this type of demand appears very limited and Plymouth is one of the few universities to offer such a specialized degree (Plymouth University, 2017), not only in the UK, but globally.

A particular problem for new destinations of adventure tourism is often the dearth of local adventure tourism skills. As a consequence, competition between local employment and global sources of employment is a challenge, as many guides and trainers are not from the destination country. Everest is a good example of this type of conflict, especially if there is over-commercialization of adventure tourism at specialist destinations. In 2013 there were industrial disputes relating to guides/Sherpas and international companies that were operating in the Everest destination (Douglas, 2013).

New technology

Technology has always had a significant impact on every aspect of society, normally improving the performance of actions, outcomes and lifestyles. Adventure tourism likewise has been changed in terms of performance and activities. AT and ODA cannot be viewed solely from its own 'gaze', but must be placed within the context of society and employment. New materials have affected the levels of performance in adventure sports and outdoor activities, such as mountaineering and surfing. Technology has improved access and acceptable conditions for more extreme experiences. A positive example is the evolution of mountaineering. Alpinism and mountaineering have been transformed through technological improvements and there are many facets to the improvements: more lightweight materials replacing older heavier equipment; improved data and information about performance, such as being able to climb Everest without oxygen – 60 years ago this would have been considered impossible. Food packaging, design of climbing equipment such as hydrodynamic ropes, breathable clothing, improved fuel performance, tracking and monitoring of climbers, communication platforms and so on have all improved the performance of participants in AT and ODA. Furthermore, the development of climbing walls and bouldering has spawned a new generation of free climbers using minimal equipment to scale peaks that were once climbed with ropes and other sundry items.

Likewise, accessibility to new destinations and locations with new designs and materials has pushed the boundaries of adventure sports and outdoor activities. Surfing 'Jaws' and big-wave surfing had always been a challenge and not possible on the boards of the 1960s, but new board design and materials together with new forms of transport, such as jet skis, have allowed surfers to actually surf these colossal waves. Consequently, big-wave riding has now developed into a subsector of mainstream surfing.

The following chapters will identify more specifically how technology has affected the AT and ODA industry and what commercial advantages there are in capitalizing on these new technical inventions. Nevertheless, there is also a paradox to technical developments, resulting in a reversal of technology, with trends returning to using older, traditional materials such as wool and wood. For example, the reinvention of balsawood boards, together with new technology utilizing natural fibres such as bamboo, has added another dimension and impetus to the surfing industry.

Sustainability

A new book on adventure tourism and outdoor activities needs to address the pressing problems related to tourism growth and in particular, sustainable development. Sustainability has been a tourist and global agenda item for at least 30–40 years and it continues to increase its significance together with that of climate change. Ethical business development through CSR (corporate social responsibility) is another treatise that businesses have to consider in the AT and ODA industry. It is asserted that these are linked and shift the product of adventure to more ethical and sustainable levels. Nevertheless, some of the practices of AT need to reflect upon the impacts that they have on the environment and the communities that they work in. AT is clearly an important sector of the tourism market and needs to address sustainable issues. Many activities will take place in milieus that are environmentally and culturally sensitive. Most adventure activities take place in nature, even though there has been a burgeoning growth in urban and cultural adventure. Consequently it is all the more important to ensure that sustainable adventure tourism activities are encouraged to be ecologically responsible and climate friendly.

Clearly there is a conflict at times between sustainable elements of a business and the need for profitability. In essence there are economic criteria that need to be met for adventure tourism companies to adopt sustainable measures:

1. reduction of costs;
2. increased revenue; and
3. ethical and moral actions (do these have an economic value?).

Item (3) above should really be first on the list for all companies but, as they operate in a market economy, it is a necessary requirement of a company to make a profit or at least break even, though for many public sector AT and educational organizations this is not necessarily an issue. Nonetheless, there are companies who advocate that a sustainable approach to adventure tourism is a profitable approach. Even adventure tourism equipment companies, such as Patagonia, try to provide the most sustainable clothing possible for the market using ethical means.

Unfortunately, this market depends upon ethical consumers, whereas current research and data on an ethical consumer is inconclusive. Just how 'price inelastic' are ethical decisions compared with economic ones (Marsh, 2013; Devinney and Auger, 2007)? In addition, the author's experience from previous research on adventure tourism companies suggests that environmental or ethical choices are often secondary when customers are buying adventure tourism products.

Climate change

As with sustainability, climate change has become an important agenda item for tourism and adventure tourism. On current predictions within the next 40 years there will be extreme changes to weather conditions throughout the world and many of these changes will affect adventure tourism destinations. These changes will increase the risk factors for some adventure tourism activities and companies need to develop strategies to risk assess what these effects might be on the company and in particular on customers.

Furthermore, companies need to be reducing their carbon footprints. Mitigation and carbon reduction are important actions needed by AT and ODA companies, to assist in diminishing the likely effects of climate change. For destinations that do not have cheap energy sources, simple measures are available to ensure reduced costs and reductions in carbon emissions. Renewable energy sources such as solar, wind and wave together with switching to vehicle fuels that have lower emissions should be part of AT and ODA companies' offsetting of carbon emissions.

Climate change for sustainable development should be considered as part of the same gamut. Sustainability is about protecting future conditions and so too is climate change; both are trying to enable resources and conditions to remain favourable for future businesses and societies. New theories relating to these two issues have suggested new concepts for tackling climate change, such as resilience and vulnerability. These are currently the concepts that are being considered as a means to ensure survival and profitability of companies in the future.

The media agenda has highlighted the importance of trying to mitigate the effects of climate change, but there are a number of challenges that AT and ODA companies face, the most important being how to mitigate carbon output and to what extent the consumers of adventure products are prepared to pay for their carbon footprints. The challenge of making consumers pay for carbon footprinting relates to issues of competitiveness and a long-held mantra of many companies: that climate change and sustainability measures reduce both a company's profitability and its competitiveness. It necessarily follows that perhaps ethical policies and practices challenge the profitability of AT and ODA companies.

This polemic does have some validity in the short run. But the sustainability and climate change agendas are very much focused upon long-term not short-term gains. It is also asserted that changing consumer attitudes into accepting more ethically produced goods at a higher cost has yet to become a reality. It is rare for consumers to examine the ethical aspects of their adventure tourism products and choices, even if they are touring in natural environments.

Conclusion

The adventure tourism market has changed immensely over the past 50 years, reflecting many aspects of change in society. Adventure tourism is now considered to be an important sector of most tourism economies. Furthermore, in many parts of the world, including developing countries, it has become a very important part of their tourism destination product. Even highly developed tourism products such as those found in the UK in Wales have recognized the valuable contribution that AT and ODA have had on tourism. VisitWales has tried to ensure that the quality and safety of the product is enhanced and protected. The importance of adventure to tourism products can be seen with special emphasis being given to this sector; for example, India designated 2018 as the year of Adventure Tourism (Indian Holiday, 2018). Issues of sustainability, new technology, lifestyle developments,

work patterns and climate change have all impacted upon the expansion of the AT and ODA product. Even the higher education sector has recognized their importance by providing qualifications both applied and academic for the adventure tourism industry.

This book will explore, in greater depth, the subjects discussed in this chapter together with the intention of making it a practical management guide to understanding the current AT and ODA market, identifying the main challenges that it faces. Adventure tourism is now an extremely important part of any destination's tourism product and has a global reach that can enhance the sustainability of a tourist destination, while providing the customer with an experience that will be remembered for a lifetime.

Questions

- How has the adventure tourism market changed over the past 40 years?
- Is 'slow' adventure tourism a new phenomenon or just simply an old one repackaged?

References

100% Pure New Zealand (2016) Jet boating. Available at http://www.newzealand.com/int/jet-boating/ (accessed 5 April 2016).

ATTA, GWU and VWC (2011) Adventure Tourism Development Index 2011 Report. ATTA, Seattle, Washington.

ATTA and GWU (2013) Adventure Tourism Market Study 2013. Adventure Travel Trade Association and George Washington University, Washington, DC.

BBC (2009) How dangerous is horse riding? Available at: http://news.bbc.co.uk/1/hi/magazine/8339097.stm (accessed 7 April 2018).

BBC (2014) World's 'first' bungee jump in Bristol captured on film. Available at: http://www.bbc.co.uk/news/av/uk-england-29819029/world-s-first-bungee-jump-in-bristol-captured-on-film (accessed 2 April 2014).

Benedictus, L.((2016) Why are deadly extreme sports more popular than ever? Available at: https://www.theguardian.com/sport/2016/aug/20/why-are-deadly-extreme-sports-more-popular-than-ever (accessed 29 June 2017).

Condé Nast Traveler (2016) The most dangerous trips in the world. Available at: http://www.cntraveler.com/galleries/2014-09-02/the-most-dangerous-trips-in-the-world/3 (accessed 5 April 2016).

Devinney, T. and Auger, P. (2007) Does what consumers say matter? The misalignment of preferences with unconstrained ethical intentions. *Journal of Business Ethics* 76(4), 361–383.

Douglas, E. (2013) Forget the Everest brawl: the real story is how Sherpas are taking control. Available at: https://www.theguardian.com/world/2013/may/05/sherpa-resentment-fuelled-everest-brawl (accessed 30 June 2017).

Grainger, L. (2016) The 10 best safaris in Africa. The South Luangwa, Zambia. Available at: http://www.telegraph.co.uk/travel/safariandwildlifeholidays/7942820/The-10-best-safaris-in-Africa.html (accessed 5 April 2016).

Indian Holiday (2018) India to promote Adventure Tourism in 2018. Available at: https://www.indianholiday.com/blog/india-to-promote-adventure-tourism/INDIAN HOLIDAY (accessed 5 March 2018).

Lepp, A. and Gibson, H. (2007) Sensation seeking and tourism: tourist role, perception of risk and destination. *Tourism Management* 29, 740–750.

Lokaantar (2017) 'Everest Green' project concludes, 5 tons of waste recovered from Mount Everest. Lokaantar, Lalitpur, Nepal. Available at: http://lokaantar.com/en/current_affairs/everest-green-project-concludes-5-tons-waste-recovered-mount-everest/ (accessed 29 June 2017).

Marathon Des Sables (2017) Available at: http://marathondessables.co.uk/ (accessed 29 June 2017).

Marsh, V. (2013) Consumers: The ethical way is an easy lifestyle choice. Available at: https://www.ft.com/content/20353c2c-b7e2-11e2-9f1a-00144feabdc0?mhq5j=e1 (accessed 30 June 2017).

PKF (2013) Promote Iceland. Long-term strategy for the Icelandic tourism industry. Extract from a Master Mapping Report. Available at : https://www.islandsstofa.is/media/1/final-long-term-strategy-for-icelandic-tourism-industry-270213kh.pdf (accessed 26 June 2017).

Plymouth University (2017) Courses, Undergraduate, FdSc Surf Science and Technology. Available at: https://www.plymouth.ac.uk/courses/undergraduate/fdsc-surf-science-and-technology (accessed 30 June 2017).

Run Ultra (2016) Marathon des Sables. Available at: https://marathondessables.co.uk/race-overview (accessed 7 December 2018).

Safi, M. (2017) Mount Everest climbers enlisted for canvas bag clean-up mission. Available at : https://www.theguardian.com/world/2017/mar/29/climbers-prepare-clean-up-mission-mount-everest-nepal-waste (accessed 29 June 2017).

Smith, O. (2016) 20 reasons why Reinhold Messner is the world's greatest living man. Available at: http://www.telegraph.co.uk/travel/lists/reinhold-messner-tribute-quotes-facts/ (accessed 29 June 2017).

Stevens, T. and Jenkins, I.S. (1993) *Managing a Safer Product*. Safety in Activity Holidays. SaiL Research Unit, SIHE, Swansea.

Synnott M 2018, Exclusive: Alex Honnold Completes the Most Dangerous Free-Solo Ascent Ever, Exploration and Adventure. Available at: https://www.nationalgeographic.com/adventure/features/athletes/alex-honnold/most-dangerous-free-solo-climb-yosemite-national-park-el-capitan/ (accessed 7 December 2018) National Geographic.

Telegraph (2000) New Zealand: The world capital of extreme sports. Available at: https://www.telegraph.co.uk/travel/destinations/australiaandpacific/newzealand/721978/New-Zealand-The-world-capital-of-extreme-sports.html (accessed 29 June 2017).

Telegraph (2004) Long ride to self discovery. Available at: http://www.telegraph.co.uk/travel/731457/Long-ride-to-self-discovery.html (accessed 29 June 2017).

UCAS (2017) Search Tool, Course: Adventure. Available at : http://search.ucas.com/search/providers?Vac=1&AvailableIn=2017&Query=adventure (accessed 30 June 2017).

Whymper, E. (1871) *Scrambles Amongst the Alps, in the Years 1860–69*. John Murray, London.

2 Globalization of Adventure Tourism

Finally, from a global perspective, adventure tourism incorporates and promotes the values of the tourism that we want – a tourism that respects cultural and natural assets and protects the most vulnerable.

(Taleb Rifai, UNWTO Secretary General, 2014)

Learning Objectives

At the end of this chapter the reader will be able to:

- analyse how adventure tourism companies operate on a global scale; and
- acquire knowledge in order to compare destinations and customers' profiles and their relationship with the development of an adventure tourism product at a destination.

Chapter Overview

Tourism is a market that has clearly benefited from world trade and globalization. The evidence certainly supports the idea that markets are now very much 'global' and that this may benefit many countries, though current evidence also suggests that such benefits are not equally distributed for every country. The 'Elephant Curve' is a classic example of how global income has been circulated and who are the winners and losers in this market (Fig. 2.1).

The same premise may be applied when considering the AT market. Globalization of tourism is a 'truism' and the current market value globally is in the region of US$7.6 trillion in 2016 (Statista, 2017) with 1.2 billion tourists (2015) now travelling the globe (UNWTO, 2016), which seems to support the notion of globalization. Yet globalization, as seen by the Elephant Curve, does not necessarily benefit every state or business and is in many cases a threat to some parts of the population. For AT and ODA the global market opens up a wide array of adventure tourism options, products and destinations. The wide variety of landscapes and climates provide a large number of scenarios for AT companies to provide for a global market. Likewise the

development of LCC (Low Cost Carrier) aircraft, especially on a more regional basis, has allowed easy and cheap access to destinations that were difficult to reach some 30–40 years ago.

The winners of globalization seem to be concentrated in the upper echelons of richer nation states and many of the poorest citizens of developing nations (Fig. 2.1). Rich nations certainly provide the demand for many AT destinations globally. The service sector employees of developed nation states also seem to have tapped into the need and desire to travel and explore more distinct and exotic (which can mean colder and culturally different) locations. The proliferation of media programmes related to adventure has also enhanced the demand for AT and OAD travel (King and Beeton, 2006; Global Traveller, 2015).

The Elephant Curve shows that competition is now very much global and therefore local companies can become exposed to global competition. Vice versa, local companies have an opportunity to compete with other global destinations. This sounds very simplistic but competing at a global level means a change in management strategy and an understanding of markets and demand. That said, there are examples of developing countries learning from developed countries in terms of AT management operations. As can be seen in the case studies in Part II of this book, indigenous people can now provide services for AT and have the advantage that, being local, they have the experience and expertise that global operations do not have. For instance, the Sherpas of Everest have demonstrated that they are in a very powerful position in providing the AT product (see Chapter 11).

The globalization of AT has presented challenges to the environment whilst at the same time raising ethical issues. Access to some of the most extreme

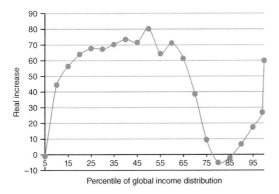

Fig. 2.1. The Elephant Curve (Milanovic).

world environments has created much debate on the ethical nature of allowing tourists to such destinations. For example, the Arctic and Antarctic are now AT destinations with a strong growth in tourist numbers visiting, even though these products are considered to be niche and extremely expensive.

> Across most of Earth, a tourist attraction that sees 35,000 visitors a year can safely be labelled sleepy. But when it's Antarctica, every footstep matters. Tourism is rebounding here five years after the financial crisis and is now growing fast, with the number of cruise ship passengers visiting doubling in a year.
> (McGuirk, 2013)

Within the adventure tourism industry, in pristine locations like these, ethical issues of globalization such as what happens to waste and human contact with wild animals need to be addressed. There are treaties for Antarctic shipping; for example, the Marine Pollution (MARPOL) Convention states:

> Annex IV of the Protocol on Environmental Protection to the Antarctic Treaty provides some respite from the impact of sewage discharges from vessels carrying more than 10 persons in the Antarctic Treaty Area. Untreated sewage cannot be discharged within 12 nautical miles of land or ice shelves, and beyond this distance, sewage which has been stored in a holding tank cannot be "discharged instantaneously but at a moderate rate and, where practicable, while the ship is en route at a speed of no less than 4 knots additionally, vessels are expected to make use of sewage record books".
> (ASOC, 2013, p. 6)

Furthermore, there are reports relating to the globalization of the AT market demonstrating its contribution to a destination's tourism products. Iceland is an exemplar of this and the exponential growth in tourism has been constructed on the basis

of nature and extreme environments, with AT playing a significant part. Nature appears to touch many aspects of the AT market from the cosseted 'soft' AT tourist to the extreme 'hard' adrenaline customer. There is also an extension of the seasons from that of summer to winter, with AT meeting the rising demand. Although summer is still considered a peak period, the 'shoulder' months have been extended to the extent that even winter is now being considered as offering potential for different products.

There is also a change in demand from the original 3 Ss (Sun, Sea and Sand). Even the products of the 3 Ss now have an extra dimension, rather than simply lying in the sun on a beach. There are usually adventure or outdoor recreation activities available for the tourist to try at a beach resort including snorkelling, (Figure 2.2) diving and parascending or riding jet skis and similar products. Although these are usually tangential to the main holiday, they certainly have an element of 'adventure' providing new opportunities for tourists to engage in adventure activities even though these could be seen rather as incidental adventure sessions.

> It is important to note that adventure tourism can be split into two categories: 'incidental holiday activities' (e.g. canyoning, white water rafting) where an adventure tourism activity may be undertaken as a one-off element of a wider holiday; and 'adventure holidays and short break holidays'.
> (VisitScotland, 2010, p. 6)

The factors of easy access, cheap flights, increased wealth and lifestyle changes have ensured that the nascent beginning of adventure tourism in the 1950s has now expanded to a global scale.

Global Adventure Tourism

Further evidence to support the growth of AT as a global industry is strengthened by world organizations such as the United Nations (UN). The 2014 Report on Global Adventure Tourism (UNWTO, 2014) illustrates the importance of AT and its prominence to the tourism industry. AT and ODA have some sound ethical aspects matching the current ethical approaches to tourism, purportedly the opposite of mass tourism (see opening quote).

Market

The global market represents a small part of the 1.2 billion or more tourists who now travel the

Fig. 2.2. Snorkelling: Red Sea Coral Reef (Source: Ian Jenkins)

world but, as has been seen, it is a significant niche market, which can provide destinations with guaranteed incomes that are not lost through economic 'leakages' found in many mass tourism market packages (where destinations can lose up to 40–50% of the income to global companies) (UNCTAD, 2013).

> The George Washington University (GWU) and Xola Consulting found that the global value of adventure tourism was USD 89 billion. The study was repeated in 2013 and found that 42% of travelers departed on adventure trips, making the sector worth USD 263 billion—an increase of 195% in two years.
>
> (UNWTO, 2014, p. 20)

The market primarily lies within developed countries and reflects the top end of the market, such as skiing and snowboarding growth. The demand comes from developed countries primarily in Europe and North and South America, representing 70% of the global market (UNWTO, 2014). The emerging markets of South-east Asia and Russia are also providing verve to AT and seeking new destinations.

It is becoming evident that:

> … adventure travelers represent a significant, growing market … Adventure tourism does not appear to be a trend specific to any one geographic area, as the results indicate similar findings in North America, Europe and Latin America, where increasingly, travelers continue to explore deeper into communities and seek to connect with nature.
>
> (Stowel and Doyle 2010).

It is difficult to obtain precise data concerning the growth of the AT and ODA market and, as with much of the economics of tourism, much is estimated. Certainly, gathering local data can provide an indication of the potential effect that AT and ODA companies have on global markets. Understanding the elements of demand is key to predicting the future. Table 2.1 gives a conceptual process for the decision making an AT holiday customer might take. Although much simplified, it does identify some key stages.

Adventure tourism remains a niche product in terms of global markets; nevertheless, research that has been done on niche markets does not mean that

Table 2.1. Six stages of travel for typical adventure tourists.

Stage	Example
Dreaming	I'd like to take a holiday sometime this year
Consideration set	I'd like to visit the Caribbean or Europe
Planning	I've decided I'd like to visit Italy; now I need to book hotels and activities
Booking	I need to pay for my trip to Italy
Experiencing	Italy is amazing
Share (can occur before, during or after the trip)	Look at the amazing trip I'm going to take/am on/just got back from

Source: UNWTO 2017 adapted from ATTA (2013)

AT fails to make a significant contribution to a destination and other aspects of the tourism market. Research completed by Jenkins (2007) showed that the concept of a niche has many understandings and that the market can, in relative terms, be in millions of tourists, given the global reach of tourism. Jenkins (2007) identified three possible scales to a niche: micro, meso and macro scale of tourist numbers.

This can be supported by global examples, where destinations have indeed capitalized upon the AT product, becoming international destinations. New Zealand and its campaign '100% New Zealand' includes the destination of Queenstown, which has been cited as possibly one of the best-known AT destinations on the global market. Its adventure imagery relates to the adrenaline experience and capitalizes upon the 'hard' adventure tourist image, attracting numerous adrenaline junkies. It also seems to fit in with New Zealand's image of an extreme destination on the edge of the world. There are authors who note that AT can be as much the destination as the actual activity, meaning that 'soft' adventure tourism can be mixed with 'hard' at the same destinations. The exponential growth of tourism at other destinations also shows linkages with AT. The growth of tourism in Iceland, for example, is reflective of the AT market. The location of Iceland in the far north and on the 'edge of the world' is seen as an 'exotic' unexplored location and the tourist boom, since 2008, has a clear connection with the isolation and extreme climate of the destination, located in the middle of the North Atlantic on the edge of the Arctic. The AT market here is growing to such an extent that the hard-core AT customers are becoming disconcerted by the Icelandic boom in tourism. A once pristine and isolated island is fast becoming a mecca for 'slow' soft AT, linked to nature (Jenkins, 2016).

The most popular destinations

Trying to identify the top adventure destinations in the world is not an easy task. By their very nature AT and ODA cover a wide range of different activities, which are sometimes destination specific. Ascertaining the top adventure tourism destinations is not a straightforward task and is dependent upon different types of criteria, such as tourist volume, new activities, combined packages and the activities offered, etc. As has been noted, there are destinations that are associated with the image of AT and seem to have a larger share of the market compared with others. For example, Queenstown in New Zealand is one of the world leaders.

Each major adventure sport may well have different destinations that attract its participants and therefore grand generalizations can be misleading. For climbing, the mountain of Everest could be seen as a very popular destination for adventure tourism, though there is debate about whether this now is really a climbing mecca or simply an adventure tourist destination. It is clearly an example of the globalization of adventure tourism at one of the world's most iconic climbing and mountaineering destinations. It has undoubtedly been popularized by commodification of the Everest experience and it is asserted that there is now a blurring of soft with hard adventure tourism at this destination. Climbing in the 'Death Zone' is by itself high risk for professional and experienced climbers; however, many adventurers who climb Everest have little experience compared with those of, say, four decades ago. The original climbers had years of experience and training, in order to scale the highest mountain in the world. Everest is possibly the most 'globalized' AT destination with such a wide mix of nationalities arriving and attempting to climb its peak.

Similarly, surfing exhibits many of these changes. For example, the North Coast of Hawaii is often cited as a top destination for surfing and AT (Bremner, 2013) and named as the home of surfing; the history of surfing emanates from this location. The waves here are, like Everest, 'mountainous' at times and not for 'soft' surfing, even though on calmer days all types of surfers are able to surf these waves.

Any attempt to evaluate what are the top global destinations for adventure tourism is complicated by the diversity of what adventure tourism now offers. The hard and soft AT options at a destination may differ and gauging what is rated as important can also differ; for example, economic spend, volume of tourists types and numbers, together with activities, can all be used to evaluative the top destinations. The list of adventure sports and activities compiled by Stowell and Doyle (2010) clearly misses some of the now more notable hard AT such as wingsuits and off-piste skiing together with snowboarding and big-wave surfing. This also tends to ignore new destinations that seem to be growing in popularity, such as the Arctic and Antarctic, which represent extreme locations; yet adventure tourists in the Arctic and Antarctic are usually in vehicles that clearly can be associated with soft AT conditions. On reflection, it is evident that currently there are very few destinations globally that fail to offer some form of adventure tourism.

A number of other considerations affect an AT tourist's decision before making the trip to a popular AT and ODA destination, including (UNWTO, 2014):

- the cost of an adventure tour;
- the cost of related products (e.g. airline tickets);
- the capacity or income of target markets; and
- marketing, which appeals to the preferences or motivations of travellers.

Nonetheless, assessments of popular destinations that draw different adventure tourists can be considered and some may be seen as more successful than others (Table 2.2). It is difficult to construct a definitive list of top destinations for AT and ODA but certain destinations (e.g. New Zealand) do appear more often, which gives some indication of popularity.

Disintermediation

Disintermediation is the removal of the traditional middle agent between the consumer and the provider. Adventure tourism is leading the way in terms of global contracts, with intermediate companies being circumvented. This means that more money is circulating in the AT destinations and not being lost through agencies. This may be explained by the AT traveller making their own arrangements, facilitated by technology and the proliferation of applications

(apps) and ubiquitous internet access. It is predicted that this trend will grow, allowing AT and ODA destinations to target demand and markets directly. Local economic benefits with global reach are the advantages of adventure tourism growth. The growth of the online booking company Airbnb is a good example of this type of technological access and success, which challenges existing supply chains and the tourism interfaces. The Airbnb app on a mobile phone is a sound illustration of this. 'The digital revolution has impacted almost everything in the world as we know it,' said James McClure of Airbnb (Bearne, 2016).

This technology is linked to adventure tourism demand, affecting AT accommodation and what consumers may purchase. Self-arranged trips are increasing in popularity and AT businesses need to be aware of local supply chains required to support this market demand. It is postulated that the AT market is more complex than mass tourism, which is based upon volume. The AT market is a niche, which means that more specific and specialized resources are needed. Furthermore, each destination may need to provide different aspects of the product mix, depending upon the landscape and climate, rather than simply the activity: trekking through rainforests, for example, is very different to glacier walking and requires different types of accommodation.

It might also be noted that omitting an intermediate company makes it more difficult to assess demand and changes to popular destinations. Nonetheless, it has its benefits, allowing destinations to target global markets directly, supporting the growth of the globalization of adventure tourism, while capturing the benefits locally.

Sustainability

Adventure tourism is said to be more amenable to sustainability and responsible tourism (UNWTO, 2014). Because an AT company usually requires local knowledge and skills to ensure that the tourist has a satisfying experience, locals and communities are integrated with the adventure product. Additionally, there is a growing demand for tourists to experience local destination cultures, adding to the adventure experience. Cultural authenticity at the locale may also be a main reason for choosing the adventure, with expectations of experiencing the cultural milieu while engaging in an adventure activity. Thus the local community has

Table 2.2. Top global adventure destinations.

Uniglobe	National Geographic	Telegraph (2016)	WYSE[a]	World Expeditions	Exodus Travel	Lonely Planet
Australia: Great Barrier Reef	**Canada**: Lake Louise (Banff National Park)	**Venezuela**: The Lost World and Angel Falls	**USA**	**Canada** (#1 Best Country 2017)	**Canada**	**New Zealand**
Egypt: Pyramids of Giza	**USA**: Moab, Utah (mountain biking)	**New Zealand**: Classic Trail	**Canada**	**Peru**: Choquequirao (#1 Best Region in 2017)	**Peru**	**Canada**
Chilean Patagonia	**USA**: Southern West Virginia (watersports, rafting)	**Australia**: Red Centre	**Australia**	**Nepal** ('Coming back stronger than ever')	**Australia**	**Vietnam**
Maasai Mara (**Kenya**) and Serengeti (**Tanzania**) Tourism Belt	**Cayman Islands**: Grand Cayman (snorkelling)	**Jordan**: Wadi Rum, 'in the footsteps of Lawrence of Arabia'	**France**	**Mongolia** ('A place like no-other')	**Bhutan**	**Slovenia**
Bolivia: Amazon forest and Inca sites	**Costa Rica**: rainforest (zip wires)	**India**: Ladakh and Stok Kangri, Himalayas	**UK**	**Ladakh** ('Welcome to "Little Tibet"')	**Madagascar**	**Nepal**
Cambodia: Angkor Wat	**Brazil**: Rio de Janeiro (hang gliding)	**Tanzania**: wild chimpanzees on Lake Tanganyika	**New Zealand**	**Iran** ('Romance in the Persian Empire')	**Serbia**	**Ecuador**
Canada: Whistler Mountain	**UK**: Isle of Bute, Scotland (hiking)	**Norway**: Polar bears in Spitsbergen	**Italy**	**Oman** ('Rich culture, ancient history, diverse landscapes')	**Uzbekistan**	
Costa Rica	**Italy**: Aeolian Islands (sailing)	**Canada**: Kermode 'spirit' bears in British Columbia	**Spain**	**Dominica** ('The Caribbean's best kept secret')	**Iceland**	
New Zealand: Rotarua	**South Africa**: Kruger National Park, (safari)	**India**: Snow leopards in Ladakh	**Thailand**	**Myanmar** (Burma) ('A taste of traditional Asia')		
	New Zealand: Queenstown (bungee jumping)	**Kenya**: horseback safari	**Argentina**	**Colombia** ('Diverse landscapes and an extraordinary culture')		

[a]WYSE: World Youth, Student and Education Travel Confederation, Amsterdam.

an opportunity to be integrated in this circular economy. The use of local resources and people, together with the landscape, are essential items in AT company products.

That said, there are clearly ethical issues relating to payment of local workers and what the customers have paid the company. If the company is non-indigenous, there is likely to be inequality in employment practices. In general, local employees will be paid less than non-indigenous managers and guides. There are polemics for both sides (local and international); for instance, the standards of living vary between the destination and the main market locations and there are arguments for differentiating wages related to average wages at destinations.

There are polemics, too, over aspects of global supply chains and the materials used in the AT products. Ethical questions need to be asked, including:

- To what extent can materials be sourced in the vicinity and what has to be bought globally?
- Who pays for the carbon footprint of that AT traveller?
- What are the energy requirements of the company?
- How is water used, monitored and recycled?
- What are the waste management practices, especially relating to plastic and human waste?

A sensitive and contentious item in globalization is that relating to the airline industry. Globalization of adventure tourism requires transport to distant destinations and air travel is the main transport service used. Yet evidence suggests that this industry contributes approximately 2–3.5% of global CO_2 (ICAO, 2017) and air transport is predicted to grow. However, there are technical developments in reducing the emission levels of engines. The paradox is that without air transport, the benefits of the globalization of adventure tourism would not exist. Unfortunately, these issues are often ignored in many adventure tourism reports but clearly conflict with the sustainable development of adventure tourism destinations.

New experiences

It seems evident that the growth of tourism and concomitantly AT is linked to the postmodernist paradigm suggesting a change to tourism and its products. As suggested in Chapter 1, developed nations now have the majority of employees working in the service economy, which from a lifestyle perspective has produced a more sedentary work force. Access to information and new trends has grown exponentially, while at the same time work still restricts access to holidays and vacations.

The growth of globalization has generated a demand for new experiences, which has effected a growth in the experiential tourist. Globalization has increased the access to new destinations and

facilitated the growth of new adventure activities. The array of different adventure activities is reflective of a more specialized market and a more tailored experience for individuals.

Traditional marketing techniques, such as basic segmentation using the Value and Lifestyle System (VALS), are now outdated and antiquated, while experiential marketing is now the new vogue in attracting customers to adventure and outdoor tourism destinations (Zantal-Wiener, 2017). The emerging 'generations X and Y' have conveyed new perspectives to the AT market together with older markets such as the 'baby boomers'. A significant part of the AT market is an older (40+) age group, which brings more monetary spend than perhaps the younger generations X and Y.

More females are also participating in adventure and they have become an important part of the adventure tourism market. This change has given impetus to expanding global adventure markets as well as an added dynamism to encouraging more women to become part of adventure tourism companies. Recent research has shown that women are becoming more prominent in leadership roles in adventure tourism (ATTA, 2017).

The aspects of virtual reality have also allowed more types of destinations and activities to take advantage of the need for new experiences together with fun parks and thrill experiences driving the need to seek more adventure (Graham, 2016). Accessibility of destinations has improved and has fuelled the global market for new experiences and extreme destinations.

Extreme sports have now become more 'mainstream', generating new demands on the AT market. Surfing is a good example of this, having moved from a fringe sport to becoming a popular soft AT activity. Its profile has been reinforced by media coverage in many areas, including advertisements that incorporate the image of surfing as an important experience, connected to the consumption of mainstream products.

It is also argued that the 'serving classes' (Urry and Larsen, 2011) in developed societies have a dynamic need to be released from their mundane and cosseted office-space, further driving a demand for thrilling and exciting leisure-time experiences to compensate for office environments. Perhaps this can be seen as a need for hyperreality experiences, a trope for postmodern adventure tourism? It seems quite common now for intensity and highs to be part of the holiday experience, especially so when related to adventure tourism, as illustrated by this comment which relates to a company that seems to offer soft AT:

> These destinations are enough to keep your heart beating fast enough and your gut recoiling at the danger you are willing to put yourself into in order to experience the 'thrill'. I do not blame you, I also love it ... and it is safer than using drugs, right?
> (Uniglobe Carefree Travel, 2017).

This seems to support the maxim that AT is about a physiological experience of thrill that lifts the customer from the mundane and into a liminal zone of excitement, regardless of whether the type of activity is hard or soft.

The move towards the experiential is not new but seems to have evolved out of the 1950s and 1960s, with key writers and philosophers of that era. Jean-Paul Sartre and Jean Baudrillard, being the more prolific writers, noted the importance of self and self-experience and its connection with the development of hyperreality, associated with technology and accessibility creating virtual worlds developing new motivations (Baudrillard, 1999). This has been capitalized upon by AT providers and it is possible to access virtual activities, effectively giving a taste of new experiences. Even the challenge of sense of smell, which is very emotive, is being used for new experiences (White, 2011). This seems to be a part of sensory and experiential marketing, which is now an important element of global product development for AT.

Local and global

Globalization is able to affect the local and the local is able to affect the global. Most developed economies have complex economies and tourism is a part of this complexity, affecting and effecting many aspects of economies. It necessarily follows that adventure tourism offers similar benefits to a country's economy. It is a truism that tourism is now an important part of any successful economy, as exemplified by the current top economies in Europe which show tourism, on average, being about 9% of GDP (WTTC, 2015).

A closer examination of individual countries such as the UK and France verifies this GDP tourism of around 9%, with obvious exceptions depending upon the size of the economic base and populations. When considering developing economies, the

dependence on tourism can be significantly higher, even rising to 50% of the overall GDP. Adventure tourism offers the local milieu the potential to benefit the local economy financially, if the supply chain remains local too (Box 2.1). Social media also seems to be a useful tool in bringing the global to the local, which is another opportunity that globalization has established; networking through social media has more or less immediate effects.

Small operators can now access the global market via social media and the internet; there is also the ability to create virtual experiences of the local. Local guides can capitalize on the extent and reach of their product to global markets, so that destinations from the Amazon to the Arctic, and many other isolated local communities, are engaging and offering AT products.

The experience of the past 70 years has shown how tourism can benefit local communities, especially for small populations, and in many cases providing an important source of employment for local people. Iceland certainly is a good example of this and the case study incorporated in Box 2.1 is representative of many tourism companies in Iceland. However, not all tourism is beneficial to destinations and locations. Globalization has expanded the cruise-ship market with dubious benefits to local communities and the environment. Some of these can be regarded as categories of adventure tourism. The Arctic and Antarctic adventure cruise ships illustrate this effect very well. The cruise-ship companies visiting these two extreme destinations do so because of the financial benefits from adventure tourism (Fig. 2.3).

In the Antarctic the impact on the locale has little, if any, effect economically as there are no permanent or indigenous populations living there. Hence, the monies are recirculated to the companies' home locations and the ethical value of tourists visiting these destinations is questionable. The environmental impacts of these cruises need to be fully assessed and re-evaluated from a sustainable and climate change 'gaze'. This market is expensive and exclusive, but has shown significant growth similar to other sectors of the AT market. The environmental sensitivity of trips to these destinations is recognized and there are associations that try to discuss and manage this type of adventure tourism. For example, the International Association of Antarctica Tour Operators (IAATO) is designed to help to control and develop Antarctic

An Icelandic farmer, whose farm was located very close to Vatnajökull National Park, was the foundation for the company Local Guide. He saw an opportunity to provide access for tourists to visit a puffin island close to the farm. The puffin tourist monies provided much needed secondary income and the idea grew that tourists might also be willing to purchase other services, such as being guided on local mountains and glaciers. Then in 1994 Local Guide was formed by Einar Runar Sigurdsson (a farmers's son), who focused on developing visits to local ice caves and ice climbing walls. Ice caves are magnificent creations of glaciers but required local knowledge to ensure safe access, so the company developed an adventure niche in this area and activity. The Local Guide Company became famous for guiding tourists to ice caves on a one-to-one basis and in small groups, providing bespoke journeys for keen photographers and adventurers. Sigurdsson was also a keen mountaineer and he offered other adventure products related to mountaineering and glacier activities.

The advent of exponential tourist growth in Iceland in 2008–2017, due to globalization of adventure tourism, expanded the company and captured more of the tourist monies, but also changed the types of products that they offered, moving towards larger tours. In 2017 Sigurdsson was keen to get back to the one-to-one tours that he used to offer. This has been helped by the creation of an artificial 'Langjökull Ice Cave Experience – Glacier Adventure', designed for large numbers of tourists, which has been seen as taking pressure off the 'real deal' of genuine ice caves and ice climbing.

The Local Guide Company is an example of exactly how the locale is benefiting from the boom in global tourism, ensuring that virtually all the monies they receive circulate directly back to the local community (most of the guides and employees are Icelandic). This seems to support the maxim that adventure tourism can be one of the most sustainable products in the globalization of tourism, as noted by the UNWTO. There is also a move by Local Guide to encouraging the repeat tourists who have been marginalized by the popular growth in adventure tourism.

Source:
http://localguide.is/
Local Guide HQ, Fagurhólsmýri 785 Oraefi Iceland
GSM +354 894-1317
Email: info@localguide.is

---

tourism and was formed in 1991 with just seven companies (IAATO, 2017).

Transnational companies (TNCs) are not usually associated with adventure tourism but, as with aspects of globalization, they are linked to AT. Compared with the typical features of TNCs (Dicken, 2015) the AT industry does have similar characteristics, but many companies are quite small and considered to be accessing niche markets on a global market, which is somewhat different to the general idea of TNCs. However, many AT companies do have a home base in developed countries, usually where their HQs are situated, while operating AT activities in developing countries, employing a variety of nationalities, including local guides and supply chains.

Adventure tourism is a global industry, as can be seen by examining the number of 'home grown' companies offering products encompassing the whole world, including the Arctic and Antarctic. As with identifying top destinations, there is difficulty in classifying the top adventure companies and a review of significant AT companies such as Exodus, KE and Wild Frontiers Adventure Consultants illustrates that many of their adventure products are at global destinations; even those with a mainly domestic market may offer some type of global package.

The Wild Frontiers website states that they offer 'more than 500 trips to 90 different countries' and, furthermore:

> Unlike the plethora of 'world specialists' who purport to know a hundred destinations, we concentrate on the locations we know and love. We don't source our itineraries from other agents, nor do we run the same tour over and over (thus creating a 'tourist circuit', spoiling an untouched region).

(Wild Frontiers, 2017)

Table 2.3 is an attempt to identify important global AT companies, but must be considered highly subjective, though a review of different sources by the author did verify some of the companies as being popular and significant contributors in the global AT market.

Fig. 2.3. Cruise Ship Visiting the Icelandic port of Akureyri. Source: Ian Jenkins.

Box 2.2. IAATO Antarctic Shipping Organizations Adventure Companies and Global Operations.

This association, formed in 1991, recognized the potential damage that tourism might do to the Antarctic (IAATO, 2017). Its mission is to develop protocols to ensure that responsible tourism occurs in this region of the world. Tourists started arriving in the Antarctic's pristine region during the late 1960s and have risen to an annual figure of approximately 34,000 tourists per year. No doubt this will continue to climb, which must have implications for environmental impacts on this fragile region.

The organization works in close cooperation with research and government agencies to discuss impacts and controls necessary, to ensure that the Antarctic remains a pristine region and to uphold the US Antarctic Treaty and concerns related to it. It encourages its members (mainly shipping companies) to ensure that responsible measures are taken when visiting this pristine region, through best practice and responsible actions.

Source:
https://iaato.org/home.

The proliferation of AT global companies challenges some of the arguments relating to disintermediation and reiterates the controlled nature of the product by a dominant company based in developed economies. Questions relating to classic tourism impacts such as the level of economic leakages for local populations need to be appraised. Major questions still need to be

Table 2.3. Top Adventure Tourism Companies' HQs (Friedland, 2017).

Company	Country
G Adventures	UK
GeoEX SanFrancisco	USA
Austin Adventures	USA
Tuska Trail Adsventure	USA
International Expeditions	USA
Natural Habitat Adventures	USA
Intrepid Travel	Australia
Mountain Travel Sobek	USA
National Geographic Expeditions	USA
REI Adventures	USA
Sacred Rides	USA
Row Adventures	USA

answered; for example: how much money is retained by local guides and the community, when compared with profits made by transnational companies?

Globalization of the AT industry also represents transport challenges (carbon footprints and effects on climate change); many of the products on offer are usually reached solely by air transport and many on long-haul flights.

Furthermore, these transnational companies are those operating in the last remaining wilderness areas, the Antarctic and Arctic, raising ethical challenges that really need to be addressed by responsible tourism operators.

Conclusion

Globalization has affected the AT and ODA industries accelerating increasing access to more global destinations. Many AT customers are from developed countries and global flows are evidently from developed countries to developing countries, which can be viewed both positively and negatively in terms of the impact on these exotic destinations. The postmodernist society has fuelled demand for different experiences caused by the humdrum office environments that most of the 'serving' classes work in. Adventure offers escape and provides thrilling experiences where experiential activities and thrill are key triggers to adventure tourism demand on a global scale. Globalization, concomitantly, also raises issues of sustainability and ethical operations of transnational AT companies.

Impacts on the locale are a significant factor of globalization, but this also offers the locale an opportunity to control the native product at a local scale. The proliferation of AT and ODA, and their availability at new and unusual destinations, means that developing countries have an opportunity to circumvent the 'middleman' while supporting the possibility of increasing disintermediation, which should allow the locale to benefit more and more from the globalization of AT.

Globalization offers many opportunities for AT to further expand and develop, but it also comes with caveats of impacts to the culture, environment and economy. In many respects AT mirrors many aspects of the mass tourist economy and AT companies should try to learn lessons from it. But as noted in the opening quote of this chapter, AT is a niche product and has the opportunity to be an ambassador for tourism 'that respects cultural and natural assets and protects the most vulnerable' (UNWTO, 2014). Let us hope that companies and customers are listening!

Questions

- To what extent is adventure tourism simply an extension of the mass market?
- How can the local benefit the global and the global benefit the local?

References

ASOC (2013) *Discharge of sewage and grey water from vessels in Antarctic Treaty waters.* Antarctic Treaty Consultative Meeting, Brussels, Antarctic and Southern Ocean Coalition, Washington, DC. Available at: http://www.asoc.org/storage/documents/Meetings/ATCM/XXXVI/Discharge_of_sewage_and_grey_water_from_vessels_in_Antarctic_Treaty_waters.pdf (accessed 6 July 2017).

ATTA (2017) *Out in Front: Tracking Women's Leadership in Adventure Travel.* Adventure Travel Trade Association, Seattle, Washington. Available at: http://cdn.adventuretravel.biz/research/ATTA_Tracking-Womens-Leadership-in-Adventure-Travel-R007.pdf (accessed 7 July 2017).

Baudrillard , J. (1999) *The Consumer Society, Myths and Structures.* Sage, London.

Bearne, S. (2016) How technology has transformed the travel industry. Available at: https://www.theguardian.com/media-network/2016/feb/29/technology-internet-transformed-travel-industry-airbnb (accessed 6 July 2017).

Bremner, J. (2013) World's 50 best surf spots. Available at: http://edition.cnn.com/travel/article/50-surf-spots/index.html (accessed 6 July 2017).

Dicken, P (2015) *Global Shift, Mapping the Changing Contours of the World's Economy*, 7th edn. Sage, London.

Exodus (2017) Top places. Available at : https://www.exodus.co.uk/?setcountry=GB (accessed 21 March 2017).

Friedland, L. (2017) Top Adventure Travel Companies in the World. Available at: https://www.tripsavvy.com/top-adventure-travel-companies-34054 (accessed 11 April 2018).

Global Traveller (2015) Social media impact in the travel industry. Available at: http://www.globaltravelerusa.com/social-media-impact-in-the-travel-industry/ (accessed 6 July 2017).

Graham, L. (2016) Virtual reality devices could transform the tourism experience. Available at: https://www.cnbc.com/2016/01/08/virtual-reality-devices-could-transform-the-tourism-experience.html (accessed 7 July 2017).

IAATO (International Association of Antarctic Tour Operators) (2017) Home. Available at: https://iaato.org/home (accessed 7 July 2017).

ICAO (International Civil Aviation Organization) (2017) Aircraft engine emissions: definition of the problem. Available at: https://www.icao.int/environmental-protection/Pages/aircraft-engine-emissions.aspx (accessed 7 July 2017).

Jenkins, I.S. (2007) Postmodern tourism niches: UK literary festivals and their importance for tourism destination development. PhD thesis, University of Swansea.

Jenkins, I.S. (2016) Research evaluating impacts of adventure tourism in Iceland. (Unpublished.)

King, R. and Beeton, S. (2006) Influence of mass media's coverage of adventure tourism on youth perceptions of risk. *Tourism Culture & Communication* 6(3), 161–169.

McGuirk, R. (2013) The Antarctic is left defenceless to tourism. Tourism booms again, but continent has no mandatory protection against visitors. Available at: http://www.independent.co.uk/environment/nature/the-antarctic-is-left-defenceless-to-tourism-8537546.html (accessed 6 July 2017).

Milanović, B. (2017) The higher the inequality, the more likely we are to move away from democracy, News Available at: https://www.theguardian.com/inequality/2017/may/02/higher-inequality-move-away-from-democracy-branko-milanovic-big-data (accessed 3 December 2018) The Guardian London.

Statista (2017) Direct and total contribution of travel and tourism to the global economy from 2006 to 2016 (in trillion US dollars). Available at: https://www.statista.com/statistics/233223/travel-and-tourism--total-economic-contribution-worldwide/ (accessed 6 July 2017).

Stowell, S. and Doyle, C. (2010) *Adventure Tourism Market*. Adventure Travel Trade Association, Seattle, Washington.

UNCTAD (2013) Sustainable tourism: contribution to economic growth and sustainable development. Expert Meeting on Tourism's Contribution to Sustainable Development, Geneva, 14–15 March 2013, UNCTAD, Geneva. Available at: http://unctad.org/meetings/en/SessionalDocuments/ciem5d2_en.pdf (accessed 6 July 2017).

Uniglobe Carefree Travel (2017) The top 10 best adventure tourism destinations in the world. Available at: http://www.uniglobecarefreetravel.com/post/view/the-10-best-adventure-tourism-destinations-in-the-world (accessed 1 September 2018).

UNWTO (2014) *Global Report on Adventure Tourism*. UN World Tourism Organization, Madrid.

UNWTO (2016) International tourist arrivals up 4% reach a record 1.2 billion in 2015. Available at: http://media.unwto.org/press-release/2016-01-18/international-tourist-arrivals-4-reach-record-12-billion-2015 (accessed 6 July 2017).

Urry, J. and Larsen, J. (2011) *The Tourist Gaze 3.0*. Sage, London.

VisitScotland (2010) Adventure travel in Scotland. Available at: http://www.visitscotland.org/pdf/TIS%2005%20adventure%20travel.pdf (accessed 6 July 2017).

White, C. (2011) The smell of commerce: how companies use scents to sell their products. Available at: https://www.independent.co.uk/news/media/advertising/the-smell-of-commerce-how-companies-use-scents-to-sell-their-products-2338142.html (accessed 3 September 2018).

Wild Frontiers (2017) Why Wild Frontiers? Available at: https://www.wildfrontierstravel.com/en_GB/wf-difference (accessed 6 July 2017).

WTTC (2015) Travel & Tourism Economic Impact 2015 Europe. Available at: https://www.wttc.org/-/media/files/reports/economic%20impact%20research/regional%202015/europe2015.pdf (accessed 7 July 2017).

Zantal-Wiener, A. (2017) How experiential marketing works: 7 enlightening tips. Available at : https://blog.hubspot.com/marketing/how-experiential-marketing-works (accessed 11 April 2018).

3 Research in Adventure Tourism

No CEO ever says, 'Damnit, we need to increase research!' I want to encourage them to do that.

Nathan Myhrvold (former Chief Technology Officer, Microsoft)

Learning Objectives

At the end of this chapter the reader will be able to:

- compare and contrast the available research techniques that will yield valid data; and
- examine and understand which data sources can provide valid data and those that can be considered unsound.

Chapter Overview

Over the past 50 years, adventure tourism has grown exponentially, which is in keeping with developments in society and tourism itself. It is interesting to consider what the predictions were for adventure tourism some 50 years ago and whether those forecasts were accurate.

It is often assumed that customer decisions and financial choices are made upon the basis of a rational individual and a process founded on valid facts and data, providing a clear evidential insight into a consumer's decision and choice. That said, could the current popular tourist destinations have been foreseen? Who would have predicted the extraordinary rise of Iceland as a major tourist destination, especially given the two key triggers: the near-bankrupting of the country in 2008 and the volcanic explosion of Eyjafjallajokull in 2010? Furthermore, it is often assumed that successful companies have made their decisions simply based upon facts, market trends and analysis. It is suggested that many businesses make their management decisions with limited knowledge and facts, basing their management decisions on the illusive concept of 'business acumen'. A quick review of accurate and detailed tourism data reveals a very limited supply of accurate data, therefore the ability to generalize with certainty, especially on a global scale, is very limited.

There is an assumption, too, that important data exists upon which to measure key business elements such as risks, be they financial or personal injury to clients. In reality data is scarce – and valid data even rarer. It is surprising how little is known about areas such as personal injury and accidents and the dissonance between perceived risk and real risk; likewise with predicting the volatility of the market and the major shocks that change consumer choice.

To illustrate this, there are very few accident databases available for adventure tourism sports or tourism. This is because accident data is rarely kept or examined by nation states, especially leisure and tourism measurements; furthermore it is usually not seen as important, compared with other areas such as industrial accidents. Most safety systems, as will be shown in Chapter 7, concern work-related accidents rather than individuals who suffer mortality or injury during their leisure time. There have been attempts to collect and measure this data but with limited success due to costs of collection. The European Union (EU) proposed such an accident database and set up EHLASS (European Home and Leisure Accident Surveillance System) in 1994 (EC, 1994). The UK Government, under the then Department of Trade and Industry (DTI), set up a similar system, but this was related to home and leisure accident data rather than leisure or tourism per se. The UK systems were known as HASS (Home Accident Surveillance System) and LASS (Leisure Accident Surveillance System). Both the EU and UK systems have been discontinued, perhaps reflecting the resources needed to collect such data.

Furthermore, there has been the development of specialized research units in tourism such as SaiL (Safety in Leisure), which was established in 1988 at University of Wales Trinity St David's. SaiL was

©CAB International 2019. *Adventure Tourism and Outdoor Activities Management* (ed I. Jenkins)

funded by the UK leisure industry and government sources to examine particular leisure and tourism accidents that were causing concern and threatening the viability of certain activities.

The SaiL Research Unit was created primarily to examine the objective risk of customers on UK waterslides (Fig. 3.1). This followed heightened articles by the tabloid press suggesting that these leisure items were very dangerous, but there were no databases that could be used to substantiate or refute these assertions. SaiL's next remit was to examine accidents in adventure tourism, due to concerns being raised by tourism agencies about the safe operations of adventure tourism. SaiL identified the many failings of the adventure industry in the UK, which sadly eventually resulted in the Lyme Bay Tragedy of 1993. The result of that tragedy prompted the UK government to heavily

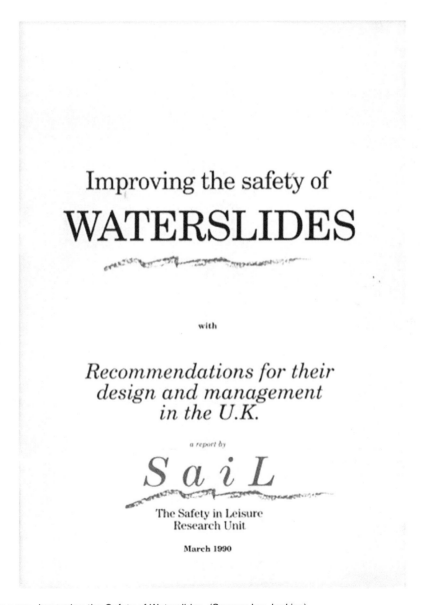

Fig. 3.1. Title page, *Improving the Safety of Waterslides*. (Source: Ian Jenkins)

regulate and license the adventure tourism industry for young people.

Both the UK waterslides and adventure tourism products in general illustrated the paucity of data relating to specific leisure and tourism activities. Data and data analysis concerning many adventure activities are rarely available and consequently companies and other agencies are presented with 'black holes' relating to facts and knowledge of their market. Measurement and comparisons are difficult to make in the adventure and outdoor industries due to a lack of coordinated databases. In most cases it is necessary for management to seek more general data from national statistics such as the UK's International Passenger Survey (IPS, carried out by the Office for National Statistics) or by purchasing databases from companies that have either collected or ameliorated different secondary data into a reconstructed database. In most cases, and at best, the available data is very general and lacks specificity. From a management and company perspective usually the 'why?' question is the most difficult to answer definitively.

Trying to bridge the gap between what we know and do not know is the *raison d'être* of research. The development of super computers and new areas of research related to Big Data (high-volume, high-velocity, high-variety data) and AI (artificial intelligence) are seen as the future for improving this data gap and it is hoped that by enlarging and joining databases, our knowledge of current phenomena should be helped. It is thought that large data sets might well be able to provide new insights into tourism and adventure experiences. There is evidence to suggest that Big Data has certainly made an impact in the financial sector, improving the prediction of markets (Eastwood, 2017).

Research is a word with a very wide remit and understanding, having many different characteristics and approaches. For example, market research and applied research are seen as different from theoretical research, even though the focus of the phenomenon might be the same. Most companies and organizations will need some form of research to guide their decisions, even if the validity and collection of it is rather tenuous. The most basic form of research is in customer feedback forms and social media reviews such as Trip Advisor. The validity and dependability of these applications are found wanting, when compared with the rigours of specific academic research methods and accepted approaches using appropriate sampling frames and random sampling methods (quantitative statistics).

Rigour and validity of data are key to providing data that can be expedient and reliable. Also the type of research methods used is very important for accuracy and validity. Unfortunately, most companies do not have the resources, expertise or time to divert to extensive data collection and analysis. This is usually why consultants or specific research units are used. They are a convenient and, in relative terms, cost-effective way of gaining valid information without expending large resources.

The problems for most companies are trying to differentiate between urban myth, hearsay or common knowledge and the validity of the facts. Supposition and reasonable guesswork are usually reinforced by other companies and operators through the sharing of information or industry conferences, yet hard data and evidence are rarely available and are limited in their use. Therefore much of the management decision process for an adventure company is made on very little definitive data or validated information.

Most companies need valid data sources or information to discern how the market is developing and changing. This could be done simply through an examination of purchasing trends and basic demographic data of the company's customers. It would provide a snapshot of the market but cannot really be generalized or used for predictive purposes. The availability of data sources for adventure tourism is limited and the reports that are published seem to be very general and lack specific details. The United Nations World Tourism Organization (UNWTO, based in Madrid) has produced strategic documents on adventure tourism but the foundation for the information appears to be quite limited and based on secondary rather than primary data. The Adventure Tourism Trade Association (ATTA) is possibly one of the leading authorities, producing reports for the AT industry, yet much of this data features in many other types of reports and predictions for AT. This elucidates once more the limited data available for management to take decisions.

What is Research and Who Does it?

Research can have many understandings, as shown by the different epistemologies and ontologies associated with it. In its broadest sense it is a process of investigation to establish facts or explanations, thereby providing new information or data on previous unknown or uncertain knowledge related to phenomena.

For the adventure tourism company, the purpose of research is usually different from that of the academic or research student. Market research is perhaps the ontology closest to what many companies will want to know and research. However, market research agencies are commercial and use techniques that will be cost effective, which might also compromise some aspects of the research that they are undertaking. These companies will not have the same scope or approach as perhaps an academic research unit, but market research units are apt to be more industry friendly and understand the requirements of many adventure tourism companies. In many cases, the essence here is time and a quick turnaround of a research question or phenomenon.

There is then the halfway house: the consultant. Consultants tend to be engaged by companies when major/demanding information is needed. They are generally experts in the field – or claim to be. Some of the larger consultancy firms who are contacted by companies are generalist but employ specialists who are able to advise, comment or collect data in the area of research being investigated. However, many large reports contain a plethora of secondary data and not necessarily large amounts of primary data. Many consultancy contracts do require specific collection of primary data and again consultants are usually used to provide the expertise needed in collecting and analysing reliable data (use of appropriate quantitative and qualitative research methods).

Research is also guided by the agencies or persons asking the questions. It involves different epistemologies in the quest to understand what we know or do not know. Research has a litany of ideological approaches relating to the collection of information and data, usually included in two distinct fields: those of quantitative and qualitative methods. In particular, the quantitative and qualitative approaches have been much debated and argued over in terms of their relevance and reliability. That said, there are clearly some techniques and approaches that have greater rigour and reliability, but will still have proponents who challenge the inferences and conclusions of the research. The combination of using both methods, which has been colloquially termed mixed methods, is now common.

Basic Rubric of Research

It is not the purpose of this text to provide detailed information on research methods, methodologies and how to collect reliable data. There are many books on this subject and the reader will need to refer to these for more detail on what might be considered a relevant research process. The idea is to whet the interest of the reader concerning research relevant to the adventure tourism and outdoor activity industry. That said, some of the more significant and relevant techniques will be discussed.

A starting point for research is having a valid question or hypothesis that needs to be answered. Defining the problem and having an achievable aim, with appropriate questions, are fundamental to obtaining relevant and useful data. For many students and managers, these issues are usually discussed and explored before starting research. Trying to identify research questions related to the global economy is usually well beyond a student's or manager's resource. Many reports restrict themselves to countries or regions, given the constraints of collecting primary data or the availability of secondary data. Practicability and efficient approaches need to be the main focus, whereas the more theoretical and ethereal questions need to be left for academics in large research units.

Approaches to research questions can be made in two formats: **inductive** or **deductive**. This relates to aspects of what we know and what we want to know.

- The **inductive** approach is used by observing different aspects of a phenomenon in the real world. This can be done by observing occurrences, then proposing what they might indicate or simply what the company or individual has experienced and then suggesting a theory or reason for the pattern (Crowther and Lancaster, 2009). This approach is seen as less valid academically but offers a much more adaptable approach to research of markets and real-world phenomena. The inductive approach is more commonly used by students, usually without them really recognizing the process. It comes from real-world observations, which are then analysed to suggest possible answers or theories for the observed occurrences (Jones and Perry, 1982).
- The **deductive** approach starts from the development of a theory or a hypothesis that then needs to be verified by collecting data or using existing

data to verify or falsify the idea. The emphasis is upon not supporting the theory but, rather, challenging it and discarding it (Crowther and Lancaster, 2009). This approach is usually noted as being more reliable.

Sources of data come in two main forms: **primary** and **secondary**.

- **Primary data** has been immediately collected from source phenomena and has not been manipulated or adjusted from its collection process (Crowther and Lancaster, 2009). It is generally more resource laden than secondary data and requires specific types of collection methods to ensure that the data is valid. Examples of this would be questionnaires collected from participants of activities or monitoring the types of people using a particular walking trail.
- **Secondary data** is usually primary data that has been manipulated, adjusted, cleaned and altered to fit a set of criteria and then represented for use. It has not usually been directly collected by the person or agency that is using it (Crowther and Lancaster, 2009). It loses some of its rigour as the source cannot be interrogated or examined and the presented data is all that can be analysed. This does raise questions of reliability, in terms of where the data came from, how it was collected and whether it can be representative of the population (a key element in reliability for prediction purposes) – for instance, data sets of government statistics, a data set of the number of passengers arriving at a destination, etc.

There are two types of primary data and methodology: **quantitative** or **qualitative**.

- **For quantitative** methods the choice is usually between judgement samples and random samples. It is generally impossible to gather data from the whole population but this really is determined by the population (e.g. total number of adventure companies in the UK) and access to each individual. A population is known as the 'complete set of things'.
  - ○ **Random sampling** is seen as the most rigorous method for gathering samples, which are likely to be representative of the population and hence can be generalized to represent the population. There are a number of methods that can be used to collect the data, the most common being Simple Random Sampling, which has fostered a number of derivatives

such as Systematic Random Sampling, Stratified Random Sampling and Cluster Sampling. Randomness has to be independent of any subjective choice by the researcher and is one of the criteria for ensuring representativeness and generalization of the population. Usually random number tables are used to choose who or what to sample, but more mechanical methods can be used, such as picking numbers from a hat.
  - ○ **Judgement sampling** is commonly used for faster collection of data but is flawed, in that it is not necessarily representative of a population. It can give a quick snapshot of a phenomenon but is not necessarily representative of it. This is usually a lot easier to administer and provides quicker results but can only be an indication of what is happening.
  - ○ **Sampling frames** are a basis for collecting data and these can range from phone books to Twitter and Facebook accounts. They are lists that provide access to individual units in a population that can be selected and targeted for information. Yet caution must be given to these sources of sampling; it must be remembered that these lists or bases are not always fully representative of the population. Many people will not be on Twitter or Facebook and with landlines becoming obsolete this excludes many people within the population. So using these sampling frames will not represent the population of a country or region. For research purposes it is important that a sampling frame should be used that is representative of a population, whatever that might be defined as by the research question.
  - ○ **Survey instruments** are utilities (questioning, observing, counting, etc.) for collecting the data and can have many different forms and styles. The most commonly used method of collecting data is the questionnaire and the style, structure and types of questions used are extremely varied, depending upon the research projects' aims and objectives. It must be remembered that a questionnaire is an instrument and not something that can be quickly thought up and applied. The key to a questionnaire is not necessarily how many questions but the length of time taken to collect the data; anything over 5–7 minutes is usually seen as too long by interviewees. But

again this depends upon the context of from whom, where and when the data is being collected. The research outcome will only be as sound as the data collected and the essential element to this is sometimes the appropriateness and quality of the questionnaire, as well as the sampling method used.

- For **qualitative methods** there has been an expanding use of this approach in the social sciences to the extent that qualitative data is Frequently used alongside than quantitative data. Behaviourist data and similar types are now accepted as just as valid, relating to evaluating and understanding the phenomenon in adventure tourism. Depth of understanding is perhaps the main axiom here rather than the generalization of data as provided by quantitative methodology. Qualitative data explores the 'why' of information rather than the description of facts and is said to provide more in-depth understanding of phenomena. Yet this type of data collection is restricted to being case specific rather than generalizations. Generalizations about phenomena are far less valid than in quantitative data collection. Prediction using qualitative methodology has much less validity than quantitative methodology. But qualitative data, if collected properly, will provide far more understanding of experience and consumption of the adventure tourism product. In many cases this is seen as an easier form of data to collect but few give thought to how it can be analysed. An hour-long interview produces a plethora of words (up to 10,000 words), which then have to be summarized into some sensible coding system or categorization so that a functional summary can be made of the data. This is not easy to do, even with the current computer programmes such as Nvivo to analyse the narrative.

In summary, it is important to have sources of data for the industry to draw on to understand and predict the changing nature of the industry and to try to identify future trends. Apart from specific consultancy reports, which individual companies might pay for, sourcing data is not straightforward or easy, and many of the available secondary databases are very limited. Furthermore, specific tourism, adventure or outdoor data is not usually available and has to be extracted from other social and economic databases. Yet there are sources and organizations that can be accessed to try to gather a more accurate picture of what the adventure and outdoor industry is doing.

Research Reports and Data for Adventure Tourism

Having précised some of the main elements of research and research methods, it is now pertinent to try to identify where companies might find sources of data and which organizations would be able to assist in the collection of specific data. The following section attempts to provide some sources that companies might wish to evaluate and use. This is not an extensive list but a sample of the types of agencies and organizations offering some data for the adventure tourism and outdoor industry.

Adventure Travel Trade Association (ATTA)

This organization is perhaps the one best known to adventure tourism providers. It seems to have a global reach and claims to represent many aspects of the adventure tourism industry and companies. It acts as a prominent association relating to adventure tourism and accompanying industries. It claims to have 1000 members in a 100 countries.

> The constituency is made up of tour operators, tourism boards, specialty agents, and accommodations all sharing a vested interest in the sustainable development of adventure tourism.
>
> (ATTA, 2017a).

There are no accessible databases but industry reports containing secondary data can be located, reflective of different aspects of adventure tourism. For example, the '2016 Adventure Tourism Development Index' or ATDI (ATTA, 2017b) evaluates leading adventure tourism companies on a global scale, together with gender and cultural research, such as the publication *Out in Front: Tracking Women's Leadership in Adventure Travel* (ATTA, 2017c). Other examples include:

- Cruise Checkpoint
- Industry Snapshot
- Adventure Travel Industry Forecast
- Attracting and Serving the US Adventure Tourist
- Women Summertime Research
- Adventure Travel Trends Snapshot
- Plastics Quick Poll
- 20 Adventure Trends to Watch
- Email Lead Nurturing for Adventure Travel Companies

- Video Distribution for Adventure Travel Brands
- What Adventure Travel Businesses Need To Know About Chinese Travelers
- North American Adventure Travelers: Seeking Personal Growth, New Destinations, and Immersive Culture
- Cost-effective Offline Marketing Tactics
- Adventure Travel Trade Perceptions of Catalonia
- Tourism Perceptions of Tuscany

As with many organizations, membership provides certain privileges relating to data access and reports. For those who are not members, it is still possible to acquire some of the reports and data, but payment is usually needed for more detailed and specific information. This organization (along with George Washington University) produced the Global Adventure Tourism Index, which is a source of information relating to countries that are developing their adventure tourism industry and markets.

UN World Tourism Organization (UNWTO)

The UN is seen as a significant source of data for many types of tourism organizations, including adventure tourism. It is unclear how exactly UNWTO collects adventure tourism data; many of the reports seem to be reflective of other organizations that provide the UN with data. However, the UN provides an overall picture of global tourism markets through its Satellite Accounts. There are UN reports published on adventure tourism, but the UN seems to be duplicating information that is already being published in a similar form elsewhere, such as ATTA. For example, the 2014 Report 'Global Report on Adventure Tourism' (UNWTO, 2014) mines outputs from ATTA. Perhaps it is time for such a prestigious organization to directly collect primary data on adventure tourism and then publish its own findings.

World Tourism and Travel Council (WTTC)

Another source of adventure tourism data that could be useful for research purposes is that of WTTC. It does have some specific research functions and will examine different aspects of the tourism market, but currently does not appear to have data specifically on adventure tourism. Once more there are no directly accessible databases for a company that wants to research the adventure tourism market. Looking at the availability of information shows that research falls into two categories, Economic and Policy, but neither has any specifics related to tourism niches such as adventure tourism (WTTC, 2017a). There is a data gateway but this provides a very limited database of simply Leisure Spending in each country (WTTC, 2017b).

North Atlantic Tourism Association (NATA)

This is an organization to promote tourism between Greenland, Iceland and the Faroe Islands. All three locations are prime destinations for the current surge of adventure tourism and outdoor activities. It states that:

> The West Nordic region is something special. Situated in the North Atlantic, the area's geographical remoteness has preserved an authentic world of wonderful cultural traditions and natural phenomena. It's a region full of things to discover.
>
> (NATA, 2018)

This organization is an example of what could be an excellent platform for sharing valuable data on adventure tourism. Its current remit is to encourage exchange of information, yet a perusal of the website and access to information is once again very limited. One would have expected to have seen some abstract of reports or information reflective of their research, but data and specific reports are unfortunately missing.

Sports or Adventure Tourism Governing Bodies

Many sports and recreational activities will have associated organizations that are their guardians. These organizations, depending upon their size and membership, can provide valid data on particular subjects relating to the adventure activities or sports (Box 3.1).

This can prove a useful resource for the manager in obtaining information, such as providing details on the participation levels of the sport or activity. Many governing body organizations related to adventure tourism are sources of data, which tend to be formed in order to benefit the members and the sport through sharing information and providing feedback on the activity, market and customers. For example, the British Mountaineering Council (BMC), which is an organization for 'climbers, hill walkers and mountaineers', is possibly one of the

This organization, established in 2009 and sponsored by VisitWales, was created to share information and data relating to the Welsh activity market, in particular the use of Wales's three national parks and linking the activity providers of these locations. It is an example of cooperation between various networks involved in adventure tourism and outdoor activities. WATO states that it is designed to 'facilitate a more structured and inclusive approach to the management and development of the outdoor sector in Wales' (WATO, 2017) which would also provide a platform for sharing information and data on specific issues affecting the adventure and outdoor industry.

However, it is evident that these organizations are trying to address the problems of the industry by creating and sharing information. For example:

The following issues all need addressing:

- What are the key factors that will inform future demand for adventure tourism & outdoor recreation over the next 10 years?

- What key factors will influence the supply of access to places for outdoor recreation over the next 10 years?
- How are national, regional and local planning and spatial frameworks likely to develop over the next 10 years and what risks and opportunities do they create in relation to outdoor recreation strategy?
- What role and contribution should outdoor recreation strategy make over the long term in relation to public health and wellbeing outcomes?'

(WATO, 2017)

This is a regional organization and will be lacking funds, so there will be little available data, but it can be a springboard to help develop research in specific fields where information is required.

Source:
http://www.wato.org.uk/worn/

---

better known organizations in the UK for mountaineering. The BMC provides a wide array of resources for members and non-members relating to aspects of mountaineering. It does engage in research and also collates information from different sources relating to different types of research, such as the effects of exposure, high-altitude climbing, outdoor participation and competencies and the effects of expeditions on individuals. Some recent examples in various sectors include (BMC, 2018):

- Access ('Crowd funding is back and it's better than ever')
- Access & Conservation ('Research shows climbers don't harm plant life')
- Clubs ('How to train novice members in your club, winter skills')
- Competitions ('British Lead and Speed Championships 2018')
- Gear ('A guide to passive protection')
- General ('Organising BMC Events')
- Guidebooks ('The Outer Hebrides')
- Huts ('Alex MacIntyre Memorial Hut AGM 2018')
- International ('Research: psychological responses to the expedition experience'; 'Concern over Everest death rate'; 'How to deal with cancelled and delayed flights')

- Medical ('Survey seeks info on medication use among Everest climbers'; 'Research project investigates the work–leisure balance'; 'Survey seeks info on pregnancy, exercise and high altitude exposure'; 'Hathersage Mountain Medicine Week')
- Membership ('Montane and BMC discount scheme')
- Press ('BMC publications: an overview')
- Skills ('Ticks and Lyme disease: what to do about tick bites')
- Walls ('Over 60,000 m logged at the Climbing4all charity fundraiser')
- Youth & Equity ('Research study: understanding outdoor practitioners competencies'; 'Youth Climbing Symposium').

Most developed countries will have similar organizations (bush walking, kayaking etc.) which can have information, databases and research reports (Box 3.2).

Adventure Activities Licensing Authority (AALA) UK

This is a specialized agency with the remit to ensure safety of young participants in adventure tourism within the UK. It was created after the Lyme Bay tragedy (1993) and was established in 1996. It has never been fully accepted by the industry and there has been a constant discourse to try to have it disbanded. It is currently still under review but continues to police the youth UK adventure industry. This is an agency that can provide advice on running safe adventure tourism but has a limited scope for available research data.

Medical Associations and Safety Organizations

A good source of accident data can be found from medical research and there are publications that can be useful for the adventure tourism practitioner. Articles and research relating to different aspects of injury and mortality in adventure sports are an excellent benchmark for assessing risks and improving management of adventure tourism and outdoor activities. Although governments have tried to provide secondary data relating to accidents, currently these have ceased. Where the state or national organizations lack coordinated data, medical research can complete some of the missing details, especially related to aspects of injury or potential life-threatening exposure to conditions, such as altitude sickness. In the UK the British Medical Association (BMA) is a source of some of these statistics and research. There are numerous articles relating to mountain sickness (e.g. 'Acetazolamide in acute mountain sickness'; 'Acetazolamide for the prophylaxis of acute mountain sickness'; and 'Identifying the lowest effective dose of acetazolamide for the prophylaxis of acute mountain sickness: systematic review and meta-analysis') and also other sports subjects ('Effectiveness of helmets in skiers and snowboarders: case-control

and case crossover study'; 'Winter sports injuries in a snowless year: skiing, ice skating, and tobogganing'; 'Surfers' myelopathy') and other stories (BMJ, 2017).

The Royal Society for the Prevention of Accidents (RoSpa) is the independent accident and safety body in the UK and has some valuable research data and reports associated with accidents and safety (RoSPA, 2017a). This is now the repository of the UK Government HASS and LHASS data sets which were originally collected by the DTI in the UK (RoSPA, 2017b). Additional current sources of online injury data include:

- AWISS (Welsh A&E data);
- EU IDB (Western European A&E data);
- HES (English hospital episode data – where patients are admitted to hospital);
- USA Injury Data (National Electronic Injury Surveillance System – NEISS);
- IBID (International Burn Injury Database);
- NHS Evidence (information for health and social care professionals);
- Association of Public Health Observatories (APHO).

This organization also provides advice relating to safety of activities. Similar organizations can be found in other countries.

Academic sources

Other accessible sources of data for adventure tourism can be found in academic research. The SaiL Report on Adventure Tourism was an instance of this and provided the industry with the only definitive details relating to adventure tourism accidents and safety in the UK. There are other research units such as the Centre for Recreation & Tourism Research, University of the Highlands and Islands (UHI, 2017). Although the Research Unit is not specific to adventure, recent publications have been focused on this niche market; for example: Northern Periphery and Arctic Programme 'Slow Adventure' Project, Nevis Landscape Partnership, Recreational Impacts Study, Norway, European Project Development.

There also are other global research establishments such as George Washington University, which is quite prolific in producing 'Adventure Tourism Industry' reports that have been incorporated into ATTA and UNWTO reports.

Academic conferences can be a valuable source of new research relating to adventure tourism. The following are examples of the type of conferences where appropriate papers are published in conference proceedings:

- Adventure Tourism Research Association (ATRA);
- Adventure Travel World Summit (Adventure Travel Trade Association);
- Balkans 2016 (Adventure Travel Trade Association);
- International Adventure Conference, Tralee 2016;
- Workshop on Adventure Tourism in Iceland (Icelandic Tourist Board).

This type of data also tends to be quite recent and usually topical. A review of the papers given at a conference can be a useful indicator of specific themes and directions that the adventure market is now taking. It is possible to contact particular authors and institutions that might provide further details on data or research and there is also the possibility of cooperative research projects.

Academic journals

Another source is journals but articles will vary and some perhaps will be less relevant to practitioners. They certainly provide a current tone on trends and research, including future developments, though there are not many adventure tourism and outdoor activities journals. Many articles are contained within more mainstream educational or tourism journals, together with outdoor education. The following are some journals that have published articles on adventure and outdoor activities:

- *Journal of Adventure Education and Outdoor Learning*;
- *Tourism Management*;

- *Journal of Tourism & Hospitality*;
- *Journal of Outdoor Recreation, Education, and Leadership*;
- *Journal of Outdoor Recreation and Tourism*;
- *Journal of Ecotourism*;
- *Journal of Sport & Tourism*;
- *Leisure Studies*;
- *Journal of Experiential Education*;
- *Adventure Journal* (a proposed (2018) journal by ATRA).

Furthermore, there are sources that try to coordinate research on adventure tourism and outdoor activities and these are useful for a quick review of some of the topics that have been researched. For example, 'Outdoor Education Research A~Z' (Greenaway, 2017) has a collection of published articles and research papers that can be accessed. How valid and rigorous these are is unclear and should be used as a helpful resource, rather than a definitive collection.

National tourist boards

Often overlooked by companies are the national and regional tourist boards. Every country has them and they are essential infrastructure to the tourism market acquiring data on particular segments or sectors of their industry. Some tourist boards will provide the industry with information on more general statistics relating to specific areas of the business. For example, VisitWales has been heavily engaged in the adventure tourism industry and it is a key product for Wales. VisitWales actively supported research on adventure tourism, with 2017 being designated the year of 'Adventure Tourism'. However, perusal of some of the reports produced by the tourist boards illustrates the importance of consultants in providing the data (Peate, 2012).

There are many other tourist boards that see adventure tourism as a significant product in their list of attractions, such as: Tourism Australia, VisitScotland, Ecuador Travel, Espania, and also the Icelandic Tourist Board. In 2016, Iceland was the top adventure tourism destination and seemed to be benefiting from the boom in adventure and the popularity of Iceland (ATTA, 2016). Yet attempting to find reports and research related to these adventure markets proves difficult and very little specific research data can be found on adventure tourism at this destination.

Consultants

These agencies and agents offer limited accessibility. They are commercial operators and it is rare to find free access to reports or data, but some do offer older or less important research as sweeteners to illustrate the type of work they perform. There are many large consultancy companies, such as (Feloni, 2017):

- Deloitte Consulting;
- McKinsey & Company;
- Accenture;
- Bain & Company;
- Booz Allen Hamilton;
- PriceWaterhouseCoopers;
- Boston Consulting Group;
- KPMG.

Many of these companies are involved in tourism consultancy containing aspects of adventure tourism. There are also many smaller consultancy teams, which provide a different perspective and are usually used by regional firms and tourist agencies.

Research Areas

Students are often bewildered trying to choose a question or problem area for a research report or project. They may spend many hours contemplating the best choice of topic and a research question to be tackled. To try to help in this process, here are some of the current topical areas and potential research projects that need answers:

- How accurate can predictions of growth in the adventure tourism market be?
- What motivates customers to seek adventure tourism activities?
- To what extent is risk an important part of the adventure package?
- What sustainable measures do companies take when offering adventure activities?
- Will adventure tourism and outdoor activities still continue to grow?
- How do companies manage health and safety to reduce risks faced by customers?
- Do adventurers really care about sustainable measures taken by companies?
- Should the Arctic and Antarctic be no go zones for adventure tourists?
- How many adventure tourists actually off-set their carbon foot print?

- Is taking an aeroplane to adventure destinations ethical?
- Why is there a demand for female only adventure tourism packages in an era of emancipation?

Many of these questions still remain not fully understood, especially with the paucity of empirical data available, and will require primary data collection. A global platform to pool adventure tourism research seems a sensible solution to the current lack of data and databases on adventure tourism. This would be an excellent way to reduce the paucity of knowledge relating to adventure tourism. Clearly the adventure and outdoor activity industry needs a cooperative research platform to share and disseminate research. But who is going to do that?

Conclusion

Adventure tourism and outdoor activities research is important for management decisions and the development of the market and the firms that operate within this market. Yet the availability and specific aspects of data are poor or non-existent. This is not unusual for a niche sector of the tourism industry, as most tourism data is general and based on secondary sources, which presents management with a challenge. In addition, the reason for the paucity of data is primarily based upon the resources available and the low return given to the high cost of collecting it. Primary data collections are infrequent, erratic and mainly engaged by academic research units or paid consultants. However consultants are usually employed based upon their expertise (personal knowledge), rather than their ability to supply or collect data.

In terms of country-specific or regional adventure research, non-governmental organizations (NGOs) are more likely to have meticulous data related to activities. The growth in importance of Big Data and AI may provide more accurate and targeted data for the industry, by combining databases and identifying nuances in the data. The effectiveness of Big Data and AI in adventure tourism is still to be evaluated in terms of its future contributions. There is evidently a need for the market to have more data available and perhaps there is also a requirement for more cooperative efforts by global and national institutions and companies to share research.

Questions

- Which research method would you use to assess a new product in adventure tourism?
- Explain why there is such a paucity of data on adventure tourism and outdoor activities?

References

ATTA (2016) Adventure tourism report. Available at: https://www.adventuretravel.biz/research/2016-adventure-tourism-development-index/ (accessed 5 October 2017).

ATTA (2017a) About Us. Available at: https://www.adventuretravel.biz/about/ (accessed 4 October 2017).

ATTA (2017b) 2016 Adventure Tourism Development Index. Available at: https://www.adventuretravel.biz/research/2016-adventure-tourism-development-index/ (accessed 4 October 2017).

ATTA (2017c) Out in Front: Tracking Women's Leadership in Adventure Travel Available at: https://www.adventuretravel.biz/research/out-in-front-tracking-womens-leadership-in-adventure-travel/ (accessed 4 October 2017).

BMC (2018) Articles Tagged as Research. Available at: https://www.thebmc.co.uk/articles/tag/research (accessed 27 August 2018).

BMJ (2017) Archive. Available at: http://www.bmj.com/search/advanced/surfing (accessed 5 October 2017).

Bushwalking Australia (2016) Overview. Available at: http://www.bushwalkingaustralia.org/overview/overview (accessed 4 October 2017).

Crowther, D. and Lancaster, G. (2009) *Research Methods. A Concise Introduction to Management and Business Consultancy*. Butterworth-Heinemann, London.

Eastwood, G. (2017) 3 Ways Big Data is Changing Financial Trading. Available at : https://www.bloomberg.com/professional/blog/3-ways-big-data-changing-financial-trading/ (accessed 7 April 2018).

EC (1994) EHLASS: Community information system on home and leisure accidents. Available at: http://cordis.europa.eu/news/rcn/2131_en.html (accessed 3 October 2017).

Feloni, R. (2017) The 9 best management consulting firms in the US. Available at: http://uk.businessinsider.com/best-management-consulting-firms-in-the-us-2017-4 (accessed 5 October 2017).

Greenaway, R. (2017) Outdoor Education Research A~Z. Available at: http://reviewing.co.uk/research/links.htm (accessed 5 October 2017).

Jones, G. and Perry, C. (1982) Popper, Induction and Falsification. *Erkenntnis* 18(1), 97–104. Available at : http://www.blc.arizona.edu/courses/schaffer/249/Darwin%20and%20Philosophers/Jones%20-%20Popper,%20Induction%20and%20Falsification.pdf (accessed 7 April 2018)

NATA (North Atlantic Tourism Association) (2018) The region. Available at: http://www.northatlantic-islands.com/the-region.html (accessed on 8 March 2018).

Peate, C. (2012) Visits to Tourist Attractions in Wales 2011. Report for VisitWales. Available at: www.tourismhelp.co.uk/objview.asp?object_id=670 (accessed 4 October 2017).

RoSPA (2017a) Accident Statistics, Other Injury Causation Databases and Information. Available at: https://www.rospa.com/resources/statistics/ (accessed 5 October 2017).

RoSPA (2017b) HASS and LASS Home & Leisure Accident Surveillance System. Available at: http://www.hassandlass.org.uk/#a2 (accessed 5 October 2017).

UHI (2017) Centre for Recreation & Tourism Research. Available at: https://www.uhi.ac.uk/en/research-enterprise/centres/recreation/ (accessed 5 October 2017).

UNWTO (2014) Global Report on Adventure Tourism. World Tourism Organization, Madrid. Available at: http://cf.cdn.unwto.org/sites/all/files/pdf/final_1global_report_on_adventure_tourism.pdf (accessed 4 October 2017).

WATO (2017) An All Wales Outdoor Recreation Network supporting and developing the outdoor sector in Wales. Available at: http://www.wato.org.uk/worn/ (accessed 8 March 2018).

WTTC (2017a) Economic Impact. Available at: https://www.wttc.org/economic-impact/ (accessed 4 October 2017).

WTTC (2017b) Leisure Tourism Spending percentage share. Available at: https://www.wttc.org/datagateway/ (accessed on 4 October 2017).

4 Customer Profile

Yet wert thou as far as that vast shore washed with the farthest sea, I would adventure for such merchandise.

William Shakespeare (*Romeo and Juliet*)

Learning Objectives

At the end of this chapter the reader will be able to:

- evaluate the profiling of customers and their adventure tourism products;
- identify the different profiles of tourists and the influence of lifestyle sports on adventure tourism; and
- understand the power of social media and the internet on customer choice and motivation in adventure tourism.

Chapter Overview

This chapter will evaluate the characteristics of the adventure tourism customer, differentiating each into market segments and looking at motivations. It will also explore the growth of lifestyle sports and the influence of the internet on propagating lifestyles and new types of adventure activities.

The tourism market has significantly changed since the heydays of the 1960s, which to a large extent was homogenized, standardized with large economies of scale. The mass tourism of the 1960s seemed to be exemplified, and was contingent upon, the expansion of leisure time and the increasing number of longer paid holidays. Demand can be further linked to most employees being employed in manual jobs, with the summer's ubiquitous 'stop-fortnight' still dominating summer holidays. Consequently, most tourism was limited to the summer season, especially in the northern hemisphere and many developing nations had yet to emerge from colonial control, with their populations being economically poor, resulting in few citizens being able to afford holidays abroad.

The current market is very different from this and there have been significant structural changes to western societies and industries, engendering new approaches to vacations and the tourism packages/products being offered. In the developed world there has been an employment shift resulting in more than 50% of workers now employed in the service economy. These jobs are predominantly sedentary with safer and more comfortable working conditions than those of the 1950s and 1960s. Furthermore, the availability of paid holidays was still very limited compared with today. Society, certainly in the UK, was also still divided by class and holidays reflected these divisions in terms of products and locations. However, there were emerging a number of tourism products and activities that crossed many of these societal mores, such as outdoor activities (walking, hiking, climbing, kayaking, etc.), based around the countryside and the use of national parks. Hiking and walking were activities that were socially mixed and the growth of new sports such as mountaineering and climbing allowed fresh recruits from all social classes to mingle, further fuelling changes to holiday expectations and experiences. The growth of television also provided a platform for enlarged holiday knowledge and choices, with many holiday programmes and documentaries providing new ideas and destinations for potential tourists.

Likewise, even the popular holiday camps of the 1960s, such as Butlins and Pontins, were offering 'activities' that could be seen as the basis for further product development into more independent sports and travel. Perhaps this was why Center Parcs became popular in the 1980s, as they offered activities, not just a sedentary destination, while capitalizing on the outdoor movement. Center Parcs' destinations were also carefully chosen in rural locations in order to have access to a wide catchment of the population.

Supporting the tourist's psychological need for more activities has been a growing health, wellness and exercise movement, compensating for the inactive lives that many citizens in developed countries experience. Governments also produced policies and campaigns to encourage exercise and fitness, which has had an effect upon the growth of adventure activities.

The idea of adventure has changed too and can now be seen simply as a 'travel activity' (car, motorbike, bicycle, etc.) to a destination with some element of risk. This to some extent explains products such as safaris and similar activities, which started to be included in the adventure tourism sector. Sitting in a vehicle, bus or car, on some of the most dangerous roads in the world has to be an aspect of adventure tourism and is exemplified by a number of television programmes (Sheref, 2016); for example, the BBC documentary 'The Arabian Motorcycle Adventures' (BBC 4, 2017; Delingpole, 2015).

There has also been a change in the scale of adventure that can be termed micro and mini adventures (Cooper, 2017). These relate to locations close to an adventurer's home; whether these can be considered adventure tourism is debatable, but certainly they can be foundations for stimulating greater national and international adventure travel. Mini adventures are part of outdoor management and education, important elements in many areas of management and educational development programmes.

Another transformation has been the rise of a more discerning consumer, with a wider experience of sporting and tourism activities, together with increasing expectations relating to the quality of products (Sung, 2004), including experiential activities whereby tourists are challenged and educated (Sung, 2004). These are oversimplifications of the changes and the mass tourism market still exists, retaining many of the characteristics of the 1960s (standardization, economies of scale, crowded destinations).

However, mass tourism has changed, with many packages adding adventure activities and thrills. Many beach destinations have a superfluity of activities such as jet skiing, parascending, diving, snorkelling, banana boating, catamaran sailing and more recent additions: stand-up paddle boards (SUPBs), surfing and kite surfing. The adventure and outdoor market has benefited from these 'one-off' activities and 'one-day adventures', encouraging consumers to engage in these adventure sports on returning home, possibly changing the next choice of holiday towards a more activity based resort (Fig. 4.1).

The concept of 'lifestyle' has also been a part of the growth of the adventure and outdoor market. The surf dude and the adrenaline junkie, jumping off mountains, have fuelled the image of adventure tourism being linked to lifestyle (Wheaton, 2004).

Fig. 4.1. Beach activities, Red Sea (photo: Ian Jenkins).

Furthermore, this has been enhanced by branding and sponsorship deals of adrenaline sports, creating images of an adventure lifestyle. Adventure equipment and clothing have become fashionable and a must-have image, similar to the growth and boom of sportswear, by companies such as Nike, Adidas and Asics.

Adventure brands such as North Face, Vaude, Rab, Salomon, Mammoth and Patagonia are common symbols of allegiance to the adventure lifestyle, worn in urban areas, demonstrating an affinity to an adventure lifestyle. Therefore, it is not surprising that the adventure and outdoor market has grown and continues to grow. Further evaluation of adventure tourism reveals a rather hazy picture of the typical profile of adventure customers. There are trends that can be identified in terms of segments (ATTA and GWU, 2013) but specific targeting of customers is somewhat imprecise, given the diverse nature of the adventure products being offered, which is reflected in the profile of adventure tourism participants.

For management, knowing the customer is key to a successful business but the profiling of adventure tourists is somewhat amorphous. As ATTA and the George Washington University noted, 'adventure travellers are younger than non-adventure travellers, with an average age of 36' (ATTA and GWU, 2013, p.2). This raises issues of segmenting with traditional marketing techniques such as geographically, demographically, psychographically and behaviourally. All of these segmentations involve various targeting techniques, none of which is exclusive, with many overlapping. Therefore just one category of evaluation for purchase is not enough to understand the purchasing behaviour of the adventure tourist. There is a need to cluster or compose composite profiles which is highly complex, especially with the data currently available (Sung, 2004). In the future it may be possible that Big Data and AI will provide some of these answers by combining large databases to form multivariate profiles of adventure tourists.

Mixed Social Profile: Splinting of the Old Marketing Mix

Niche markets combined with mass tourism products

The phenomenon of niche markets in tourism was fashionable in the late 1990s and early 2000s (Jenkins, 2007). A number of tourist organizations and quangos (UK and Ireland) and others cited niche markets as the new way ahead for both strategic and product development which would incorporate the niche markets of adventure activities. Some tourist boards saw these products as very important, in order to encourage tourists to visit their destinations (e.g. Wales, Scotland and Ireland). There is evidence to support adventure tourism as being a niche market, even though there is still confusion relating to an exact definition of what constitutes a niche product or market (Jenkins, 2007). Some tourist organizations still pursue the idea of marketing and targeting niches. For example, the Maltese Tourist Board has targeted a number of clear market niches (Malta Independent, 2014).

The definition of a niche market can have many connotations, ranging from strategic developments (tourist boards and government policies) through to specific products (canyoning, surfing, climbing, wingsuits). It seems evident that a niche contains three specific elements: specialized, specific and small (Fig. 4.2). 'Small' is a relative concept and can include many millions of consumers. The concept of niche has many different spatial perspectives too, especially in current economic global markets. Most of the current demand for adventure tourism comes from the regions of Europe, North America and South America (UNWTO, 2014). But the emerging developing countries are also starting to become involved in growing the market of adventure tourism, which means that the adventure niche will continue to grow in numbers of customers.

Outdoor activities and adventure tourism have similar niche traits and could be considered to be the antithesis of the mass tourism market. Yet connections are present between mass tourism and adventure tourism; many mass tourists now want more than a sedentary experience while on holiday. They will engage in some form of activity reflective of adventure activities, at least for part of the holiday. It is suggested that steady growth of soft adventure tourism may well be linked to the developments of this nature from the mass tourism market.

Many activities in outdoor adventure are specialized and specific, reflecting some of the characteristics of a niche product (Jenkins, 2007). They are also targeted to specific groups, though some of the soft adventure products can be seen as being more universal, especially activities such as horse riding, glacier walking and rafting (ATTA and GWU 2013).

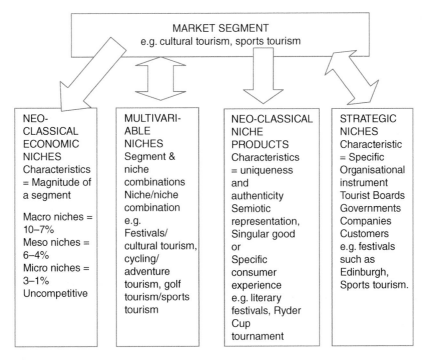

Fig. 4.2. Types of niche (Jenkins, 2007).

Many are adventure experiences that tourists would like to say they have taken part in (social kudos), with tourism companies capitalizing upon the appeal of this niche, especially in the context of family holidays. Family adventure markets are growing and initial research in Iceland by the author (Jenkins, 2016) identified operators focusing on this market.

The old marketing techniques of targeting geographical areas are less efficient and there is a need to use more sophisticated techniques. The ATTA and GWU report identified growth regions of the globe where market growth is occurring. Undoubtedly, the use and development of social media by outdoor companies has enhanced the reach, but definitive evidence is still required to demonstrate the success of this marketing strategy. Connecting to social media is similar to the old form of 'word of mouth', which is still a very powerful marketing tool; indeed current social media sites (Trip Advisor, Lonely Planet and others) are able to capitalize upon this. The review process by customers of adventure may have produced increasing demand for particular outdoor and adventure activities.

As will be seen below, the specifics of targeting customers is still somewhat nebulous and the author has found that companies are not really precisely aware of their potential customer base. Generalities of customer profiles abound, especially elements of age, social standing and lifestyle.

A challenge for niche marketing is identifying how to target customers. The experiential evidence seems to be still gut feeling and business acumen as the main factors for niche targeting of customers. This is not really pertinent, especially with the vast array of data that is available which could be used more effectively for specifically targeting customers. The difficulty is obtaining access to databases and then linking them, which is where Big Data might make an impact on the adventure market.

Another issue relates to the array of activities included under the product umbrella of adventure tourism. A growing number of activities have developed and evolved from the more typical outdoor activities of the 1960s and 1970s. Surfing has evolved a number of specialized sports that are now purchased by adventure customers, such as wind surfing, paddle boarding, kite surfing and surf skiing. Terra firma and aerial activities have followed the pattern of water sports, splintering and developing into composite activities. It is suggested that the market is becoming ever more specialized, which has cost implications for providers and companies. Companies offering single outdoor adventure activities do exist, such as those offering horse riding and surfing, but more often adventure companies offer a wider array of products to meet customer demands.

Older adventurers: SKIs (Spending the Kids' Inheritance)

The baby boom of the 1950s and 1960s is now affecting the tourist market, with many adventurers being a lot older than in years gone by. They have a different perspective upon financial matters and how they will spend their money, usually with far more disposable income than previous generations. Similarly, their holiday experiences and what is considered to be a quality experience are different; hence their expectations of an adventure product are noticeably altered and more experiential than those of their parents. They seem to be a lot fitter, indicating that age deterioration has shifted a generation (at least 10 years). Fifty has become the new 40 and so on through the ageing process. The perception of adventure tourism sports being activities participated in by young volatile men and women has become rather a cliché (though the largest segment may well be under 35 years) (ATTA and GWU, 2013). The adventure tourism market now encompasses many 'grey tops' who are also seeking adventure and excitement (Naidoo *et al.*, 2014).

There is a growing element of the adventure tourism market now made up of older profiles of customers and inevitably a lot of these have more money than the 'young guns'. Yet age will affect activities and there is evidence to suggest that it is soft adventure tourism that is being developed for these customers, which might explain the growth of this category of the adventure tourism market.

Younger profile: different activities

The younger profile of adventurers is associated currently with Generations X and Y, having different expectations to the Baby Boomers (Reynolds and Hritz 2012). They have grown up, as with all generations, in a different environment to that of their parents; they are technologically savvy and expecting a more diverse and exciting experience

from their activities. Many of this generation have seen the exploits of a wide range of adventure and sporting events being pushed to the limit; moreover skateboarding, surfing , BMXing and snowboarding will be familiar and, with these activities, affinities closely linked to adventure tourism lifestyles. It would also be expected that younger adventurers would be buying into hard adventure tourism. Inevitably, there is a need for physical performance to be optimal in many of the hard sports such as climbing. However, caution needs to be raised here as older adventure tourists will still be undertaking some of these hard adventure sports well into their middle and senior years. For example, Ranulph Fiennes and Reinhold Messner are still pushing the limits of adventure.

In terms of company profits and economic sustainability, the younger market may well not be as profitable as that of the Baby Boomers; nevertheless, there are companies that have made a profitable income from the younger market and continue to do so, such as Contiki and TopDeck (Box 4.1).

Adventure Lifestyle

What does seem evident is that greater numbers of tourists are being attracted to the adventure tourism product, which is supported by a number of studies advocating that growth is exponential. Lifestyle adventure tourism (surfers and climbers) is perhaps a rather limited part of the growth market now being experienced, but must be seen as relating to the infrastructure and supply side of the market. Many guides and instructors are employed in the adventure and outdoor sector and their main motives are not monetary gain but the job itself. As will be seen in Chapter 10, there has been a growth in university and vocational courses to match the developments of adventure tourism. These courses have produced graduate instructors who want to work in the adventure and outdoor industry. These employees are very much examples of a performatory lifestyle choice. Seasonality has always been a challenge to the tourism market, in particular the aspect of permanent employment, and adventure tourism is no exception to this, with many adventure guides and instructors having to find other types of work in the low season. This has now changed and it is quite common for many guides and instructors to be employed throughout the year, especially in adventure tourism and particularly those offering more domestic tourism products in Europe.

Box 4.1. Contiki

Contiki is a company that perhaps epitomizes the spirit of adventure. It is a company that provides holidays for the 18–35 age group and clearly has the spirit of adventure. Its latest marketing statement (2018) says that they have no strap lines but simply a lifestyle: 'Most companies have taglines, slogans and jingles. At Contiki, we have a way of life. It's called #NOREGRETS.' (Contiki, 2018).

This seems to reflect the current experiential aspects of the adventure market and certainly sees the 'experience' as the main driver for customers to embark on one of their products. It provides 300 holidays over six continents and was developed from a start-up based in the UK for Australians and New Zealanders to holiday around Europe on an adventure lifestyle package. Contiki has an array of categories of adventures (Independent Outsider, Discoverer, High Energy, Camping, In Depth Explorer, Sailing, Cruise & Beach, Short Trips & Festivals, and Winter & Ski), presenting new dimensions to the marketing of the adventure niche.

The company grew out of a personal adventure trip to Europe by a New Zealander in 1961, which gave him the idea of providing European trips for Anzacs which he started in 1962. Globalization has now changed Contiki's UK base to HQ in California. Contiki employs 278 people and has a business turnover of $38.5 million. Its chief competitor is seen as TopDeck but others also feature such as Peek, Vayable, Musement, Seek Sherpa, Dashbell, Get Your Guide, Klook, Viator (Owler, 2018). This is a difficult market to capture as the disintermediation of the market is exemplified by many of this age group, characterized by single, lone travellers vehemently opposed to organized tourist infrastructures, not wanting packages.

Source:
http://www.contiki.com/destinations/europe

Furthermore, the professionalization of many areas of the adventure tourism industry, such as mountaineering, surfing, snowboarding, sailing and other extreme sports, has helped to fuel the ambitions of many potential employees seeking to earn a living out of being employed in an adventure or outdoor activity.

To a lesser degree this has been helped by the advertising and marketing policies of companies who have used experiential marketing to attract potential customers to take part in adventure tourism and outdoor activities during their leisure and holiday times. Lifestyle and its emotive imagery is a key element in participating in adventure travel and undertaking outdoor sports and activities (Reynolds and Hritz, 2012). It is argued that there are also supporting elements and social constructs that help to fuel this demand through lifestyle magazines connected to health, exercise and travel. In addition, more specialized magazines on adventure and outdoor activities have further encouraged participation in these products, such as *The Great Outdoors*, *National Geographic* and *National Geographic Adventure*. These help to develop latent demand for adventure and outdoor activities. In addition, lifestyles have their own 'adventure tribalism' further segmenting and targeting markets, though adventure tribes are not mutually exclusive (surfers and snowboarders often have mutual interests).

According to Target Media Group (TMG, 2015), 'lifestyle' involves classifying people according to their values, beliefs, opinions and interests. There is no one standardized lifestyle segmentation model; instead market research firms and advertising agencies are constantly devising new categories, which will best help target possible consumers of their clients' products. One example of a lifestyle classification model is that developed by the advertising agency Young & Rubican called 'Cross Cultural Consumer Characterization' (4Cs for short). This classification model is presented in Table 4.1, which illustrates some of the more general lifestyles that can be identified for target marketing and perhaps many can be transferred to the adventure and outdoor market segmentation. In the same way that mountaineers and sailors are tribal, surfers have their own symbolism and culture reflected in the branded clothes that they wear and the lifestyle choices they make. Yet it is clear that more research is needed in terms of surrogates (types of products they purchase) of definitive lifestyle profiles for the AT and ODA industries.

Eco adventure tourists

Eco adventure is perhaps a peripheral area of the adventure tourism market. Ecotourism is becoming more closely linked to adventure and many of its

Table 4.1. Segmentation by Lifestyle Source: the 4Cs (TMG, 2015).

Classification	Characteristics
Resigned	Rigid, strict, authoritarian and chauvinist values, oriented to the past and to Resigned roles. Brand choice stresses safety, familiarity and economy (Older)
Struggler	Alienated, Struggler, disorganized – with few resources apart from physical/mechanical skills (e.g. car repair). Heavy consumers of alcohol, junk food and lotteries, also trainers. Brand choice involves impact and sensation
Mainstreamer	Domestic, conformist, conventional, sentimental, passive, habitual. Part of the mass, favouring big and well known value for money 'family' brands. Almost invariably the largest 4Cs group
Aspirer	Materialistic, acquisitive, affiliative, oriented to extrinsics – image, appearance, charisma, persona and fashion. Attractive packaging more important than quality of contents. (Younger, clerical/ sales type of occupation)
Succeeder	Strong goal orientation, confidence, work ethic, organization – support status quo, stability. Brand choice based on reward, prestige – the very best. Also attracted to 'caring' and protective brands – stress relief. (Top management)
Explorer	Energy – autonomy, experience, challenge, new frontiers. Brand choice highlights difference, sensation, adventure, indulgence and instant effect – the first to try new brands. (Younger – student)
Reformer	Freedom from restriction, personal growth, social awareness, value for time, independent judgement, tolerance of complexity, anti-materialistic but intolerant of bad taste. Curious and enquiring, support growth of new product categories. Select brands for intrinsic quality, favouring natural simplicity, small is beautiful. (Higher Education)

precepts. Furthermore, ecotourism can be regarded as a niche tourism product, associated with the exploration of wilderness or rural locations, which is also a part of the soft adventure market. Ecotourism involves walking, hiking, trekking and camping (ATTA and GWU, 2013), similar to adventure tourism. The ecotourism customer's profile will be somewhat different to the adventure tourism market overall, with a propensity towards an older age profile of 35–54 years (Patterson, 2007). Yet many older customers now participate in adventure tourism and outdoor activities.

Adrenalin and slow adventure customers

Hard adventure tourism is a smaller part of the adventure tourism market, representing some 4–8% of the market, differentiated upon the adventure tourism generating regions (ATTA and GWU, 2013). It is associated with the adrenalin junkies that proliferate on YouTube and 'Extreme' TV channels. From an image perspective, adrenalin-fuelled activities are useful marketing experiences to attract potential adventure and outdoor consumers. Hard adventure is a very limited sector of the market and very specialized which from a management perspective provides limited profits, through tailor-made small group expeditions can be extremely profitable, especially where the activities offered

are iconic, such as summiting Everest. The author has also noted this at other destinations such as Iceland, where personalized expeditions to ice caves are very lucrative for certain companies.

As with all products, monetary returns depend upon the customer type and the activity being participated in. Some hard adventure companies clearly have profitable businesses and the clientele are on average spending large sums of money. The average spend for an adventure tourist is approximately $3000 whereas specialized trips to adventure locations such as the North and South Pole can be up to ten times that amount: $23,000–45,000 (Polar Cruises, 2018) In addition, trips to Everest have grown exponentially and they are expensive for the adventure tourist who wants to reach the summit. A customer would have to pay up to $65,000 to attempt to get to the summit, with no guarantees of success (Adventure Consultants, 2018). These adventure customers are elite adventure tourists linked to the hard adventure tourist market but are not necessarily reflective of the overall profile of hard adventurers.

It is suggested that many adrenalin junkies are not commercially viable for specialized companies. They are usually individuals with limited access to money for adventure trips and devise their own itineraries (disintermediation), staying in low-cost accommodation which contributes little financially to the local economy. It is also suggested that they would not use a commercial company to access their destination or adventure activity.

The soft adventurer is currently a very lucrative market (UNWTO, 2014). Linked to changes in the mass tourism market is a tourist who has a propensity to dip into adventure activities, especially adventure sports. As discussed, many ordinary tourist package holidays now offer adventure activities as a part of the package; even the expanding cruise ship market has mini aspects of adventure with climbing walls and when calling at ports the availability of different types of adventure sports being offered, as demonstrated in this quote:

> Today's Caribbean adventure cruise ships are geared up to active passengers and children being on board. A number of cruise ships have now gone overboard with activities and adventure sports available for children and family members of all ages.
>
> (Active Caribbean, 2017)

The inference is that the average tourist will want some 'adventure' while on holiday and many adventure companies are beginning to target this, especially from a family perspective. There are now day trips to adventure destinations where a tourist can take part in soft adventure tourism. In Greenland there are daily flights from Iceland offering this type of one-day adventure package, which are less expensive than other trips to Greenland.

Targeting Customers

Attracting customers is vital to maintain a company's profits and existence. As has been shown, globalization has provided companies with a platform for a larger reach. Table 4.2 illustrates the process that customers may use in looking for and booking an adventure holiday. Social media is now considered an important marketing tool for enticing customers to participate in activities. The internet and online bookings are the dominant categories in this table, yet the more traditional processes are still valid and relevant. Visibility, the quality of websites with blogs, including social media support, are now indispensable requirements for most companies and organizations. Knowing the experiential triggers for attracting customers to the website are important; and once customers have reached the site, it is important to maintain their attention and ensure that they find the right material to engage them in the adventure product. That said,

Table 4.2. How do adventure travellers prepare for their trips? (% represents the probabilities of picking each choice) Source: GWU, 2010

Process of preparation	%
Research online	23.2
Consult friends and family	17.8
Book airfare/hotels online	11.4
Consult magazines/newspapers	8.7
Visit a travel agency	8.1
Purchase a guide book	7.5
Book through travel agent	5.8
Watch a travel programme about destination	5.6
Will not prepare before leaving for the destination	5.2
Visit destination marketing or tourism promotion organizations	4.1
Book through a tour operator	2.7

there are questions that need to be answered. For example, what is the information that adventure tourism customers are looking for? To what extent is the product price sensitive? Other factors may also influence decisions such as the image of the activities, access and spatial location of the activity, reputation and customer reviews.

A website is a window into the company that should offer a virtual reality of the company and it is essential that companies actively evaluate the effectiveness of the website. Yet very little data is available to appraise a website's effectiveness.

'On spec' or speculative sales can be found at some destinations and are used as another marketing channel. In Reykjavik, many adventure tourism companies have shops in the city centre and along the main tourist street. Their HQ adventure operations are actually elsewhere in the country or city but these physical retail outlets are seen as successful lures for their products. Most of the trade here seems to be 'face to face', rather than booking through the internet (Fig. 4.3). Clearly a connection to a member of staff is an important asset for ensuring the transaction of the tourist in purchasing their adventure products.

Internet advertising is now seen as being another conduit to attract customers, helped by the analytics of the cookie and data analysis used by companies to profile customers, so that many adverts are pushed to potential customers. Again the data relating to the effectiveness of 'push' advertising is not freely available and it is difficult to evaluate the effectiveness of this marketing channel for management.

Fig. 4.3. Adventure tourism companies located on Laugavegur, Reykjavik (photo: Ian Jenkins).

YouTube and viral marketing are other methods used by companies to attract customers. Embedded within websites, there are usually customer experience videos or other links to YouTube videos that have been filmed by the company or customers who have participated in the activities.

The diversity of marketing and targeting networks also has a downside in terms of customer feedback and customer reviews. Sites like Trip Advisor, Trivago and Expedia are regularly used by tourists to review their experience, which has both a positive and negative effect, especially when negative comments are cited. There are two issues here: (i) responding to negative comments; and (ii) trying to establish the validity of the narrative. It seems that online reviews are good for business, depending upon how these are used and presented. There are a number of reasons for this (Hanratty, 2015):

- People have a degree of trust in peer reviews.
- Online reviews are good for search engine optimization (SEO).
- They generate feedback.
- They open up a channel of communication.
- User-generated content (UGC) can be generated.
- Bad reviews are good too.
- They help consumers with product selection.

Other aspects of marketing relate to supplementary product purchases of customers who choose adventure travels. Knowing the key purchases of these customers could create an entry point for other advertising and targeting. For example, adventure equipment and gear purchase can be a trigger or an indication of potential trips or intentions to take an adventure or outdoor activity. Adventure destinations may engender a conglomeration of adventure tourism companies and adventure gear and equipment retailers, creating a critical mass. The challenge is matching the retail gear purchase data to actual outdoor activities purchased.

Directories of adventure tourist companies

Another important element in reaching customers is associated with outdoor or adventure tourist directories and associations. As noted in Table 4.2, a significant main process for purchasing an adventure holiday is online research; concomitantly consumers will review the market to identify which companies and packages are available. Being part of adventure tourism bodies and associations is verification to the tourist of quality and professionalism, as there is an assumption that an association ensures certain standards and reduces the risk of poorly run or unsafe activities. An important issue here is reputation and good standing, which must attract more customers than those that have dubious reputations.

Partnering with other tourism operators or accommodation

Adventure tourism does not operate in a vacuum. It is part of the global tourism market and therefore needs to be supported by other tourist infrastructure and superstructure. This provides an opportunity to access more adventure tourists through partnerships. There are hotels that offer their products in combination with other tourist activities; likewise adventure and outdoor activities can provide offers to accommodation providers. Partnership of marketing can also cut the costs and increase awareness of how to attract more potential customers.

The linkage with equipment and gear manufacturers to outdoor activity companies is a useful marketing tool. Icelandic Mountain Guides, for example, are linked to 'Mountain Equipment and Rab to Íslensku Alparnir Outdoor Specialists' (IMG, 2016). This is not unlike the sports market that supports and sponsors different national teams in order to advertise their branded equipment and gear.

Partnering also offers a wider reach for the adventure and outdoor company to contact the customer who would not normally be looking for these types of activity. Providing information presented to ordinary tourists enables the potential to release latent demand.

Sponsorship

Sponsorship provides an opportunity to widen the appeal of adventure tourism to new customers by providing finance and gear to individual explorers or companies. However, individual explorers seem to benefit more than particular adventure companies from sponsorship deals.

Companies that offer ethical adventure for certain disadvantaged groups can benefit from sponsorship, as shown by Big City Mountaineers (BCM, 2018), which has a large number of sponsors connected to some high-profile companies for their expeditions. Big City Mountaineers uses the wilderness to change lives through mentoring. There are numerous sponsors who support this company and their funding depends upon the type of expedition being provided (Table 4.3).

Table 4.3. Sponsors of Big City Mountaineers

Summit Level ($50,000)	Ascent ($25,000)
Backpacker Magazine	Vasque
Jan Sport	REIcoop
Polartec	The North Face
Sierra Trading Post	Stanley
	Columbia
	Sole

Reaching new customers through sponsorship seems to be limited to equipment and gear manufacturers. For example, Sir Ranulph Fiennes had just one sponsor for his expedition to the South Pole: Karrimor (Karrimor, 2016); whereas Ivan Braun, artist turned mountaineer, who in 2016 attempted the ascent of Everest without oxygen, has had a number of equipment sponsors, such as North Face, Friluftsland, Outdoor X-perten, Edelrid, Haglöfs, Recoverit (Braun, 2016)

It is difficult to evaluate the benefits of sponsorship that an adventure expedition will have on a company but it is contended that this method of attracting new customers has to be connected to something exceptional and different from the normal adventure tourist activities. It is really a specialized form of enticing customers and is not one that is applicable to most companies.

Psychological profile of customers

This form of segmentation of customers is difficult to use when trying to locate customers in geographical space. An a priori concept of adventure tourism engenders an image of an adrenalin junkie, pushing the limits, with high risk outcomes but also psychological rewards. Psychological profiling of customers has been used for some time and is linked to earlier tourism markets. The idea is supported by theory, probably the most renowned being that of Plog's Psychographic model of tourist motivation (Murphy, 1985).

Plog's premise was based upon perceived risk and familiarity of tourist products at destinations. The Allocentric risk takers will choose holidays in destinations that are undeveloped and newly discovered, equated with high psychological risk and lacking much of the tourist infrastructure and superstructure that mass tourism destinations have. On the other hand, Psychocentric behaviours have aspects of the timid stay-at-home tourist, where adventure is to be avoided. The mass tourist market is to be found in Midcentric profiles and these tourists encompass characteristics of both Allocentric and Psychocentric classifications (Page, 2003).

An analogy can be made to Plog's model and similarities applied to those of the adventure tourist and outdoor activity market. The adrenalin junkies who seek hard adventure are akin to the extreme Allocentric tourist. They have a motivation to experience thrills through fear and risk taking. They require activities that are high risk and could result in fatality. These extreme adventurers are a very small minority even within the sector of hard adventure, such as cave divers and base/wingsuit jumpers, experiencing high mortality levels and using isolated and unusual physical features.

The main adventure market is more like the mass market profile with most customers wanting some element of risk but with this being minimized and controlled. This would give them some adrenaline rush, but with the knowledge that they are relatively safe (soft adventure). There is evidence that many companies see this type of adventurer as the primary market for adventure tourism and outdoor activities, including families. Certainly, there seems to be an increasing demand for more experiential holidays with some elements of risk, which helps to explain the increasing growth of soft adventure tourism.

Trying to use personality profiling of adventure tourists is complicated. The problem relates to locating these individuals through the current available marketing and advertising networks. Demographic profiling is possibly easier in terms of targeting and then trying to categorize personality types. The essence of the problem lies with attempting to use surrogates for personality types and then targeting the customers that purchase these products.

Another marketing approach might utilize the 'Sensation Seeking Scale', developed by Marvin Zuckerman in 1979. This uses four personality traits to evaluate individuals and could be applied to explore those currently engaged in the different products of adventure tourism. An adaption of the traits is as follows (Zuckerman, 1979)

- Thrill and adventure seeking: linked to outdoor activities with high thrill element and experience.
- Experience seeking: choosing to mix with individuals, who challenge the social conventions of society on the fringes of society.

- Disinhibition: connected to extreme elements of the party scene and drug taking, pushing social mores to the limits, has elements of uncontrollable situations.
- Boredom susceptibility: unable to accept boring situations and always needing to be stimulated. Likes environments which have constant change and new situations.

For a manager, the problem is establishing the viability of these categories and also the reliability and stability of the profiling. It could be argued that adventure tourism is reflective of some members of society who need to have new sensation-seeking experiences, which adventure tourism can offer, so there might well be a link with changes in the psychology of an individual, in response to the need for new exciting experiences. In the UK there has been a move to link wellbeing with adventure and outdoor activities and in the past even psychologically damaged individuals such as war veterans experiencing post-traumatic stress (PTS) have used adventure sports to help recover, surfing for Vietnam Vets being one example. There are challenges with such a categorization, including: do individuals change from one profile to another and are profiles mutually exclusive?

There have been studies using Zuckerman's model to assess profiling of adventure tourism customers, but with mixed results. As with all psychological profiling, how these individuals are reached and targeted in cyber or physical space is a complex problem.

Big Data and Artificial Intelligence

Big Data is seen as a useful addition in helping to understand many aspects of tourism, including identifying new demands and products. Adventure tourism may benefit from fine tuning and amalgamating data; Big Data might be able to provide new insights into customer profiling and marketing. There are suggestions too that Big Data will be able to help develop new products garnered from the information collected and reoriented, based upon present consumer choices (Future Foundations, 2016). Big Data is not a new cure-all and, like most new tools, it relies upon the way it is applied and quality (validity and reliability) of the data. It has the potential for many types of applications that could be used for adventure tourism and outdoor activity markets. Linking databases such as adventure holidays and consumer purchases (types of food, clothing or hobbies) might provide an approach to new types of targeting of adventure tourists.

However, the citations in journals and magazines on Big Data now seem to have peaked and the new perspective is towards AI based upon Big Data. The focus is upon cognitive developments of learning, using machines such as IBM's Watson.

Conclusion

The profiling of adventure tourism consumers still remains rather general and lacks specificity. The proliferation of the internet has created opportunities for adventure tourism and outdoor activity companies to use this new form of access and advertising. The most noteworthy process for accessing new adventure tourism consumers is related to websites and other electronic material, and the future will continue to see this marketing area expand, yet its effectiveness is still being evaluated. Moreover, social media platforms will continue to be influential in creating demand for adventure holidays.

Different types of profiling and lifestyles of customers have also emerged, but rather than simplifying the market they have created more dispersed profiles of consumers. The advent of new types of data and techniques such as Big Data and AI may have a significant impact on understanding adventure consumers and meeting their lifestyle needs, but the evidence is still not available to verify the effectiveness of these new approaches.

Questions

- In what way does lifestyle affect the adventure tourism market?
- What theories of customer profiling can be used to explain the potential targeting of customers to the adventure tourism product?
- Why is it a complex process to successfully target adventure tourism customers?

References

Active Caribbean (2017) Cruise Adventures: Caribbean Adventure Cruise with Activities. Available at: http://www.activecaribbean.com/leisure-activities/caribbean-cruises-with-adventure-activities-for-all-the-family/ (accessed 10 October 2017).

Adventure Consultants (2018) Everest. Available at: https://www.adventureconsultants.com/expeditions/seven-summits/everest/ (accessed 13 March 2018).

ATTA and GWU (2013) Adventure Tourism Market Study 2013. Adventure Travel Trade Association and George Washington University, Washington, DC.

BBC 4 (2015) The Arabian Motorcycle Adventures. Available at: http://www.bbc.co.uk/programmes/p02hcrfr/p02hcqj3 (accessed 10 October 2017).

BCM (Big City Mountaineers) (2018) Sponsors. Available at: http://www.bigcitymountaineers.org/sponsor (accessed 10 December 2018).

Braun, I. (2016) Past sponsors. Available at: http://www.ivanbraun.dk/past-sponsors/ (accessed 11 May 2016).

Contiki (2018) The No Regrets Travel List. Contiki, Guernsey. Available at: https://www.contiki.com/uk/en/no-regrets-travel-list (accessed 27 August 2018).

Cooper, J. (2017) Easy expeditions: 30 great 'microadventures' for spring. Available at: https://www.telegraph.co.uk/health-fitness/body/easy-expeditions-30-great-microadventures-spring/ (accessed 10 October 2017).

Delingpole, J. (2015) Arabian Motorcycle Adventures review: enthralling and constantly surprising. Available at: https://www.spectator.co.uk/2015/02/arabian-motorcycle-adventures-review-an-enthralling-and-constantly-surprising-documentary/ (accessed 10 October 2017).

Future Foundations (2016) Big Data Insights for Travel & Tourism Available at: https://www.wttc.org/-/media/files/reports/special%20and%20periodic%20reports/wttc_big_data_report_final.pdf (accessed 12 May 2016).

GWU (2010) Adventure Tourism Market Study. George Washington University, Washington, DC.

Hanratty, C. (2015) 7 reasons customer reviews are important for your tourism website. Available at: https://www.trekksoft.com/en/blog/why-customer-reviews-are-important (accessed 12 October 2017).

IMG (Icelandic Mountain Guides) (2016) Trekking Tours. Available at: http://www.mountainguides.is/practical-information/equipment-lists/trekking-tours/ (accessed 11 May 2015).

Jenkins, I.S. (2007) Postmodern Tourism Niches: UK Literary Festivals and Their Importance for Tourism Destination Development. PhD Thesis, University of Swansea.

Jenkins, I.S. (2016) Interviews with adventure tourism providers in Iceland. Research evaluating tourist impacts of adventure tourism in Iceland. (Unpublished.)

Karrimor (2016) Karrimor SF sponsors Sir Ranulph Fiennes Expedition. Available at: http://www.karrimorsf.com/news/9-latest-news/37-karrimor-sf-sponsors-sir-ranulph-fiennes-expedition.html (accessed 11 May 2016).

Malta Independent (2014) Developing Malta's tourism niches: a targeted approach. Available at: http://www.independent.com.mt/articles/2014-07-31/news/developing-maltas-tourism-niches-a-targeted-approach-6033113094/ (accessed 12 March 2014).

Murphy, P.E. (1985) Tourism: a Community Approach. Routledge, London.

Naidoo, P., Ramseook-Munhurrun, P., Seebaluck N.V. and Janvier, S. (2014) Investigating the motivation of baby boomers for adventure tourism. *Procedia – Social and Behavioral Sciences* 175, 244–251.

Owler (2018) Contiki Revenue, Funding, Number of Employees, Competitors and Acquisitions. Available at: https://www.owler.com/company/contiki (accessed 13 March 2018).

Page, S.J. (2003) *Tourism Management Managing for Change*. Butterworth Heinemann, Oxford.

Patterson , C. (2007) *The Business of Ecotourism: The Complete Guide for Nature and Culture Based Tourism Operators*. 3rd edn. Trafford Publishing, Oxford.

Polar Cruises (2018) North Pole 90 Degrees North – The TOP of the world. Available at: https://www.polarcruises.com/arctic/destinations/north-pole (accessed 13 March 2018).

Reynolds, Z. and Hritz, N.M. (2012) Surfing as adventure travel: motivations and lifestyles. *Journal of Tourism Insights* 3(1), article 2. Available at: https://core.ac.uk/download/pdf/10683779.pdf (accessed 10 October 2017).

Sheref, I. (2016) Terrifying video shows men risk DEATH on the world's most dangerous. Available at: http://www.express.co.uk/travel/articles/678015/viral-video-men-driving-dangerous-Pangi-Valley-india (accessed 10 October 2017).

Sung, H.H. (2004) Classification of adventure travelers: behavior, decision making, and target markets. *Journal of Travel Research* 42(4), 343–356.

TMG (2015) *How Business Categorizes Consumers*. Target Media Group, Newark, New Jersey. Available at: http://www.tmgnj.net/tag/4cs/ (accessed 12 April 2018).

UNWTO (2014*) Global Report on Adventure Tourism*. United Nations World Tourism Organization, Madrid.

Wheaton, B. (2004) *Understanding Lifestyle Sports, Consumption, Identity And Difference*. Routledge, London.

Zuckerman, M. (1979) *Sensation Seeking Beyond the Optimal level of Arousal*. Taylor & Francis, London.

5 Product Development

The most efficient way to produce anything is to bring together under one management as many as possible of the activities needed to turn out the product.

Peter Drucker (management consultant and author) (Drucker, 2001)

Learning Objectives

At the end of this chapter the reader will be able to:

- differentiate how geographical space and technological developments have affected the adventure tourism market; and
- appraise how postmodernist theory is able to explain changes in the adventure product through changes in technology and consumer tastes.

Chapter Overview

Products are simply the merchandise that is offered to customers by companies for purchase. Adventure tourism and outdoor activities are no different from other areas of the tourism industry. They are similarly affected by preference and technology changing the types of holidays available. However, the array of adventure tourism products currently offered presents a sea change from those emerging in the middle of the last century.

The locations for adventure are key features in changing the dynamics of the product, as the destination can be as important as the activity itself. As will be seen within this chapter, spatial locations can be drivers for adventure and outdoor products, even those of urban landscapes. Product development in clothing and equipment has also made vast strides as regards the types of expeditions and holidays offered by adventure tourism companies. To illustrate this, Portaledge, the hanging tent that can be pitched on a cliff face, has become a familiar feature of many climbing adventures and new clothing materials have helped to make adventure far more comfortable than the woollen tweed suits worn by the first Alpine climbers.

An important element in helping to foster new products in adventure tourism and outdoor activities has been the evolution of management training using adventure as the vehicle to bring together teams within companies. The growth in hen and stag parties has seen many groups purchasing adventure tourism packages to enjoy their fraternal experiences. Consequently the growth of multi-activity products has grown to meet this demand, which is also related to short breaks, weekends and domestic tourism demand.

New products such as boot camps, wellness centres and family activity holidays, together with a boom in fitness and health-related products, have developed composite activities between adventure and health. The ubiquitous fitness watch measuring the recommended '10,000 steps a day' exemplifies the changes to the outdoor market and the new products developed. Instagram and Facebook broadcast the many and varied activities that adventurers now participate in, further encouraging other adventurers into experiencing a wide range of adventure products.

These are some of the issues that this chapter will discuss and explore. As noted in earlier chapters, adventure tourism and outdoor products are now essential elements in most countries' tourism packages. The task is to maintain the customer's interest in the products which, as with all tourism products, are somewhat quixotic. There are the physical supporting items of the holiday such as equipment, clothing and digital footage, but the actual experience and memory still remain temporal and spatial, challenging any attempt in recreating the same experience, meaning that it is just as fragile as it has always been. The physical landscapes, the group of participants and the nature of the activity all combine to change the dynamics of any adventure product.

Geographical Spaces: Playgrounds for Adventure Products

Adventure tourism would find it difficult to operate without 'space'. It is a given that different destinations provide different physical challenges for adventure activities, though with contemporary developments in virtual reality one could argue that an adventure could be had without a physical space: risk, activity and adventure are all in the mind. However, adventure usually means movement/activity of some kind in geographical space, so the environment in many cases is the key sensory perception to the nature of adventure. Geographical space and adventure tourism destinations are key to the adventure tourism experience. Yes, simulation of artificial environments can be created such as 'snow domes' and 'climbing walls' but the actual feeling of being amongst nature and wilderness is difficult to recreate virtually. The natural landscape is the very fabric of adventure tourism. For example, the Matterhorn (Fig. 5.1) is not the same as Mont Blanc (Fig. 5.2), yet the adventure activity may be homogeneous in terms of skills used in the physical activity, unlike the experience. It is argued that this is a reason for the development of 'new' locations offering similar activities, as there is a need to experience the 'physiognomy' (features associated with the physical layout of elements within the landscape) (Dunning *et al.*, 1992) of these geographical locations; engaging in a very different natural landscape brings with it different challenges for the chosen activity. Hence, location is a very important factor in the adventure experience. The following sections provide a brief overview of adventure and outdoor product development.

Mountains and glaciers

Mountains are part of human history and society and are geographical/geological features that resonate with adventure: the urge to reach the summits of mountains has been a primordial presence in the human race. The unreachable or unclimbable provide the challenge and the greatest challenge was Everest, the world's highest land mountain, which finally yielded in 1953 but this conquest was far from ending mountaineering or the human need for continuous adventure. Mountaineering and climbing have progressively developed since the start of the Alpine movement in the 18th century and there

have been many product innovations fuelling demand for adventure. With the invention of the ice axe and crampons came the opportunity to climb mountain faces that were until then thought to be unclimbable (Douglas, 2015). The Alpine movement laid the foundations for the sport of mountaineering and the spirit of adventure; and once all the best known peaks had been conquered, new ones were sought in other locations around the globe.

Climbing has also fractured into other more specialized areas of the sport such as bouldering, where new techniques and styles could be practised in relative safety at low-level rock faces. This in turn has grown into a sport in its own right, with even children's playgrounds exhibiting bouldering walls and climbing apparatus. The development of climbing walls is clearly linked to the growth of mountaineering and climbing. They have mushroomed in popularity and nearly every sizable city in the UK will have some form of climbing wall, allowing different techniques and styles to be practised in relative safety. The UK boasts nearly 400 climbing walls (UKC, 2016), which have grown exponentially and there is now a representative Association of British Climbing Walls (ABCW, 2016).

The climbing of Everest has engendered the commercialization of mountaineering in general and increased the commercialization of Everest itself for tourist climbers/adventurers (Jones, 2016). Tourist climbers at Destination Everest are now 'big business' and allied to the growth of climbing and the accessibility that tourism transport has provided. In many cases climbing Everest can be seen as a form of 'Disneyfication'. The Disneyfication of Everest creates new adventurers, who it seems do not fully understand the real risk or dangers of climbing the world's highest mountain. The climbing of Everest by tourists has become an industry in itself, no longer a sport, but a tourist 'bucket list' for those who have the money or inclination. In many respects this seems to have removed the mystery and spirituality of climbing the world's highest mountain, reflecting the quick fix and tick list tourism of the 'tourist gaze' and the new adventure tourism market.

New products have emerged in the adventure market connected to mountains and their physical features. Many mountains have to be climbed by traversing glaciers and glaciers themselves have become a product for adventure. In Iceland the

Fig. 5.1. The Matterhorn (photo: Ian Jenkins).

Fig. 5.2. Mont Blanc (photo: Ian Jenkins).

growth of glacier walks has been related to the growth of tourism; and just like the Disneyfication of Everest (Jones, 2016) there seems to be a similar phenomenon of adventure on glaciers. Glacier walks are advertised as offering adventure and clearly those who are unsuspecting of the risks and dangers are likely to find themselves in trouble. In Iceland there are numerous tragic examples of adventurers disappearing on glaciers. As noted here:

> A German tourist unfortunately fell to his death in Vatnajökull glacier a short while ago while exploring an ice cave with a professional guide. Sadly, not the first casualty of this nature in Iceland ... Glaciers should be feared and treated with utmost respect at all times by people. They move, break, melt and harden at any given moment and no guide, no matter how knowledgeable, can predict such things in advance.
> (Total Iceland, 2014)

Yet 'glacier walks' are offered to most people regardless of their abilities in climbing or mountaineering. Glacier walks are for all ages (including children) and the development of ice axes and crampons have allowed this product to be sold as an adventure for average tourists.

> Glacier hiking and ice climbing, like many things in Iceland, are once in a lifetime opportunities for most travellers. Many people in the world may never even get the chance to attempt either of the two. But after at the very least attempting both of them, one feels accomplished and humbled at the very same time. Accomplished for having done something active and unique, humbled by the beauty and awesomeness of nature. These were both feelings I was lucky enough to retain after a trip to the Sólheimajökull glacier.
> (Tummolillo, 2011).

Another product development relating to glaciers is that of visiting ice caves (Fig. 5.3). There have been a growing number of adventure tourists wanting to visit ice caves because of the surreal world which they find deep within a glacier. Some of the pictures are incredible and in many cases photographs do more justice to the experience than just the naked eye. Again the growth of adventure tourism to glacier caves has mirrored the growth of tourism per se and demand has grown exponentially. In Iceland,

Fig. 5.3. Icelandic Ice Cave (Photo: Þorvarður Árnason).

as with glacier walking, ice caves have become so popular with ordinary tourists that they have become somewhat commodified. The creation of gigantic ice caves in glaciers reflects the commodification of wilderness and mountain areas for soft adventure. Iceland has one such cave created by an Icelandic bank. 'This ice is money,' says Addi, knocking on the tunnel wall, 'and it's safer here than in the bank' (Rogers, 2015). There is also a huge array of natural caves created by glaciers and these present a more authentic experience for the adventure traveller.

Mountains and glaciers present other opportunities for adventure, many using mechanical devices. Snowmobiles and 4×4 trucks or off-road vehicles (ORVs) are other new adventure tourism products developed to attract adventure tourists. Many vehicles are similar to 'circus' big cars, having high suspensions and huge tyres. Expeditions in these vehicles can be included in adventure tourism, even though the physical activities and skill levels are somewhat minimal compared with more active climbing or skiing activities. Yet the perception of adventure is still there with thrills (fear) and different experiences making up the components of adventure on a glacier.

Air

The atmosphere is an adventure space that offers many different types of exploits developed from the basic premise of flying. Historically, gliders and light aircraft have been the main devices of this area of adventure tourism, but now have splintered into many other types of activities and experiences. Hang-gliding (popular in the 1960s) has evolved into paragliding and microlights but the most adventuresome and high risk (Beaumont, 2016) is that of wingsuit flying, which has now become quite a familiar sight on the Extreme channel and YouTube even though it is associated with high mortality rates. Mountains make great bases to launch into the air and many other aerobatic adventure activities also are launched from mountains, such as heli-skiing and paragliding.

Wingboarding is one of the latest products to emerge on to the extreme adventure front. This is where a board rider is pulled behind an aircraft and surfs the air. It is still very much in the developmental stage but will no doubt have a number of extreme adventurers participating very soon, as with wingsuits. The participant is strapped to a wing and once airborne can perform aerial tricks (Quick,

2014). It will be interesting to see if this new sport becomes popular in the future.

Rivers

Rivers, like mountains, are adventure features used by many tourists, meaning that it is no surprise that adventure tourism has also expanded the number of activities using this physical feature. There has been accelerated participation in certain sports such as river rafting, which is now a common adventure activity on many fast-flowing rivers, usually in mountainous locations. As with glacier walking, there has been a move to attract families to participate in rafting, which has helped to expand the market.

Canyoning is a fairly recent addition to adventure (it began 20–30 years ago) and it is a ubiquitous activity for many adventure tourism companies. It requires a multitude of different skill sets, but offers a relatively safe and exciting adventure product with popular customer appeal. For many adventure companies in the UK, canyoning is an indispensable product. Canyoning also offers many different types of physical landscapes that can be used in the activity, mixing climbing, bouldering and swimming as well as allowing access to parts of rivers that might well not be navigated by other water activity sports, such as canoes or rafts. Many of these activities can be found close to waterfalls where the passage downstream is fast and exciting (Fig. 5.4).

Another composite sport and new addition to river adventure activities is river boarding, which is akin to boogie boarding down the river on a foam surf board with the adventurer wearing fins. It is certainly offered in Queenstown, New Zealand, and also found at many other adventure centres around the globe.

New Zealand has also developed the idea of the jet boat to navigate rivers and is part of the soft adventure palette on offer to adventure tourists. The adventurer is a neutral participant simply relying on the experience of the drivers to ensure a thrilling experience. There are alternative versions of this in other countries which appear to emulate the theme park experience; for example, Jet Boat tours of Ramsey Island in West Wales (VisitWales, 2018).

Oceans/seas

Oceans are wildernesses where many adventures have taken place. Numerous different types of adventures and adventure activities occur on oceans, ranging from around-the-world single-handed

Fig. 5.4 Canyoning: the Neath Valley, South Wales (photo: Ian Jenkins).

yacht races to crossing oceans in rowing boats or other types of transport. As with rivers, coasteering has become a popular adventure activity on shore lines and exhibits many of the characteristics of canyoning, providing companies with a good supply of customers and income. The latest adventure products are the growth of cruise ships to remote locations such as the Antarctic and Arctic. The original pioneer for ocean adventure has to be Thor Heyerdahl (Klein, 2014) who with his *Kon-Tiki* expedition in 1947 became the first crew to sail on a papyrus raft from South America to Polynesia. Indeed the sea continues to provide many adventure activities, often adaptations of older sports. For instance, stand-up paddle boards, kite surfing and big-wave surfing are all derivatives of surfing. Likewise with sailing, there are newer faster boats pushing speed and distance to the limit.

Deserts

Deserts too are used as adventure settings for different products (Leadbeater, 2015). The locations offer many challenges which appeal to AT and ODA customers. Technological developments have not necessarily produced new activities but rather an adaptation of sports or activities that naturally occur in deserts. Camel riding (Fig. 5.5), marathon running, sandboarding, 4×4 riding, motorcycling, etc. are some of the more common activities found in these extreme locations.

Deserts, like mountains, offer an array of different landscapes (Table 5.1) and environments. They have many different physiognomies (Table 5.1) which prescribe the types of adventures likely to be engaged in. Most perceptions of deserts are those relating to developing countries but many are to be found within developed countries; Spain could be considered to have mini deserts such as the Monegros Steppes, Aragon (Guardian, 2015); the USA has many different types.

Many activities in deserts are related to aspects of survival and survival techniques, especially where water and shelter are normally limited or non-existent. Formal transport is usually not used; rather, alternative methods such as camels and pack animals or air transport are utilized. New types of products are being developed in deserts, focusing on aspects of survival, and companies together with countries have exploited this niche. For example, as noted in Chapter 1, the Marathon des Sables, a race over 250 km, celebrated its 33rd year in 2018 (Marathon des Sables, 2017).

Fig. 5.5. Camel riding in the desert. (Source: Ian Jenkins)

Table 5.1. Types of desert. (Source: National Geographic, 2018)

Type	Description
Subtropical	Found in hot regions of the globe and have little precipitation, very high temperatures in the summer and still dry in the winter with lower temperatures
Coastal	Usually located on western coast of continents, between latitudes 20–30°. The wind direction prevents the moisture from the sea moving inland and creating precipitation
Cold winter deserts	Sometimes known as semi-arid deserts, have long dry summers with cold winters and limited precipitation, often related to the 'rain shadow effect'
Polar	Extreme cold and dry air with very little precipitation. Most falls as snow and freezes

Jungles

In contrast to deserts, jungles have a plethora of water and vegetation and they are connected to ecotourism and sustainable tourism developments. However, adventure tourism is popular in these types of terrain; many expeditions are closely connected to eco-lodges and association with indigenous populations. In terms of actual activities these again are more reflective of staple adventure tourism products: hiking, kayaking or boating and similar activities. By its very nature, movement through jungle is greatly restricted and the use of motorized vehicles and similar products is limited or non-existent. Geographically, jungles are located in the equatorial regions of the planet and, as with deserts, adventure products are usually linked to survival activities. Soft adventure products dominate at these locations interspersed with a few hard adventures such as cave diving; for example, using cenotes or sink holes of the Riviera Maya in Mexico (Under the Jungle, 2017).

The Poles

As with the commercialization of Everest, the North and South Poles are offered as one of the most extreme challenges for adventure tourists; indeed travelling to these geographical locations are important adventure products. Prior to the current boom in holidays to these locations, the historical legacy of expeditions such as those of Amundsen, Scott and Shackleton have encouraged tourists to seek similar experiences. Emulating the routes and conditions of these adventures are new products for today's adventure tourism. It seems that these locales are still a sanctuary to only a few real adventurers and although there have been many technological developments there are still limited numbers of adventure tourists travelling to these destinations.

Types of adventure activities are few, primarily nature and landscape treks with few adrenalin-pumping activities featuring in this pristine environment. Consequently it could be argued that even given the extreme climates at the Poles, adventure is primarily linked to soft adventure activities. For many it is described and understood as the 'last wilderness on earth', raising ethical questions of whether adventure tourism should be allowed in these regions at all.

However, camping and trekking are growing in the Polar wildernesses and companies offer these activities to customers who have no previous experience of camping and hiking. Again this commercialization of pristine wilderness suggests a Disneyfication of Antarctica and the Arctic for commercial exploitation by adventure companies. Sadly pressure from the adventurer's bucket list appears to be increasing pressures on these regions (they are hardly destinations) and for the foreseeable future the Polar Regions will be exploited for commercial gain to the detriment of their pristine environments.

Urban

Urban adventure products challenge the perception of wilderness and its association with adventure tourism; it takes another perspective whereby elements of risk and exploration are also involved. The types of products on offer are varied, including exploring the underground sewers of major cities such as Paris and London and cycling tours. Cycling is somewhat more contentious but the association with adventure can be found, and cities do offer cycling as an urban adventure, for example in Glasgow, Scotland.

Base or BASE jumping (an acronym for Building, Antenna, Span, Earth) would be included in urban adventure but offering this as an official tourist product would not be viable, as base jumping is considered illegal in many cities. Yet as a fringe of urban adventure in cities, base jumping does occur, usually on newly constructed buildings – the Shard in London being one (Slawson, 2016).

In essence the concept of urban adventure tourism is somewhat limited and spending a weekend or a week participating in adventure activities in an urban destination would be very limited. Yet many urban locations use the tome of adventure as a marketing strap-line, further expanding the definition of adventure tourism.

Technological Developments

As mentioned in the introduction to this chapter, technology creates change and is an important energizer for developments to tourism and concomitantly adventure tourism products. Technology developments have affected materials, construction, communications and design, all of which affect enjoyment on adventure and outdoor activities. Warmth/heat protection, food, water and shelter have all been affected by technological improvements (Voith, 2009), which have been incorporated into much of the merchandise on offer.

Warmth

Hypothermia and heat exhaustion are two serious risks for adventurists in the wild and technology has been successfully used to improve survival. The introduction of Gore-Tex was significant and this fabric has now become a standard for waterproofing and breathability, both problems relating to older material used such as plastic and wool. Gore-Tex has led the way for the development of other similar types of material on the adventure market, such as PrimaLoft, Climashield and Thermolite (Voith, 2009). Also wicking material is used to take sweat away from the body and there have been important technological advances here to reduce the likelihood of hypothermia, by removing perspiration away from the body. Materials such as Coolmax, Cordura and eVent fabric (Voith, 2009) are new scientific improvements. Specialist materials such as neoprene have also been used for adventure activities such as surfing and kayaking, allowing these adventurers to explore new environments that have previously been inaccessible.

Thermal sleeping mats, together with emergency blankets and bothy tents (which in the former case were developed from space technology and are now used in adventure survival equipment), have also helped to reduce heat loss.

Food

Dried food and special energy foods are examples of advancements in technology helping to improve nutrition and expedition nutrition. These have replaced the antiquated tins (still useful but weight laden) which were first introduced in 1812 and used on many expeditions of the time, such as those of Scott and Shackleton; these were quite revolutionary then, extending food for years (1–5) rather than weeks (Geoghegan, 2013). Some 200 years on tins are still being used, but the newest technological change has been in dried food and food nutrition. Yet a close examination of the types of food used on extreme expeditions, such as Everest, demonstrates that technological advances have not in fact been that significant. A review of literature relating to expeditions identifies even the 'old tin can' as an effective food source as well as the use of more traditional dried foods such as pasta and porridge. The focus is upon the nutritional value of food consumed and its performance effect, rather than the scientific developments in food processing (MountEverest.net, 2017).

Shelter

Temporary shelters have been the staple of many expeditions in adventure/outdoors and, as with tins, these have changed from using heavy materials such as canvas, requiring expedition support teams to carry them, to lighter, more advanced materials. The tent is perhaps the most popular temporary shelter and the array of types of tents available is extensive and specialized; for example, popup tents (self erection), pneumatic erection tents, suspension tents and the old manual erection tents. It is apparent that design is the area that has been most affected by technological developments. A myriad of forms and shapes have been developed as a result of technological advances in new materials. Table 5.2 itemizes some of the more popular fabrics used by tent manufacturers.

Lighting

The advent of halogen and LED lighting has transformed light sources in adventure tourism and

Table 5.2. Tent fabrics (Graystone, 2017).

Brand fabric	Fabric type	Manufacturer's description
Coleman WeatherTec	Polyester	Waterproofing tech.
Kampa WeatherShield	Polyester	Kampa WeatherShield is the waterproofing treatment Kampa applies to their polyester tent fabrics, which come in a variety of thickness and hydrostatic head ratings
Hydrofilm	Polyester	Hydrofilm is the name Jack Wolfskin tents have given to their polyester groundsheets
Outwell Outtex 100% Ripstop Cotton	Cotton	Cotton with a weave to reduce the chance of rips
Outwell Airtex	Polycotton	Treated to help water droplets run off the tent
Outwell Outtex 6000-3000	Polyester	A polyester-based fabric, typically the Outtex 6000, that has a weave to give it the appearance of polycotton or canvas on the outside of the tent. The fabric is also thicker and Outwell claims it is tougher, so it should last longer
Robens HydroTex® LT 40D	Nylon	A nylon ripstop flysheet with a silicon external coating and a PU internal coating
Robens HydroTex HD	Polyester	75D (fabric weight) polyester 185T (thread count)
Robens HydroTex DP	Polyester	68D (fabric weight) polyester 190T (thread count)
Robens HydroTex 5000	Polyester	Polyester with a 5000 mm Hydrostatic Head
Robens HydroTex Polycotton	Polycotton	65% cotton / 35% polyester. Breathable with a light water-repellent treatment
Vango Protex70	Polyester	70D polyester
Vango Protex 150	Polyester	150D polyester
Vango Protex Cotton	Polycotton	A blend of cotton and polyester

outdoor activities, together with the use of solar battery rechargers which have improved the availability of quality lighting while on expeditions. The main technological developments have been towards small size, light weight and high light luminosity, as well as more durable usage levels for rechargeable batteries.

Communications and navigation

One of the most significant advances in adventure technology has been communications. The mobile phone and satellite phone provide adventurers with close contact to base camps and friends. Satellite phones are now standard pieces of kit for around-the-world adventurers, polar explorers and expeditions. Global positioning system (GPS) devices have also boomed, to the extent that old map-reading skills are being lost or diminished, creating problems for rescue teams (who are being called out to find lost tourists), especially if the GPS is not working and the adventurer has to use a map (if they have one). GPS devices do malfunction and lose battery power, which has now led to some safety agencies re-emphasizing the reliance upon old skills of navigation, based upon compass navigation.

Social media, computers/mobile phones

As will be seen below, the idea of hyperreality is starting to play a significant role in the development of adventure tourism products, though juxtaposition to this is a return to enacting past adventure experiences, which might also be associated with the growth of slow adventure tourism. Hyperreality products attempt to give adventure tourists virtual experiences of adventure and expedition conditions. The developments of headsets giving the illusion of a virtual world may have many new perspectives for adventure tourists. Rather like the simulators (more mechanical than cerebral) of the 1970s and 1980s, these new types of virtual products transmute the senses, offering virtual experiences without actually entering a real world. Another aspect of the current market is the idea of authenticity and even though hyperreality perhaps has potential for adventure tourist play, in truth it is not able to replace reality and that experiential feeling of climbing or surfing. It is suggested that hyperreality might have a place in marketing products, rather than duplicating or replacing adventure tourism:

While nothing can compare with actually standing on the edge of the Grand Canyon gaping into the chasm's shadowy depths, or wandering Yellowstone's trails listening to steaming geysers and bubbling mud pots, or drinking in the misty air of the Great Smoky Mountains, a new digital tool can get you closer than ever before – right at home!'

(Redal, 2012)

Experiential and Psychological Factors

The notion of postmodernism has impacted upon the concept of experiential adventure tourism. Experiential marketing is a new approach for attracting adventurers to adventure products (Dio, 2016). It seems evident that markets have splintered into submarkets and niches, making access to consumers more difficult and specialized. Experience has always been a part of any tourist product, but the emphasis is upon differences and exaggeration of the emotions and senses in experience. This seems to be closely connected with postmodernist hyperreality (Baudrillard, 1999). This is a product that is in essence more than real, temporal and illusionary.

The emergence of extreme sports is an aspect of this type of experiential paradigm, though it is evident that history is littered with risk takers and adrenalin junkies. That said, the emergence of new adrenalin experiences that have controlled aspects of risk appear to be increasing, perhaps reflecting the illusion of risk in adventure tourism. One such instance is Europe's longest zip wire situated close to Snowdonia National Park of Wales UK (ZipWorld, 2017). The author has had a number of comments made to him about this from adventure tourism companies, who see one future adventure market in these areas (national parks), with tourists using innovative adventure products encouraging the illusion of risk but with activities that are relatively safe, while surrounded by natural landscapes.

The development of bungee jumping is an example of experiential adventure (with limited risk of injury but immense sense of risk). It has matured in popularity and is still a staple for many operators, as exhibited by Queenstown, the centre of extreme sports in New Zealand. In many aspects jumping off a bridge or crane while attached to an elastic band is clearly hyperreality – not an everyday experience but it is statistically relatively safe.

The new extreme sport of wingsuits can be included in the category of hyperreality and experiential adventure. The notion of humans flying has always been a fantasy and many Hollywood films show superheroes flying, again reflecting a hyperreality experience. Jumping off a mountain whilst wearing a winged suit, thus emulating flight, must be a form of hyperreality, yet compared with bungee jumping the objective risk (deaths per jumps) is very high.

In essence, adventure activities seem to be pushing the boundaries of reality in order to provide experiences that are not obtained by normality. Climbing Everest might also be put into this category as a meta-experience and the number of tourists paying to do this seems to be another aspect of hyperreality in tourism. Everest is the highest mountain in the world and until recently was the preserve of a very few professional climbers. This seems to have been transformed into a new hyperreality for tourists who can pay to be guided up the world's highest mountain. It is a real experience but very far removed from normality. The perceived and objective risks seem to play a part in the drive and desire for this experience. The 'Death Zone' on Everest is named for a reason and the objective risk is high: one in ten climbers on Everest die. Is this a risk understood by tourist climbers? It is suggested that this is a high objective risk and would be unacceptable to most climbers, yet the adventure tourist seems to have a warped illusion of their invincibility and reality. Or do they?

It is also argued that the growth in adventure products and services appears related to the reduction of risk in Western society (perhaps also explaining the adventure tourist's need to climb Everest). Again this is related to aspects of experience and what customers perceive as risky, even if it is not. Fright, rather than fear, is perhaps the difference for most soft adventure tourists (low-level fear). It is suggested that the perceptual risk (fright rather than fear) of the adventure activity is the main experiential reason for engaging in these activities, which will vary depending upon the activity chosen. As will be discussed in Chapter 7, risk in adventure tourism is a 'product' of the package and a crucial motive for a customer; without it (real or unreal), adventure tourism and outdoor activities would lose much of their product appeal.

Conclusion

Product development is what companies do and AT and ODA are no different to any other sector. Adventure tourism and outdoor activities have changed significantly over the past 50 years and have been affected by many societal and technological developments. Postmodernism is a useful lens to examine the changes through market and customer demand. It seems evident that tourism products and markets have splintered into many different forms, including adventure tourism and outdoor activities. Even within the niche area of adventure tourism, further splintering has occurred and there have been many new developments from 'vanilla' activities such as surfing, sailing and climbing. These changes have been effected by a number of variables, including technological enhancements allowing greater access and use of new types of equipment in extreme environments, which in turn have pushed the envelope of most adventure sports.

With an intensifying and growing market have come cheaper products, through economies of scale and changing production techniques, further fuelling demand. The playgrounds for adventure tourism are physical features at tourist destinations, with every part of the globe accessible to adventurers, including the Earth's Poles and the highest mountains. This has led to the commodification and loss of authenticity of many adventure destinations and sports such as mountaineering. Societal changes linked to working practices have also fuelled the demand for more thrilling and exciting experiences, offering minimal risk and high thrills (fright rather than fear), which can be seen in the concept of the hyperreality of adventure products. Climbing Everest and wingsuiting and bungee jumping are emissaries of this notion. Even less risky and relatively safe adventure can be advertised as thrilling but safe for all the family, including zip wires, glacier walking and rafting, all connected to the current growth in soft adventure tourism products.

Questions

- What are the key factors that have led to changes in adventure tourism products?
- How important are technological changes in effecting new developments in adventure tourism?
- What is meant by the Disneyfication of adventure tourism and outdoor activities?

References

ABCW (2016) Home Page. Available at: http://www.abcwalls.co.uk/ (accessed 8 June 2016).

Baudrillard, J. (1999) *Share The Consumer Society: Myths and Structures*. Sage, London.

Beaumont, P. (2016) Wingsuit flying's most deadly summer leads to soul searching. Available at: https://www.theguardian.com/sport/2016/sep/02/wingsuit-flyings-most-deadly-summer-leads-to-soul-searching (accessed 27 July 2017).

Dio (2016) Virtual reality experiences, market tourism boards, convention and visitors bureaus. Available at: https://diousa.com/blog/virtual-reality-experiences-market-tourism-boards-convention-visitors-bureaus-travel-industry/ (accessed 17 October 2017).

Douglas, E. (2015) *Mountaineers: Great Tales of Bravery and Conquest*. Dorling Kindersley, London.

Drucker, P.F. (2001) Will the corporation survive? *The Economist* (Special Report), incorporated into: Drucker, P.F. (2008) *Management: Tasks, Responsibilities, Practices* (revised edn), Harper Collins, New York.

Dunning, J.B., Danielson, B.J. and Pulliam, H.R. (1992) Ecological processes that affect populations in complex landscapes. *Oikos* 65(1), 169–175.

Geoghegan, T. (2013) The story of how the tin can nearly wasn't. Available at: http://www.bbc.co.uk/news/magazine-21689069 (accessed 17 October 2017).

Grayston, G. (2017) Tent fabric: which is best? Available at: https://www.getoutwiththekids.co.uk/family-tents/tent-fabrics-best/ (accessed 26 July 2017).

Guardian (2015) Adventures in the world's deserts: readers' tips. Available at: https://www.theguardian.com/travel/2015/sep/24/desert-adventures-readers-travel-tips (accessed 28 August 2018).

Jones, J. (2016) Behold Mount Everest, reduced to adventure tourism. Available at: https://www.theguardian.com/commentisfree/2012/may/30/mount-everest-nature-adventure-tourism (accessed 27 July 2017).

Klein, C. (2014) Thor Heyerdahl's Kon-Tiki Voyage. Available at: http://www.history.com/news/thor-heyerdahls-kon-tiki-voyage (accessed 27 July 2017).

Leadbeater, C. (2015) The best desert holidays and tours. Available at: https://www.telegraph.co.uk/travel/activity-and-adventure/The-best-desert-holidays-and-tours/ (accessed 10 December 2018).

Marathon des Sables (2017) Regulations 2018. Available at: http://www.marathondessables.com/en/marathon-des-sables-maroc/2018 (accessed 13 October 2017).

MountEverest.net (2017) Food. Available at: http://www.mounteverest.net/expguide/food.htm (accessed 17 October 2017).

Quick, D. (2014) WingBoarding: an extreme aerial sport inspired by a Disney cartoon. Available at: https://newatlas.com/wingboard-extreme-sport/34181/ (accessed 6 March 2018).

Redal, W. (2012) Take a virtual hike in our National Parks! Available at: http://goodnature.nathab.com/take-a-virtual-hike-in-our-national-parks/ (accessed 17 October 2017).

Rogers, J. (2015) Inside Langjökull's Ice Cave: The Glacial Cavemen. Available at: https://grapevine.is/travel/travel-featured/2015/05/20/inside-langjokull-ice-cave-the-glacial-cavemen/ (accessed 10 December 2018).

Slawson, N. (2016) Base jumper's audacious leap from top of the Shard stuns onlookers. Available at: https://www.theguardian.com/uk-news/2016/mar/12/base-jumpers-audacious-leap-from-top-of-the-shard-stuns-onlookers (accessed 13 October 2017).

Total Iceland (2014) Death on a glacier in Iceland. Available at: http://totaliceland.com/death-glacier-iceland/ (accessed 13 October 2017).

Tummolillo, S.A. (2011) Glacier hiking: ice axes, blood, and rainbows. Available at: https://grapevine.is/travel/organized-tours/2011/06/17/ice-axes-blood-and-rainbows/ (accessed 10 December 2018).

UKC (2016) Directory – Indoor Walls. Available at: http://www.ukclimbing.com/listings/?t=wall (accessed 8 June 2016).

Under the Jungle (2017) Cavern diving. Available at: http://www.underthejungle.com/en/cavern-diving/ (accessed 13 October 2017).

VisitWales (2018) Venture Jet. Available at: Waleshttp://www.visitwales.com/attraction-search/attraction-search-results/attraction-search-details?id=1503592&latitude=1&longitude=1 (accessed 6 March 2018).

Voith, M. (2009) New fibers and membranes make outdoor gear lighter and more comfortable. *Materials For Adventure* 87(40), 15–21. Available at: http://cen.acs.org/articles/87/i40/Materials-Adventure.html (accessed 26 July 2017).

ZipWorld (2017) The nearest thing to flying: Velocity 2. Available at: https://www.zipworld.co.uk/adventure/detail/velocity (accessed 17 October 2017).

6 Management Issues

There is nothing so useless as doing efficiently that which should not be done at all.

Peter Drucker (management consultant and author)

Learning Objectives

At the end of this chapter the reader will be able to:

- understand and examine the complexity of management issues related to the running of a successful adventure organization; and
- analyse and prioritize which management themes are more important than others to the success of an adventure tourism organization.

Chapter Overview

This chapter presents the overall management principles for successful adventure tourism, covering the key operational and management procedures required to run an effective and sustainable company. It builds on all the chapters in this book which are in themselves parts of management strategy or have effects on management decisions.

Management, like adventure, has a multitude of connotations and definitions; its meaning is perhaps as nebulous as that of adventure tourism. It also raises questions of how important management is to the success of a business compared with the product being sold. There is a belief that many adventure tourism companies are started by those who had an interest or hobby in adventure tourism and/or outdoor activities, suggesting that they do not necessarily have management experience or any particular management skills (Donaldson, 2016).

Furthermore, there appears a trend in that some adventure tourism companies are eventually taken over by what can be described as business people with management acumen. Some successful companies that are now household names were started by people who just wanted to offer adventure activities to tourists, using their own experiences as a starting point. One notable company is Adventure Consultants, cited as being one of the first companies to take customers to the summit of Everest. The logistics of taking clients up the highest mountain in the world, by its very nature, must involve careful management of resources and personnel to ensure that resources and customers are able to reach the summit successfully. Perhaps it could be experience that engenders and evolves into the management of a company? There are several treatises that suggest that successful management cannot be taught, rather it is something that has to be experienced or is innate.

With the accelerated growth of AT there has been increased competition for both resources and customers. Consequently, there is a need to manage and control destinations regarded as honey pots (popular locations with large numbers of tourists). AT activities at these locations put pressure on natural landscapes, frequently causing overcapacity and damage. Management of resources is a key issue and directing activities and resources at destinations is important to its success. Competent management of tourists and activities will have a minimum impact on the environment whilst maximizing the customer experience.

Sustainable management principles are now essential and should already be high on a manager's priority list, ensuring that the use of resources reflects sustainable principles, as set out by a number of agencies and specifically the Global Sustainability Tourism Council (GSTC) and similar organizations (GSTC, 2018).

In essence, management is the use of human and capital resources to maximize the main aims and objectives of the adventure company or outdoor organization. The aims and objectives will differ depending upon the culture and philosophy of the company or organization (private or public sector). But, as with any attempt to define a concept, there are many different perspectives gleaned from different definitions.

Management is about people and styles of management differ depending on the personality and philosophy adopted by the manager. The particular style and philosophy of management can be both an advantage and disadvantage in how a company is run. There is also an assumption that companies are administered by either a board or a number of directors, with managers enacting the philosophy and aims of the company or organization. However, there is wide variation in the structure and philosophy of companies inevitably affecting management style. Pertinent literature seems to identify at least six styles of management, ranging from employee management control through to an autocratic management model.

Another management challenge is developing new products based upon old activities or creating new activities. New activities present management with challenges related to ensuring standards and quality. There will be little information relating to running these products and it may be necessary for managers to create in-house rules and regulations to ensure the quality of the customers' experience.

There are also positive and negative management practices. A successful company is rarely poorly managed and usually has a number of management attributes that are competent in dealing with certain areas of the business of an AT company or organization. Good management should be the aspiration of all companies, yet in many cases, especially with small self-starter companies, the level of management experience may be very limited. Poor management usually results in failure of the company, certainly in the long term.

Management Principles

Management covers many different areas of an adventure organization; it might even include leadership, though there are many who suggest that leadership is very different to management (Zaleznik, 2004). In essence, management is the control and development of human and resource capital, ensuring that a product or service meets a customer's expectations, as well as achieving the aims of the company or organization (Page, 2003;

Eagles and McCool, 2004). The following is a quote from John Kotter of Harvard University:

> Management is a set of processes that keep an organisation functioning. They make it work today – they make it hit this quarter's numbers. The processes are about planning, budgeting, staffing, clarifying jobs, measuring performance, and problem-solving when results did not go to plan.
>
> (Ratcliffe, 2013)

This is just one perspective of management but seems to cover many of the key features enabling successful management. Deciding which is best for an adventure organization really relates to what is effective for the company to deliver the adventure product effectively. However, team motivation has to be a primary aspect of any management approach and whether this is done from leading from the front or back is a personal choice of the manager.

Consulting firm Hay/McBer identified six management styles (Cardinal, 2015):

- autocratic directive;
- authoritative;
- affiliative;
- participative;
- pacesetting; and
- coaching.

There are a number of areas that managers need to control but these are not definitive or exclusive. They will also incorporate the immediate operational aspects of a company or organization (day-to-day) and long-term future prospects (strategic). Inevitably, managers will have employees to support them in delivering the aims and objectives of the AT or ODA to the customer. With large organizations the manager will be directed by a board or director/s who should be guiding the targets and evolution of the company. The two are not necessarily exclusive and management has power to influence the decisions made by the board or directors. The typical management actions are as follows (Page, 2003):

- operations environment (day-to-day);
- work environment;
- guiding and planning and designing future developments;
- leading or strategic;
- creative thinking;
- engaging resources;
- staff development and coaching; and
- organizational synergy.

There is also the need to manage the organization from two types of environments, internal and external, which will have different dynamics but will affect each other. Economic shocks such as the recession of 2008 will inevitably have implications for turnover and the number of staff at an organization and will impact internally upon a company in many ways. Efficiency drives and reducing costs may have effects upon structures, such as staffing and equipment purchase, but should never really affect safety standards (though safety is usually overlooked in periods of constraint as it is an unseen cost).

Internal management will affect how the external environment is approached, and the external environment will include aspects of marketing, supply chain, customer experience and safety. Effective communication and organizational structures need to be in place to ensure that employees know exactly what needs to be delivered to ensure the successful running of the adventure tourism company. The author, while pursuing research projects, has met a number of managers who have explained that their staff knew the procedures; however, during casual walk-arounds it was obvious that procedures were not being followed. Having internal staff codes and operational procedures is important but, as with safety, staff need to enact them and be vigilant of changes. Hence the need for managers to monitor staff to ensure that procedures are being properly enacted.

Organization of a Company

Depending upon the size of the company it will need to be organized into various departments or sections. Regardless of size, management principles are the same and will need to control human and material capital. These are not necessarily distinct areas but interrelated to deliver a product that is successful. There are myriad organizational structures, depending upon the size of the company and the philosophy.

There are also essential elements that every company will have to action: marketing, finance, supply chain, recruitment of staff, staff training, delivery of activities, product development and maintenance of equipment and transport and so on. These elements should be incorporated into how a company is organized and managed. Management structures and organizations have many models and approaches.

A variety of structures can be used to manage and organize adventure tourism and new concepts on the formation and control of structures. Morgan (2015a–e) suggested innovative approaches to control and management with the development of five possible assemblies:

- the traditional hierarchy;
- flatter organizations;
- flat organizations;
- flatarchies; and
- holacratic organizations.

The traditional model (Fig. 6.1), or hierarchy, 'is a very resilient management structure that has been so embedded in how we work that most organizations around the world are having a tedious time getting rid of it' (Morgan, 2015a). It is a model whereby directives are sent from the top to the bottom, without much integration and more akin to the dictatorial style of management, which may well stifle innovation and be slow to change to markets and customer needs.

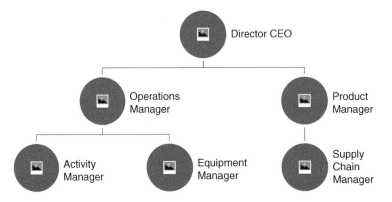

Fig. 6.1. Traditional Model (Morgan, 2015a).

'Flatter' organizational structures are another model where there is more communication between managers and staff and also between senior management and the directors or board. As Morgan notes, 'In flatter companies there is still a strong focus on communication and collaboration, improving the employee experience, challenging the status quo around traditional management models, and the like' (Morgan, 2015b).

The third model is a more compact structure with closer lines of communication so that management is visible and seen. 'Flat' structures are not really feasible for large companies and relate primarily to small and medium-size enterprises, especially those that are new. These would be linked to many of the smaller adventure tourism companies with fewer than 20 employees. The challenge with this structure is keeping focus and cohesion, as hierarchical structures do not exist, allowing factions and friction to develop.

'Flatarchies' are a juxtaposition of two polar-opposite structures having structure but also fluidity within teams. Figure 6.2 provides an idea of the structural format of this type of model. It is used by companies (e.g. Google) that see innovation as important but with a need for some managerial direction, whilst also encouraging innovation.

An adaption of the traditional model has led to the development of the 'holacratic' concept. This is a style that replaces individuals in hierarchical positions with groups or departments, thus reducing the dictatorial nature within the department but which may increase tensions between departments. It has some structure but allows individual departments a degree of creativity and democracy regarding how the company is run and decisions about its future. 'The basic goal with this structure is to allow for distributed decision making while giving everyone the opportunity to work on what they do best' (Morgan, 2015e).

A review of the organizational structure of these models shows them to be adaptations of current structures related to the size of the company and the management's philosophy. Adventure managers need to be flexible in changing the style of approach, matching human and material elements to delivering a product that provides customer satisfaction.

Personnel Development and Training

Personnel are the most important resource of a company's operations. AT and ODA companies cannot operate without employees, especially those with activity experience and skills. As with most

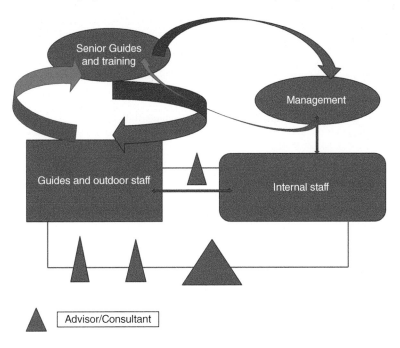

Fig. 6.2. Flatarchies Model (Morgan, 2015d).

evolving industries, academic and vocational courses tend to follow demand and AT is no different. In the UK there have been a number of academic courses related to the AT and ODA industries, in particular management courses that were developed with the idea of producing graduates skilled in management. This is in addition to a number of vocational qualifications in AT and ODA that can be obtained during these management courses (Box 6.1); for example, diving and climbing qualifications from sports bodies such as the Professional Association of Diving Instructors (PADI, 2018) and the British Mountaineering Council (BMC, 2018).

Adventure tourism and outdoor education courses were designed and redesigned to provide not only personnel but also to supply managers for these companies. Consequently management modules are a part of some of these higher education courses. This implies that when graduates complete their courses, they will be able to take part in some management aspects of AT companies, as well as being instructors and guides for various activities.

There is also a need for companies and organizations in AT and ODA to ensure that all personnel have the correct skills for the tasks to which they are assigned. This is not always the case and there are occasions observed by the author where staff were expected to organize and deliver activities for which they were clearly not equipped to supervise competently.

It is a management responsibility to ensure that employees are matched to the tasks for which they have appropriate qualifications and experience; this can include the need for companies to provide in-house training for activities that cannot be outsourced to other training companies. Sound management principles include regular training sessions and tracking renewals of qualifications.

Good management also inspires commitment and hard work from employees. As a manager, this usually means sometimes leading by example. However, there is a danger that this can then develop into dictatorial control and employees need to be given a level of responsibility matching their ability. An overbearing management can stifle creativity and commitment; there needs to be a certain level of trust between the employees and management.

Gender equality is now an essential aspect of personnel management and the move to support more females in adventure tourism has grown (Fig. 6.3). It has been demonstrated that females perform equally well as their male counterparts in the AT and ODA field, but they are not yet equally rewarded in AT. There are now processes to ensure more equality for women and the AT sector is improving the number of women who are leaders and managers within the AT and ODA industry (Box 6.2). ATTA has produced research and a report on this area and it is very encouraging to see that in the future more women will be holding and performing similar roles to those of men (ATTA, 2017).

Box 6.1. Management training.

This was a phenomenon that grew in the 1980s and 1990s and declined during the 2008 recession and financial crisis. It still has its place in the adventure niche for companies and also in terms of training adventure staff within a company or groups of tourism organizations. There are interesting examples of this being applied to adventure staff and the AdventureEDU programme at the Adventure Travel Trade Association (ATTA) is a good example of application for sustainable management and staff development. AdventureEDU 'provides training for governments, associations and individual companies seeking to deliver the best adventure travel experiences in a safe and sustainable practice' (ATTA, 2018) and they provide workshops for staff to attend, even providing training for specific destinations. Of particular interest is that which focused on Greenland

and Iceland, countries that have experienced an exponential growth in tourism: Iceland, with a population of only 320,000, now has over 2.1 million tourists (which could be considered as 'overtourism'). The training programme specifically targeted skills and management for safety and risk as well as building sustainable adventure communities.

Many management training courses provided by adventure companies are related to specific activities, providing employees with development skills in areas such as leadership, team building, talent management, change management, strategy, performance management and coaching (COTW, 2018).

Training given by outside organizations can provide a fresh insight into team dynamics and management of staff motivation, both of which are important management issues.

Fig. 6.3. Female adventure management student (photo: Ian Jenkins).

Box 6.2. Gender equality

Gender equality is now an important issue in AT and ODA and this seems to be changing, with more females being guides and managers within the industry. There are now sound illustrations of women being employed and starting their own businesses and achieving new feats in adventure tourism. The 3 Sisters Adventure Trekking Company in Nepal is a good example of this and the Empowering Women in Nepal (EWN) initiative (TIES, 2015).

Recent research has shown that AT has more females, with 38% on the boards of companies, generally more than for business, but prejudices still exist as well as different pressures to those on men, 'such as motherhood, chauvinistic attitudes … and a lack of female role models' (ATTA, 2017). Research shows an improvement in equality but there is still a dominance of males in adventure sports. In terms of leadership, research has shown that on average the numbers of females and males in leadership roles are equivalent.

The growth of female-only adventure companies also underlines this current division in adventure and the role that each gender has in approaching adventure tourism.

The press has a tendency to be biased against female explorers, especially if they have families. The death of Alison Hargreaves illustrated this, with the press suggesting that she was selfish and should have been at home looking after her children (Boggan, 1995; Barnard, 2002).

Reviewing the list of current female adventurers is impressive but the names do not stand out compared with those of male adventurers, again emphasizing the lack of media coverage. Perhaps the most notable on this list is Ellen MacArthur, the yachtswoman, who is known for long solo journeys. But many of the others cited by various sources are not that well known outside their activity circle.

Another aspect of sound management is ensuring that employees have their career aspirations mapped out and met by the company or organization.

It is also evident that in the case of AT the monetary rewards for staff are not the main motive for employment and therefore managers need to review what other fringe benefits can be offered, to ensure that employers feel they are contributing to staff development. Staff training will therefore vary depending upon the size and nature of the company.

Corporate Social Responsibility (CSR)

The World Bank and other prominent organizations have noted the need for the tourism industry to embrace CSR and it is evident that AT and ODA also needs to do so (Grenna *et al.*, 2006).

CSR seems to be a euphemism for sustainability and many of the characteristics of sustainability can be found within CSR. CSR is a move towards more ethical procedures by a company or organization, ensuring the protection of natural and social environments, such as the protection of wildlife while on adventure holidays (Fig. 6.4). (Many of the management issues relating to CSR are dealt with in Chapter 11.) A common allegory is that companies that adhered to CSR criteria might well lose a competitive advantage, but this view now seems to be fading in favour of companies gaining a competitive advantage by embracing more ethical principles.

Employee wages should be of a fair and reasonable level and ought to be related to the risks and conditions undertaken by employees. This is not always the case, especially those destinations in developing countries, e.g. Sherpas in Nepal (see Chapter 11). There are growing pressures on companies to ensure that resources are climate friendly, which usually means local supply chains and low carbon emissions.

The supply chain is an often overlooked feature of management. In AT and ODA this might not be so important compared with more global companies, but it still presents the management with ethical decisions relating to who supplies them with goods and services. This needs to be balanced with the cost of the goods; buying local does not always mean less expensive and sometimes may not be cost effective.

Management also needs to evaluate the ethics of running activities at certain destinations, especially those that may challenge cultural values of sacred landscapes; for example, Maori sites in New Zealand. Management of ethical issues is now an important success criterion for many AT companies, especially linked to destinations that have environmental and social constraints. It is then sometimes necessary to manage the access to the resource and coordinate with other AT companies to ensure competent management of adventure at a destination.

A number of companies have expanded CSR to include working with destination non-governmental organizations (NGOs) and local communities to improve their environment and living conditions. A review of the larger and more successful adventure companies shows them to have incorporated some of these aspects into their operations (Box 6.3).

Competitive Markets: Outdoor Competition in Local Areas

Globalization of adventure tourism is now challenging competition at the local level (Dicken, 2015). Management of competition is an essential element in running a successful company. It is somewhat different from the local authority ODA organizations that are often publicly owned in the UK, which

Fig. 6.4. Local whaling safari poster, Iceland (Source: Ian Jenkins)

have different customers to those of more commercially oriented companies. This will change the focus of management and priority. Even so, local authority ODA providers are under constraints of efficiency drives, especially following the economic crisis of 2008, and finding additional income is often a management priority.

Inevitably a competitive element of any company will be the price of the product being offered, which will have to be set closely to match competitors. There is a need to offer clients other advantages, including the company's reputation in the market, which can support higher prices paid by the customer. Cutting prices to undercut the competition is not a long-term strategy for success.

There is also a difficulty in deciding who the company's direct competition is and how to manage this. AT and ODA is now an expansive market and differentiated by a number of products and companies. It is also expanding in terms of new activities as well as global destinations and the management's raison d'être will direct the aims and objectives of the company. For example, global destinations are offered by some companies whereas others are more regional or national. Furthermore, there are many local and regional companies whose sole remit is to operate within a local radius.

Management of competition must focus on marketing and the quality of the service and products being offered. It is much more than advertising and the use of social media platforms, even though this has now become a ubiquitous and desirable

requirement, if a successful marketing strategy is to be designed. Much has been written about the impact of social media but there is now a surfeit of hard evidence of its success in helping managers to attract more adventure tourism customers (Moorman, 2015).

Viral marketing has been successful in stimulating new interest in a company's product. It seems closely related to aspects of word-of-mouth marketing, which was heralded in the last century as being extremely important to the success of a company's product. 'Viral marketing exploits existing social networks by encouraging customers to share product information with their friends' (Leskovec et al., 2007). Currently, social media platforms offer immediate marketing opportunities for companies and organizations, with the human-interest story still being one of immediacy with emotional appeal, complementing experiential marketing.

Maintaining a competitive image is also an important part of management and decisions are increasingly made based upon the available information found on the internet. A company's image is important and social media platforms such as Trip Advisor have become important information sources for decision making by companies and management; negative comments are also an important aspect of quality control of the product (Aula, 2010). However, perfect knowledge of the market by consumers is still a long way off, so managing reviews on these types of sites is an important aspect of quality control.

Financial Management

Managing this aspect of the company is essential and not always discussed in adventure literature. Finance is key to the delivery of the product and affects so many other aspects of the company. The available resources dictate the quality of the product and the strategy of the company; and being solvent and profitable are fundamental aims for any AT and ODA organization. Larger companies will have employees who have financial skills but ultimately it is the manager who has to decide how and where the resources will be used. There are many considerations to ponder and the following are some of the main sources of expenditure:

- buildings;
- vehicles;
- employees;
- adventure equipment;
- office equipment;
- services;
- insurance;
- marketing; and
- subcontracting.

Income is far more simple but even within this area there are different products that can generate income, such as:

- customer sales;
- shares;
- sponsorship;
- equipment and food sales;
- accommodation rentals; and
- grants.

These very basic headings of expenditure and income can be further divided into different sections such as capital and revenue costs.

The above items are the main components of an adventure centre but there are some vital issues that management needs to manage, the main one being cash flow. This is vitally important to success and often overlooked by new start-ups. It is merely managing outgoings and balancing income.

Often new start-ups and sole traders will simply look at the prices of the competition and then undercut them. It may well be that new companies have lower overheads and therefore can charge less for the activity, but the lowest cost is not always seen as the best product for a consumer. Low cost can reflect low quality and poor experiences. The essential component of financial management relates to ensuring that costs are lower than the income, but also knowing the range of prices that could be charged by a company. Profit margins are a relative issue and determined by the directors and managers being affected by a number of factors. Of significance are the brand image, the current market situation, geographical operations, type of activities on offer and availability of staff and equipment, etc. It is suggested that a company should:

> ... look in particular at your quality promise. Would you characterize yourself as: (1) Highest quality, no expense spared. (2) Value for money: good quality and prices are moderate. (3) Budget: no frills, appealing to a wide market. (4) Customer Audience: targeting intellectuals looking to engage deeply and have a learning experience, or possibly targeting more active, adventuresome trips with less cultural emphasis.
>
> (Beckmann, 2016)

As shown, the task is to match costs to income and although this is not always possible there may be a need to ensure that the activities continue, even if there is not enough cash to fund them. These should be rare occurrences and often such situations are dealt with by banks allowing a loan or extended overdrafts. However, these are not automatically available and will depend upon the company's profile, such as length of trading time, trading track record, well managed accounts, the outstanding income, actual orders and what future orders are likely to be. Usually loans are conditional on assets and a charge may be made on these by the bank for security.

Table 6.1 is a very simple example of costing an activity, which would then be multiplied by other products and bookings to give an overall profile of immediate costs, not forgetting the income and costs listed above. The £180 in Table 6.1 is residual

Table 6.1. Example of cash flow: canyoning.

	Cost (£)	Income (£)	Profit (£)
Staff: 1 guide, 1 assistant	180	(12 people @ £50): £600	
Minibus hire	80		
Fuel	20		
Equipment hire/cost	100		
Access to site	20		
Insurance (per day)	20		
Totals	420	600	
Profit			180

profit but this has to be offset by all the other elements of the list above of expenditure and income. This means that the actual profit on this activity might be a loss, depending upon the aggregate income from activities over the year.

Financial management for small and medium-size enterprises (SMEs) is usually the responsibility of the manager and it is rare that financial experts are used in a company, unless it is of some considerable size. Simple accounting systems and spreadsheets are used, as more sophisticated structures are expensive for small companies. The financial aspect of the company is an essential element of management that needs to be maintained and monitored on a regular basis. For some companies the manager and directors will have daily knowledge of the cash flow. Furthermore, accounts are in essence a success barometer for a company and close liaison with them is an essential requirement to ensure the health of the AT and ODA company.

Risk Management: Health and Safety

How do customers know that an adventure company or organization is safe? It still remains the case that there is little accessible information indicating to consumers that AT and ODA companies are operating safely, except for the assumption that all companies have to abide by state health-and-safety regulation, which depends upon the country where the activity is taking place. State health-and-safety legislation is an attempt to assure customers that a company is operating safely, but is generic rather than specific to each company and many aspects of adventure products are not precisely covered by these laws.

From the author's research and experience within the adventure industry there is an expectation that, if a customer has paid for a product, it should be relatively risk free and safe. Consequently, companies that fail to ensure this safe environment are often more likely to have numerous accidents and even customer fatalities (Piekarz et al., 2015). High accident levels and deaths of customers are not conducive to business success (truism) and the evidence highlights that deaths of customers usually relate to loss of income and eventually bankruptcy, aside from the trauma for the customer's family and relations and the prospect of a civil law suit.

Chapter 7 on health and safety explains the main principles that all AT and ODA operators should be observing to ensure that the risks to customers are reasonable (minimum risk environment). This means that higher-risk activities will have higher threats to a customer's safety, yet from a management perspective this is acceptable if the company is sanctioning a higher level of safety management. The very nature of adventure is about risk, perceived or real, and AT products do have activities that provide greater risks than other types of leisure activities, meaning that there are no guarantees of the customer's safety. Unfortunately, this is not always appreciated by the customer, hence the need to ensure, wherever possible, that all reasonable precautions are taken to maintain a level of safety that is commensurate with the activity, such as an appropriate ratio of instructors to clients (Fig. 6.5).

In developed countries there has been a growth in litigation, especially for businesses where incidents (injury or loss of property) have occurred to customers. It is now more likely that companies will be sued if injury or death occurs while participating in an activity.

Customers who originate from developed countries will expect a higher level of care than a global destination may offer, especially if it is in a developing country. It is the manager's responsibility to ensure that all due care has been taken to minimize risks (Piekarz et al., 2015). A common misconception among managers is that written waivers are guarantees of abdicating responsibility; under UK law they simply indicate that the customer may need to be aware of risks.

Further Considerations for Management

Legislation in different countries

Adventure tourism and outdoor activities are global products and this means that companies and hence managers may be operating in countries where the legislation in respect of adventure tourism and its customers may be very different. Management needs to ensure that the company meets all the legal aspects of the destinations, including health-and-safety conditions. The manager needs to consider employee working conditions and other aspects of operations such as taxes and purchase of materials. Liaison with destination organizations will be essential before setting up operations and selling products to consumers at global destinations.

Fig. 6.5. Adventure management: students leaning to surf (photo: Ian Jenkins).

Influence of associations, cooperatives and forums

Key sources of data and information are invaluable assets for a manager and knowing where to gather the precise information is extremely important for successful operations and future developments. Information is a resource and thus has cost implications, so that anything which improves the knowledge base of operations or future developments of the company has to be beneficial to the company's management.

What is usually missing for the manager is primary data that can be specifically used by an organization (see Chapter 3). The major industry associations and forums will have secondary data but this is very general, so there may be the need for management to collect specific data; the decision must be made either to spend resources on the company's own data collection or to employ a consultant. Consultants are usually employed, because the resources used to collect a company's own information are far more expensive than the cost of paying a consultant.

Being a member or setting up forums or cooperatives are useful management sources that allow the exchange of information and data relating to many aspects of a company's or organization's operations.

Conclusion

The chapters in this book are about management and the issues that affect management decisions. There is much debate about how to manage effectively and how management decisions affect an organization. In its simplest form it is really about ensuring that a company or organization meets its aims, which from a commercial perspective are usually about profit or, at the very least, breaking even. Adventure tourism management functions are the same as for other companies and organizations and encompass the efficient running of the organization. Globalization has provided a new platform and the need to manage resources further afield is a new challenge for many of the larger SMEs, as many of their operations are located outside the country of their headquarters. The management function is to ensure that capital and human resources work effectively together, assuring that a quality product is delivered that also provides full customer satisfaction.

Questions

- What are the key factors that make an adventure tourism company successful?
- To what extent are governing bodies a valid source for delivering a quality adventure tourism product?

References

ATTA (2017) *Out in Front: Tracking Women's Leadership in Adventure Travel*. Adventure Tourism Trade Association, Monroe, Washington.

ATTA (2018) AdventureEDU. Available at: https://www.adventuretravel.biz/education/adventure-edu/ (accessed 15 March 2018).

Aula, P (2010) Social media, reputation risk and ambient publicity management. *Strategy & Leadership* 38(6), 43–49.

Barnard, J. (2002) 'I loved her because she wanted to climb the highest peak. That's who she was.' Available at: http://www.theguardian.com/world/2002/aug/28/gender.familyandrelationships (accessed 28 August 2018).

Beckmann, C. (2016) Adventure Travel Trip Pricing – Part One. Available at: https://www.adventuretravelnews.com/adventure-travel-trip-pricing-part-one (accessed 20 March 2018).

Better Places (2018) Responsible Tourism Policy. Available at: https://www.betterplaces.nl/responsible-tourism/ (accessed 27 August 2018).

BMC (2018) Qualifications explained. Available at: https://www.thebmc.co.uk/qualifications-explained_0 (accessed 14 March 2018).

Boggan, S. (1995) K2: the final hours Available at: http://www.independent.co.uk/news/k2-the-final-hours-1597003.html (accessed 7 August 2017).

Cardinal, R. (2015) 6 management styles and when to use them. Available at: https://www.huffingtonpost.com/rosalind-cardinal/6-management-styles-and-when-to-use-them_b_6446960.html (accessed 12 April 2015).

COTW (2018) Home Page. Available at: http://www.callofthewild.co.uk/ (accessed 15 March 2018).

Dicken, P. (2015) *Global Shift Mapping the Changing Contours of the World Economy*, 7th edn. Sage, London.

Donaldson, M. (2016) The rise of the cool: starting an adventure travel company blog. Available at: https://www.idealsvdr.com/blog/starting-an-adventure-travel-company/ (accessed 7 August 2017).

Eagles, P.F.J. and McCool, S.F.A. (2004) *Tourism in National Parks and Protected Areas, Planning and Management*. CABI, Wallingford, UK.

Grenna, L., Hilbruner, R., Santi, E., Scuppa, G. and Vereczi, G. (2006) *Communication and Sustainable Tourism. Proceedings of the Global E-Conference and Summer Speaker Series on The Role of Development Communication in Sustainable Tourism*. World Bank Organization, USAID, UNWTO, Washington, DC.

GSTC (2018) *GSTC Criteria: The Global Baseline Standards for Sustainable Tourism*. Available at: https://www.gstcouncil.org/ (accessed 19 April 2018).

Lechner, F.J. and Boli, J. (eds) (2008) *The Globalization Reader*, 3rd edn. Blackwell Publishing, Oxford, UK.

Leskovec, J., Adamic, L.A. and Huberman, B.A. (2007) The dynamics of viral marketing. *ACM Transactions on the Web* 1(1), Article 5. ACM Digital Library, Association for Computing Machinery, New York. Available at: https://cs.stanford.edu/~jure/pubs/viral-tweb.pdf (accessed 14 March 2018).

Moorman, C. (2015) Measuring the impact of social media on your business. Available at: https://www.forbes.com/sites/christinemoorman/2015/01/18/measuring-the-impact-of-social-media-on-your-business/#206acc1c15e5 (accessed 14 March 2018).

Morgan, J. (2015a) The 5 Types of Organizational Structures: Part 1, The Hierarchy. Available at: https://www.forbes.com/sites/jacobmorgan/2015/07/06/the-5-types-of-organizational-structures-part-1-the-hierarchy/#2f1c79f75252 (accessed on 14 March 2018).

Morgan, J. (2015b) The 5 Types of Organizational Structures: Part 2, 'Flatter' Organizations. Available at: https://www.forbes.com/sites/jacobmorgan/2015/07/08/the-5-types-of-organizational-structures-part-2-flatter-organizations/#4f7e1e3b6dac (accessed 14 March 2018).

Morgan, J. (2015c) The 5 Types of Organizational Structures: Part 3, Flat Organizations. Available at: https://www.forbes.com/sites/jacobmorgan/2015/07/13/the-5-types-of-organizational-structures-part-3-flat-organizations/#5a20801e6caa (accessed 14 March 2018).

Morgan, J. (2015d) The 5 Types of Organizational Structures: Part 4, Flatarchies. Available at: https://www.forbes.com/sites/jacobmorgan/2015/07/15/the-5-types-of-organizational-structures-part-4-flatarchies/#268128396707 (accessed 14 March 2018).

Morgan, J. (2015e) The 5 Types of Organizational Structures: Part 5, Holacratic Organizations. Available at: Available at: https://www.forbes.com/sites/jacobmorgan/2015/07/15/the-5-types-of-organizational-structures (accessed 14 March 2018).

PADI (2018) PADI Course Catalogue. Available at: https://www.padi.com/courses (accessed 14 March 2018).

Page, S. (2003) *Tourism Management*. Butterworth Heinemann, London.

Piekarz, M., Jenkins, I. and Mills, P. (2015) *Risk and Safety Management in the Leisure, Events, Tourism and Sports Industries*. CABI, Wallingford, UK.

Ratcliffe, R. (2013) What's the difference between leadership and management? Available at: https://www.theguardian.com/careers/difference-between-leadership-management (accessed 7 August 2017).

TIES (2015) *Empowering Women through Adventure Tourism & Sports*. The International Ecotourism Society, Washington, DC. Available at: http://www. ecotourism.org/news/empowering-women-through-adventure-tourism-sports (accessed 7 August 2017).

VAA (2010) Virgin Group's Corporate Responsibility and Sustainable Development Report 2010. Available at: http://cdn0.virgin.com/doc/sustainability-report/lo_res/Virgin_Sustainability_Document_2010_Lo.pdf (accessed 14 March 2018).

VAA (2018) Responsible Tourism. Available at: https://www.virginholidays.co.uk/who-are-we/responsible-tourism (accessed 14 March 2018).

Zaleznik, A. (2004) Managers and leaders: are they different? *Harvard Business Review* 82(1), 74–81.

7 Risk and Safety Management

The dangers of life are infinite, and among them is safety.

(Johann Wolfgang von Goethe)

Learning Objectives

At the end of this chapter the reader will be able to:

- demonstrate a clear understanding of the importance of safety within the adventure tourism product; and
- interpret which aspects of safety should be prioritized in order to maintain a safe adventure tourism product.

Chapter Overview

Adventure is risk. Much media coverage relating to extreme sports has a narrative that includes the likelihood of incurring fatal or serious injury but also lauds the human capacity to challenge and conquer high-risk environments. Yet the ability of an individual to objectively assess likely risks is influenced by external sources of information from friends, colleagues, television and newspapers, creating subjectivity when assessing risk and risky environments. Furthermore, the growth of service sector employment, together with safer working environments and practices, have created 'pampered' western societies. Taking personal responsibility for our actions has lessened and there has emerged a blame-related and increasingly litigious society. This has contributed to recognition that the control of risk and safety is an important component of a competent management and a successful adventure tourism organization. This contrasts with developing societies where death, injury and disease are commonplace and life expectancy rates low.

It is asserted that adventure is a necessary part of our lives, making us feel alive. Only when we are faced with the potential for injury or death do we actually appreciate our safe existence and how fortunate we are. As has been discussed earlier in the book, adventure differs for each individual and will vary depending upon the personality and social circumstances of the tourist.

Safety can be seen as the antithesis to risk and adventure, which perhaps holds true for the adrenalin junkie and explorer. Such individuals rarely have a death wish even though some of the activities they participate in have high objective risk with a high probability of death. At the other end of the adrenalin scale are the slow adventurers whose needs as tourists have low objective risk with maximum emotional gain. One could say that slow and soft adventure tourism is a lot safer and possibly one of the reasons that some tourists engage with these products, but evidence suggests that we are poor at assessing risks, especially in environments that are new and alien to us. A classic illustration of this is at the famous Jökulsarlon glacier lake in Iceland, where tourists have been rescued from near-drowning or hypothermia, clearly not aware of the risks and ignoring warning signs (Figs 7.1 and 7.2).

What is evident is that companies that experience customer deaths have a tendency to fold and cease trading. There is clear evidence of this in the chronicles of adventure tourism development. One example is the company OTT, which guided tourists up Everest and changed its name after losing a customer, which also resulted in a protracted legal case taking a number of years to settle (Douglas, 2001).

It is evident that risk and safety go hand in hand and are not oxymorons but actually symbiotic in ensuring that customers maximize their adventure tourism experience. A successful adventure tourism package should comprise a balance of both qualities in proportion to the type of risk being offered.

The growth in the compensation culture emanating from the USA is increasingly being seen in the UK and Europe and is focused on monetary gain from injury and loss. This has affected parts of the

Fig. 7.1. Warning notice (Source: Ian Jenkins).

adventure tourism and outdoor activity markets and has also been fuelled by the media, who have, at least in the UK, previously challenged the safety of adventure centres and their regulation. Certainly, research of the adventure tourism market in the UK confirmed these concerns (Stevens and Jenkins, 1993). However, the current market seems to have made companies nervous and unsure of how to manage potential monetary claims by customers. It seems that an accident (defined as an unfortunate occurrence that occurs by chance) rarely occurs and there is usually someone who is responsible or an agent other than the customer that has caused the incident.

Litigation, Criminal and Civil Negligence, Health and Safety Law

For the past 30 years there has been an increase in litigation relating to accidents. There has also been a growth in accidents related to leisure and tourism activities, punctuated historically by major disasters such as Heysel (Belgium, 1985) and Hillsborough (UK, 1989) and other football stadium accidents, highlighting the potential for injury during leisure and sporting activities. The AT sector has also not been immune to these accidents. The deaths of 19 adventurers who were canyoning in Switzerland in 1999 (Lashmar and Karacs, 1999) and the whale-watching tragedy in Tofino, British Columbia, Canada in 2015 where six fatalities occurred (BBC, 2017), are both examples of adventure going wrong. Claims for negligence were filed against both companies, followed by calls to tighten safety standards. This also seems to have been linked to the quality of products and at the same time growing concerns to improve levels of safety in tourism and leisure activities. Again it is argued that a quality AT product is also a safe one ('safe' does not exclude risks). Further pressures have come from an expansion in adventure activities and outdoor activities.

Fig. 7.2. Tourists walking on icebergs, Jökulsarlon, Iceland (Source: Ian Jenkins).

Negligence is certainly not a new phenomenon in the legal systems of the USA and UK, but has increased in importance with ever larger pay-outs to victims of accidents. In addition, there has been a change to legislation in certain countries, especially within the European Union, which introduced the process of 'strict liability in tort'. This has meant that it became easier for plaintiffs to seek justice for harm caused by third parties or companies. Furthermore, changes to national safety legislation have meant more proactive and stricter control of risks and hazards by firms.

The Lyme Bay tragedy was a turning point for adventure and outdoor safety in the UK (Box 7.1). The events that led up to this tragedy were those of company complacency and poor safety management (Stevens and Jenkins, 1993). In many ways it was inevitable that a tragedy occurred, given the approach to safety taken by some adventure companies.

If there is evidence to suggest that negligence has been the cause of an accident, two procedures are usually followed: in the UK, these are criminal and/or civil litigation. Prior to the Lyme Bay tragedy, criminal prosecutions were historically difficult to secure. Usually the procedure involved examining the possibility of a criminal prosecution, which, if successful, increased the success of a civil prosecution (normally used for compensation to the victims or victims' relatives). Civil litigation is primarily concerned with monetary compensation and associated with the extremely large amounts of money paid out to accident victims. Criminal prosecution is much harder to secure and has to establish an action that is 'without reasonable doubt', whereas the maxim for civil prosecutions relates to the 'balance of probabilities', meaning in essence that a 51%/49% balance is enough to secure a successful verdict.

Most accident claims caused by adventure and other leisure tourism activities are to be found in

The tragic death of four teenagers while participating in outdoor activities could have been avoided had the St Albans Adventure Centre acted responsibly. Safety in Leisure (SaiL) research at the time, 1990–1992 (Stevens and Jenkins, 1993), found that many companies had varying degrees of safety standards and there was a need to ensure that a competent system for validating centres was in operation. There were private industry organizations or federations which did undertake safety assessments and the St Albans Centre had been vetted only weeks before the tragedy. However, many parents at the time were not able to judge which might be a safe centre for their children to attend.

As a result of this ineffective vetting, staff and instructors at St Albans were not appropriately trained or skilled to take children on the sea in kayaks. Consequently, due to their lack of appropriate activity qualifications and skill levels, they made simple mistakes, such as not informing the Adventure Centre of their route and when they would arrive and having no means to call for assistance or alert the Centre to any mishaps. The activity's risk assessments did not appear to exist; the weather and sea conditions were, that day, unsuitable for novice kayakers; and the coastguard had not been informed of the route.

Furthermore, staff who had recently left employment at the Centre had written to the manager and director, sometime before the accident, about the poor safety standards of the Centre, forecasting that a fatality was likely.

At the trial the director was found guilty of 'gross criminal negligence' and was given a custodial sentence, unprecedented for a case like this. This case was also significant as it was the first time that a 'controlling mind' of a company had been identified in causing criminal negligence.

The failure of the adventure industry to regulate itself effectively meant that the UK government devised an inspection system which was brought in for all centres wishing to offer outdoor activities to children. The Activity Centres (Young Persons' Safety) Act 1995 created the Adventure Activities Licensing Authority (AALA) to ensure that a similar tragic incident did not occur again and up until today none has (HSE, 2017).

---

the civil courts, but successful verdicts can be extremely costly for a company if they lose the case, even to the point that a company may have to close, due to significant costs and pay-outs to plaintiffs. Most companies and providers are fully aware of their liabilities and the need to ensure maximum protection to customers. The 1980s and 1990s created a fear factor throughout the adventure and outdoor industries, together with an unclear understanding of what exactly should be seen as a competent delivery of adventure activities. It is often forgotten that the courts will examine the actual activity and the level of voluntary risk that a consumer is assumed to have taken on. So higher-risk activities, such as base jumping and climbing, will have higher levels of personal responsibilities.

Negligence can be defined as failure to provide a duty of care to the adventurer, based upon a reasonable and prudent person, and a failure to ensure that appropriate actions have been taken, or no omissions made, which would have led to injury or loss for the customer.

The essential element is founded on what is considered 'reasonable'. Usually under civil action the test of reasonableness is that of an average person and the knowledge which would be needed while managing the activity. But this does not mean the average person in the street; rather, the test relates to what, for example, an average guide would be expected to have done related to knowledge, skill and common sense. Another expected attribute is foreseeability and whether the incident could have been foreseen given the circumstances. It is therefore the responsibility of the company or provider to act proactively on assessing risk and actively ascertain what is required, rather than wait until an accident occurs (Box 7.2). It is important to be fully aware of the risks and safety procedures of the specific activity.

Negligence has a number of different elements: intention to act badly or harm; actions that are deemed inappropriately performed; and non-action or omission. Each of these conditions can be seen as negligent, depending upon what a reasonable person would have done given the same circumstances. For example, failure to attempt to save someone who is drowning or has been badly injured are situations that could be deemed negligent (dependent upon the conditions and equipment available). However, one would have expected guides and instructors to have been trained in

Box 7.2. Adventure World, Lauterbrunnen, Switzerland

Switzerland is well known for adventure tourism, especially climbing and mountaineering. The new sports of adventure tourism are also found in Switzerland, canyoning being one, which in 1999 resulted in 21 deaths.

The cause of the incident was linked to poor weather conditions and a flash flood generated by a lightning storm higher up the valley that flooded the valley, causing a wall of water to sweep the adventurers away. There were three guides with the group and, as far as we know, they were appropriately qualified. The evidence suggests that they were warned by the authorities of the expected storm but chose to assess the risk as being acceptable or minimal. Unfortunately, the slogan that the company used was 'Much fun – no risk', perhaps a moniker that has significance today. 'No risk' just does not exist and sadly the risk here proved to be extremely high. Deaths of customers usually result in companies ceasing to exist and this was the case with Adventure World.

The Swiss authorities prosecuted the company and found the managers guilty of manslaughter.

As with the UK Lyme Bay incident, a review process established that there was a need to improve safety standards in these activities and, 10 years on from the tragedy, the Swiss authorities introduced new certifications under the umbrella of Safety in Adventures (SIA, 2018).

Safety in Adventures requirements:

- Employees must be trained, experienced and possess appropriate personal aptitudes.
- Equipment must guarantee the maximum safety to users.
- All activities should be planned out and action plans identified for emergency situations.
- Self-testing and regular evaluation of the conditions for safety are required.
- Third parties involved in any activity should meet the same requirements.
- All checks and assessments must be recorded.

As a result of these new procedures the fatality rate is similar to that of road traffic statistics, suggesting that standards have improved and an incident like 1999 is less likely to occur.

---

emergency situations and therefore it is necessary to demonstrate that they performed all that could be deemed reasonable and prudent to help the customer. Implicitly, if by attempting to save one customer others are endangered, then decisions have be taken regarding the many. This does not mean that all reasonable actions should involve risking one's own life in order to avoid negligence; rather, the focus is on the concept of what is 'reasonable' and what society would consider as normal actions taken to prevent an accident or injury.

Civil actions in the UK, Europe, USA and Australia are usually undertaken using the legal concept of Tort, which derives from the French word meaning a 'wrong'. New Zealand approaches accidents in adventure tourism in a different way in order to protect customers from negligent actions and subsequent compensation claims (Box 7.3). It is also interesting to note that New Zealand is a destination known for its adventure tourism.

Risk Assessments

A key transformation in maintaining a minimum-risk environment (MRE) in adventure tourism and outdoor activities safety has been the introduction of risk assessments. These are seen as key elements in a safety tool kit and have been introduced by legislative changes to safety and also industry codes of practice. They were established following inquiries into disasters and an identification of the factors that failed to create a safe environment. In Europe, the most significant impact has been the Framework Directive of 1989 which made risk assessments compulsory across all occupations (Cabinet Office, 2010). This was subsequently introduced into the UK in 1992, under the Management of Health and Safety at Work regulations, and embellished the 1974 legislation of the Health and Safety at Work Act (Piekarz *et al.*, 2015).

What is a risk assessment?

According to the UK government's Health and Safety Executive (HSE, 2016), risk assessment is about 'identifying sensible measures to control the risks in your workplace' and requires that you should 'think about what might cause harm to people and decide whether you are taking reasonable steps to prevent that harm'.

Box 7.3. New Zealand: No Fault Compensation System

Malpractice in New Zealand has a process unlike that in the USA and UK. Compensation for injuries and negligence are dealt with by government funds and therefore waiver the right of the injured party to sue a company or person for negligence, which completely replaces the common law system. The government has a system of compensating for injuries based upon aspects such as loss of employment and permanent effects of the injury.

This does not lessen the responsibility of a provider or company to ensure a 'duty of care' or a standard of care that is considered reasonable. Criminal negligence exists in New Zealand and adventure tourism companies and their personnel can still be held responsible for any negligent acts caused by a company or its employees. The outcomes relate to custodial sentences rather than compensation to the victims. There are also arguments to suggest that, as with other developed economies, customers are less willing to accept injury or fatalities and that there is now a lowering threshold of what the public consider acceptable. This has decreased the bar in terms of what may be considered negligent, so even though the civil aspects of negligence are unlikely to affect companies, criminal courts still require companies and individuals to be accountable (Charlish, 2004).

Risk assessment is about reviewing what might go wrong and the likelihood of it happening. Personnel or guides need to be fully aware of the activity being undertaken as well as the known risks and how these can be minimized. There is a misnomer concerning common sense: it is considered to be universal but this is not always the case and companies must not assume that employees have common sense. Some form of training is usually required before employees undertake risk assessments.

Risk assessment definitions can be adapted to a generic approach for adventure tourism, which might be a systematic process of evaluating the magnitude of risks related to hazards of the activity or activities that are likely to result in loss or injury, within an acceptable time frame (Box 7.4). The assessment should then enable immediate procedures and actions that will minimize the risk to an acceptable level for an activity.

Risk assessment should be carried out on a regular basis and it is recommended that in companies with over five employees, documents should be kept showing how the risk assessment was completed and the actions taken to reduce risks. Documentation can also be a form of protection in relation to negligence claims. However, the author has seen companies who fail to act on the recommendations of their own risk assessments, leaving them open to negligence claims.

The overall aim of a risk assessment is to try to achieve a minimum-risk environment. It is not possible to eliminate all the risks (which, sadly, challenges the moniker of Adventure World, Switzerland – see Box 7.2 above). But even with high-risk activities there must be attempts to minimize the level of risk. There are also a number of approaches that can be used for a risk assessment. There is no universal system and there is a wide variety of different methods, but these are all subjective assessments and will include human fallibility (Piekarz *et al.*, 2015).

Hazards in Risk

Hazards are not separate from risk and are a potential source of harm. They are not solely related to physical objects either, which is the common misunderstanding of a hazard. Water in a swimming pool can be considered the major hazard but has more than one possible effect on injury or fatality. Drowning is the main risk but others exist, such as water on the side of the pool that could increase the risk of slipping. How people behave in the swimming pool is also a hazard that might contribute to slipping or drowning.

There are different types of hazard, including: (i) physical hazard; (ii) moral hazard; and (iii) morale hazard.

Physical hazards

As has been discussed above, these are the most commonly understood form of risk identifications and recognized by most AT companies' risk assessments. They are likely to be the visible aspects of the physical hazard, such as the weather conditions, sea state, rock climbing routes, etc. Weather is a hazard depending upon the conditions that can

Box 7.4. Variety of risk assessments.

Although every company or provider is expected to carry out risk assessments on their activities, the model or process will differ notwithstanding the validity of each. The apophthegm is to minimize the exposure of risk to customers while participating in the activity.

Numerical approaches use a matrix table to evaluate the activity and its components. For example, in surfing, a key aspect of risk is exposure to water, relating to sea state, temperature, rip currents and size of waves. These variables would be given a numerical rating to assess which has a higher risk of causing harm. Others may include the number of surfers, board type (foam boards are usually used for beginners), etc. The table would then have scores for each of the hazards which, when processed, would produce a likelihood scale of causing harm or death.

Although this seems quite 'factual', there is considerable subjectivity in establishing the likelihood and severity of the hazard. Hence most risk assessment tables are indicators and only as rigorous as the ability of the person who has constructed them. There are many variations of numerical assessments, many emanating from manufacturing industry risk assessments (Piekarz et al., 2015).

Qualitative risk assessments do not have numerical scales but are related to a report-style review of likely potential areas of harm and numerical evaluation is usually absent. The process is to identify hazards and assess what risks these will have for the activity and the consumer. These focus more around discursive techniques, perhaps using staff members to identify areas of potential harm (Piekarz et al., 2015).

---

be a source of harm. It is an a priori assumption that hypothermia (risk) is caused by the natural hazards of wind and rain and exacerbated by inappropriate equipment that a customer may be supplied with.

Drowning is a water risk and the equipment and skill levels of the customer when entering the water increase or reduce the risk (Fig. 7.3). Risk assessments would evaluate these hazards and create a programme to minimize injury or fatality with these foreseeable outcomes.

There are less obvious hazards that are tangential to the common understanding of a hazard; for example, not leaving a planned itinerary with an organization or person so that if the adventurer fails to return or contact someone, they have provided information relating to where this person had planned to be. A planned itinerary reduces the risk, increasing the likelihood of being rescued. Lack of information can be seen as a hazard.

Moral hazards

This category relates to human actions rather than any physical element as a source of harm. Not developing a safety programme to ensure the minimization of risks could be viewed as a moral hazard, especially if the omission was deliberate because of a languid approach or a careless attitude towards management. In essence, it is acting without due regard to ethical behaviour (unreasonable). In civil cases, aspects of negligence

include a test to evaluate the moral behaviour of the plaintiff. Moral hazard can be linked to the three types of tort negligence: malfeasance (harmful act), misfeasance (careless act) and nonfeasance (lack of action).

Morale hazards

This type of hazard is one that few adventure tourism organizations may have considered. It relates to the attitude of company employees and their behaviour in the workplace. Some disasters can be attributed in part to this; for example, the sinking of the *Herald of Free Enterprise* in 1987 in Zeebrugger, Belgium (Bell, 2017). In the latter case, the Inquiry's findings showed that the bow door of the ferry had not been closed and hence not sealed when the ship left port. A number of reasons were attributed to the sinking, and one of the reasons (apart from the formal checking system to ensure that the doors were shut) was the attitude of the employees, who were overworked and lacked motivation to double check that the doors had been shut (Holmes, 2017).

The morale of employees is an important part of any safety programme and a safety system may well fail where employees lack motivation due to poor working conditions or an unsympathetic attitude of the management. To some degree, this may be due to a lack of tenacity by staff to be vigilant and ensure that the safety system is operating appropriately.

Fig. 7.3. Danger sign: rip currents (photo: Ian Jenkins).

High-risk Activities and Vulnerable Customers

There are many misnomers relating to adventure tourism activities, especially those of high risk and involving children. Customers who engage in high-risk activities have some responsibility, which means that they have assumed some degree of risk for the activity. But this does not mean that AT companies can be complacent. A higher-risk activity also implies that the company needs a higher level of care, such as closer supervision, higher ratios of staff and specific training or qualifications.

When children are involved in adventure and outdoor activities, a much higher level of supervision and control is required. Under UK law, if a child is under the age of 18 the adventure guide is, de facto, *in loco parentis*. This is why the UK AALA regulations were introduced and specifically apply to those operators providing adventure activities for children. Other countries also have this approach where children are usually more highly protected than adults.

A review of sports and recreational databases shows some interesting patterns in the UK. As discussed, it is still very difficult to obtain an accurate picture of risk and injury in adventure activities and much of the data relies on estimates, related to number of accidents and population statistics. UK mortality data of sports during the 1990s showed that the highest number of deaths was related to horse riding and the highest mortality rates of females were in this sport. The author has tested this perception of types of sport that have high mortality a number of times on students of AT and certainly horse riding is not seen as one of the main mortality rates in the UK. Climbing, aerial sports and boxing were indicated as sports resulting in high mortality (distorted perceptions in some cases, especially boxing, as there are only a few deaths).

Research on adventure tourism in the UK by Stevens and Jenkins (1993) found that there was evidence to suggest that the companies or operators who were providing high-risk activities were particularly cautious in their preparation and accident records. This supports the premise that operators of higher-risk activities are often more vigilant and better prepared.

Stevens and Jenkins (1993) also identified that most accidents at adventure tourism centres and companies occurred in free time and not while participating in the adventure activity, especially if staying several days or overnight in AT operator-owned buildings. Trips, falls and other accidents were the most common and very few reported accidents related to the activities in which the customers engaged. This is not to say that there are no serious injuries to customers participating in adventure activities but rather that, sometimes, fewer precautions are taken when the risk of the activity is lower. Companies should not assume that their customers are competent even with ubiquitous sports equipment such as bicycles: there are cases where companies have been sued because they assumed customers could ride a bike.

Health and Safety Regulations

An adventure tourism operation is required to abide by the health and safety laws and regulations of a country and these will vary depending upon the destinations. The 1970s saw the foundations being laid for many of the health and safety regulations found in developed countries, certainly within the UK and many other European countries. The EU has added to the amount of health and safety legislation and different aspects of health and safety management, increasing the volume of regulations and laws relating to safe operations of companies and organizations. As has been noted, the most important change is the requirement to have regular risk assessments, which was included in the EU Directive of 1989 (Directive 89/391/EEC) (OSHA, 2017).

The introduction of the Health and Safety at Work Act in 1974 was an important milestone for health and safety in UK work environments. Until then there had been disparate aspects of legislation relating to specific industries. Risk assessment was incorporated into this legislation to a certain extent but it was not explicitly identified. Many other countries at this time, especially those associated with the UK, also started to develop similar legislation controlling health and safety at work (Piekarz *et al.*, 2015).

How health and safety affected customers of companies was less clear, especially tourist and adventure activities. It is contended that much of the new legislation of the 1970s covered aspects of health and safety at work and tangentially would include members of the public who purchased a company's or organization's product. A pertinent question is: why was there a need for specific legislation such as AALA regulations affecting adventure activities?

Table 7.1. New Zealand Codes of Practice (Supportadventure, 2017).

	Sources of good practice	
Adventure activity	Activity Safety Guidelines (ASG)	Other sources (such as related ASGs, standards, codes of conduct or practice, factsheets and guidelines)
High rope course crossings	High wire and swing	MBIE Factsheet: Zipline attachment safety, 2013
		Outdoor Activities: Guidelines for Leaders, 2009 – high ropes course
High wire crossing	High wire and swing	MBIE Factsheet: Zipline attachment safety, 2013
Kite surfing		Yachting New Zealand Safety Regulations Part 1
Mountain biking		Outdoor Activities: Guidelines for Leaders, 2009 – mountain biking
		Queensland adventure activity standards – mountain biking
		Western Australia adventure activity standards – mountain biking
Mountaineering		ASG: Heli-skiing
		Outdoor Activities: Guidelines for Leaders, 2009 – mountaineering
		MSC alpine skills manual
		MSC guidelines and recording standards for weather, snowpack and avalanche observations
		MSC avalanche awareness in the New Zealand backcountry
Off-road vehicle driving – vehicles (not motorbikes) with engines greater than 50cc or weighing more than 1000 kg	Related	ASG: All-terrain vehicle
		Automotive Training and Events Association 'Code of Practice, 2012'
		Queensland adventure activity standards – four wheel driving
		Western Australia adventure activity standards – four wheel driving

If the primary legislation and codes of practice had been working effectively, would the AALA legislation have been necessary? In fact, there have been moves to repeal this legislation, as the 1995 Act was seen by some in the industry as heavy handed and unnecessary. However, even though the Young Persons Act is being readied to be repealed, the AT industry has hesitated, amid fears of another Lyme Bay tragedy occurring, especially if there are no inspections and validations of centres.

Codes of Practice

There now seems to be a move away from legislation and heavy policing of adventure and outdoor activities towards more reasonable and sensible approaches to managing adventure activities. Legislation is costly, not only for the state but also in terms of companies who are usually expected to pay a fee for compliance and also other aspects of implementation, such as employing consultants or other experts to advise them on the most appropriate ways to run an activity.

Codes of practice are in effect substitutes for legislation and are really a benchmarking system assuring the customer that a company is complying with the correct operational appropriate standard.

However, governing bodies for new AT activities (Table 7.1) are less likely to be established, meaning that there will be periods where an activity will lack a coherent standard of practice or delivery. This in turn results in managers of AT and ODA operations having to consider the idea of constructing a code or procedures to be operated in a prudent manner. Coasteering and canyoning are examples of this. When new adventure activities emerge, help might be sought from other organizations, especially health and safety agencies, which may provide advice on what would be considered necessary for a minimum risk environment.

For example, in the UK, the Royal Society for the Prevention of Accidents (RoSPA) is a respected NGO, allowing it to offer authoritative comment and recommend safe operating procedures, as well as making recommendations to minimize the occurrence of accidents. Many of RoSPA's members will sit on safety committees and would therefore have experience in evaluating the appropriate nature of a new procedure or action for an innovative AT activity. Consultants also play a part here as experts and should be used to advise a company, especially if they work within similar fields to that of the activity being proposed. A consultant also helps to spread some of the liability for risk.

Another approach would be to contact adventure guides or experts in the activity field or develop a focus group approach to the design of an operating document (Box 7.5). The Welsh adventure tourism market created a discussion forum when coasteering was first being implemented by local companies. Forums of local or regional companies are useful to share information and review what are reasonable precautions and actions needed to deliver an activity within a competent and safe environment. These forums are also important for coordinating activities at destinations that are becoming congested and overused. There are several examples of these in the UK which have been created to help facilitate a better customer experience and develop better working relationships for the commercial operators at the destination (Pembrokeshire Coastal Forum, Brecon Beacons Local Access Forum, Wales Activity Tourism Organization).

Another scheme to create safe practices for new activities would be a company's own guides and encouraging operational staff to discuss the requirements when a new activity is introduced. Either way, it is necessary for a company to show some systematic development of establishing a safety system to protect its customers, even if there are no guidelines or standards available.

Governing Bodies

In terms of the assessment of risks and managing a safe product, it can be difficult for AT and ODA operators to identify what is best practice, especially if the AT company is offering multiple activities rather than specializing. This is particularly important when a new AT activity combines a number of different sports, producing a new AT experience.

Governing bodies can be crucial in providing guidance and regulations for managers on how an activity should and will be provided (Table 7.2), including guidance on safety and appropriate qualifications for each instructor. They may also provide codes of practice for delivering this activity, which will be seen as the baseline for assessing negligence.

If there are no governing bodies relating to the activity, other practical means need to be used to try to establish internal codes of practice or guidelines for the activity (see last section).

Staff Training and Assessments

Safety policies and programmes are a key element in an AT company's health and safety tool box. But they are simply a piece of paper with written guidelines and instruction. Personnel and employees are the company's actors and vitally important to ensuring that these instructions, policies and strategies are imparted and acted upon. In fact, the staff are a company's safety programme and how they behave and perform reflects the company's ability to manage safety and reduce risks. Many, if not most, tragedies are connected to human error and these are often related to poor safety

Table 7.2. Adventure and outdoor activities: national governing bodies, UK (Inside Papertrail, 2017).

Activity	Governing bodies
Archery	Archery GB
Canyoning	UK Canyon Guides
Caving	Association of Caving Instructors
	British Caving Association
Climbing and mountaineering	Association of Mountaineering Instructors
	British Mountaineering Council
	British Association of International Mountain Leaders
	British Mountain Guides
	Mountaineering Council of Scotland
Cycling	British Cycling
	British Schools of Cycling
	Mountain Bike Coaching UK
	Cycling Association of British Cycling Coaches
Orienteering	British Orienteering
	British Schools Orienteering Association
Snowsports	Snowsport England
	Snowsport Scotland
	Snowsport Wales
Watersports	British Canoe Union
	Canoe Wales
	Canoe Scotland
	Canoe Association of Northern Ireland
	British Kite Surfing Association
	Royal Yachting Association
	British Water Ski
	Surfing Great Britain

management where staff are unprepared, incompetent or simply unaware of how to create a safe activity environment.

Management training of staff and assessments have implications on a number of levels. Training is time off the job and a cost to the company. Getting staff to be enthusiastic about safety and risk management is another challenge. Training is often viewed as a chore rather than part of the company's or provider's product. As has been discussed earlier, safety is a very important aspect of profitability, especially in the long run.

Companies need to approach safety training in positive and creative ways, to ensure that personnel are fully aware of the importance of safety and the operation of safety within the activity they are engaged in. There are a number of ways in which this could be used to help with staff training, such as:

- web-based assessment tests (these have become quite popular);
- spot-check evaluations;
- management checks at destinations and activity locations;
- mystery guest visits at activity location;
- multi-guide away-days with local companies sharing experiences; and
- peer assessments.

Qualifications and Experience

The emerging AT and ODA industry had little coordination and consistency of safety in its nascent years, which meant that customers could not choose a provider based upon any universally recognized safety standards or guarantee safety (Stevens and Jenkins, 1993). In addition, there were challenges in verifying the competency of the guides and staff for the activities they were delivering. Many had no first aid qualifications and in some cases the guides were not appropriately qualified (Stevens and Jenkins, 1993). The key to competent guides and instructors relied upon governing-body qualifications for adventure tourism activities. It was evident from the number of tragedies during these emerging years that guides and instructors were not always qualified for the adventure activity they managed.

With many types of governing bodies now providing appropriate qualifications and courses, the current industry is able to verify and check potential employees before employing guides and instructors. Furthermore, there is a requirement to ensure that these qualifications are up-to-date and to verify renewal at the appropriate time. Many adventure qualifications need refresher courses, ensuring that knowledge and skills have not been lost. Consequently AT and ODA managers should have a recording system to monitor qualifications of employees and ensure that regular updates and refresher courses are undertaken.

Experience is another area of adventure tourism that needs to be carefully evaluated. A common aphorism is that a person who has learnt on the job probably does not need to take qualifications to supervise an activity effectively. There seems some common sense in this assertion and one would consider that those who have had experience in supervising and guiding activities are more likely to be competent compared with newly qualified guides. Nevertheless this raises the question of what is more relevant and useful.

It is not acceptable to assume that a long period of experience is immediately equivalent to the same level of qualification offered by a governing body. It is possible that instructors can be employed without a competent level of skills and knowledge for the activity, though this is very unlikely. The maxim here is to exercise caution and have secondary sources to validate the competency of guides when required. Further assessments and onsite evaluations may be required to confirm competence of a member of staff.

Training Customers: the Foreseeability Principle

With the rise of the litigious society a new approach is needed when assessing customers' competence for adventure activities. As with the concept of common sense, companies should not assume that customers have average skill levels, even for activities such as riding a bicycle (as mentioned earlier). Staff should ensure that all customers are given some simple instructions relating to aspects of the equipment to be used, even if the customer asserts that they are experienced and know how to use it. In more hazardous conditions and activities, more intense assessments are needed, such as when snow climbing. Furthermore, when on location it is necessary to identify possible hazards and risks in a balanced and reasonable manner, and to point these out to customers. This should be done not to alarm, but from an educational perspective. The premise for this is to try to illustrate the 'foreseeability' principle, which is one of the tests used to assess negligence. In essence, prevention is better than cure.

Most legislation relating to accidents and injuries is based upon a person or company behaving in a responsible and sensible manner. Therefore, there is a need to be explicit, especially relating to certain activities carrying a high risk.

Conclusion

It is impossible to provide a completely risk-free environment for adventure. Adventure is associated with risk and stepping out of mundane safe environments is a primary motive for adventure tourism

and outdoor activities. Yet the sheltered societies of the western world do not prepare the customer for these objective risks; furthermore, fatalities while taking part in adventure and outdoor pursuits are not that infrequent, which raises the spectre of whether these incidents are accidents or negligent acts. The judgement will be grounded upon the premise of preventable outcomes and an evaluation of the level of control and foreseeability that was exercised by the manager. This level of control and risk minimization will relate to the objective risk of the activity. Pro rata, higher risks and vulnerable customers will require closer supervision, advanced qualifications and higher control levels. Companies need to ensure that staff have appropriate qualifications, experience and motivation for the activity it provides and that staff (including the manager and director) provide a standard commensurate with that of a 'reasonable and prudent person'. If this level is reached, the customer has received an appropriate level of care for the activity provided and the company has delivered a minimum risk environment.

Questions

- To what extent should safety be a key priority in the adventure tourism product?
- Evaluate the process of ensuring that an adventure tourism product can be made as safe as possible.

References

AAAS (2017), The Australian Adventure Activity Standards: a national approach to safety outdoors. Available at: http://australianaas.org.au/ (accessed 7 March 2018).

BBC (2017) Leviathan II whale-watching tragedy caused by breaking wave. Available at: http://www.bbc.co.uk/news/world-us-canada-40268008 (accessed 18 October 2017).

Bell, B. (2017) Zeebrugge Herald of Free Enterprise disaster remembered. Available at: http://www.bbc.co.uk/news/uk-england-39116394 (accessed 19 October 2017).

Cabinet Office (2010) Common Sense Common Safety. Available at: https://www.gov.uk/government/uploads/system/uploads/attachment_data/file/60905/402906_CommonSense_acc.pdf (accessed 29 April 2016).

Charlish, P. (2004) The Astrid Andersen Case. *International Sports Law Review* 4, 85–96, Sweet and Miaxwell, London. Available at: http://shura.shu.ac.uk/674/1/fulltext.pdf (accessed 18 October 2017).

Dacey, J. (2009) Adventure sports safer ten years after tragedy. Available at: https://www.swissinfo.ch/eng/adventure-sports-safer-ten-years-after-tragedy/986566 (accessed 18 October 2017).

Douglas, E. (2001) Death on Everest. Available at: https://www.theguardian.com/theobserver/2001/nov/11/focus.news (accessed 18 October 2017).

Holmes, G. (2017) Zeebrugge ferry disaster, 30 years on: deadly failings behind one of UK's worst peacetime maritime tragedies. Available at: http://www.independent.co.uk/news/uk/home-news/zeebrugge-ferry-disaster-ms-herald-of-free-enterprise-uk-30-years-on-maritime-tragedy-killed-a7583131.html (accessed 19 October 2017).

HSE (2016) *Controlling the Risks in the Workplace*. Health and Safety Executive, London. Available at: http://www.hse.gov.uk/risk/controlling-risks.htm (accessed 29 April 2016).

HSE (2017) Information for the public. Available at: http://www.hse.gov.uk/aala/public-information.htm (accessed 18 October 2017).

Iceland Monitor (2016) 'Totally irresponsible' tourists go iceberg-hopping with their kids at Iceland's Jökulsárlón lagoon. Available at: https://icelandmonitor.mbl.is/news/nature_and_travel/2016/02/15/totally_irresponsible_tourists_go_iceberg_hopping_w/ (modified 18 April 2016, accessed 30 March 2018).

Inside Papertrail (2017) List of National Governing Bodies for Adventure Activities in the UK. Available at: http://blog.papertrail.io/national-governing-bodies-adventure-activities/#.Weo12ItSzIU (accessed 20 October 2017).

Lashmar, P. and Karacs, I. (1999) Swiss river disaster: black wall of water swept down the gorge, crushing everyone in its path. Available at: http://www.independent.co.uk/news/swiss-river-disaster-black-wall-of-water-swept-down-the-gorge-crushing-everyone-in-its-path-1109256.html (accessed 18 October 2017).

ORC (2009) *Adventure Activity Standards (AAS) Guidelines for Dependent Groups, Legal aspects (Version 3. May 2009)*. Available at: https://outdoors-victoria.org.au/wp-content/uploads/2014/12/AASLegalAspectsMay09.pdf (accessed 20 October 2017).

OSHA (2017) *The OSH Framework Directive*. Available at: https://osha.europa.eu/en/legislation/directives/the-osh-framework-directive/the-osh-framework-directive-introduction (Accessed 20 October 2017).

Piekarz, M., Jenkins, I.S. and Mills, P. (2015) *Risk and Safety Management in the Leisure, Events, Tourism and Sports Industries*. CABI, Wallingford, UK.

SIA (2018) *Safety Concept*. Safety In Adventure, Berne. Available at: https://www.safetyinadventures.ch/en/safety-concept/safety_concept.htm (accessed 28 August 2018).

Stevens, T.R. and Jenkins, I.S. (1992) *Safety on Waterslides*. Safety in Leisure (SaiL), Swansea, UK.

Stevens, T.R. and Jenkins, I.S. (1993) *Adventure Tourism as Safer Product*. Safety in Leisure (SaiL), Swansea, UK.

Supportadventure (2017) Adventure activities – sources of written good practice information. Available at: http://www.supportadventure.co.nz/system/files/150410%20Good_Practice_Resources.pdf (accessed 21 October 2017).

8 New Adventure, Old Adventure

Then one day, when you least expect it, the great adventure finds you.

Ewan McGregor (Adventure in You, 2017)

Learning Objectives

At the end of this chapter the reader will be able to:

- illustrate the dissonance that exists between different adventure tourism products and market expectations; and
- apply a clear understanding of the stimuli influencing the adventure tourism market and how these are being adapted to meet customer demand.

Chapter Overview

Perhaps the greatest changes to the tourism market have been those of consumer expectations, lifestyle and new opportunities provided by technology developments. Additionally, the advent of cheaper air transport to a large variety of destinations has widened the horizons of both tourists and adventure tourists, and currently the low-cost carriers such as easyJet, Ryanair, WoW and JetBlue continue to increase access and demand for tourism. Concomitantly, adventure tourism has been affected by these elements, which means that new opportunities were being presented to the consumer. Also media coverage of different types of adventure and adventurers has raised expectation and ambitions.

This evolution of AT over the past 50 or so years has developed new types of adventure tourism products. This is partially true, but many activities that are now found in the AT industry have a long history of development and participation, suggesting that it is misleading to think that older adventure products have become moribund. Adventure is still adventure and it has to some extent become a metaphysical experience and perhaps in some senses liminal. Adventure is in essence a 'psychological experience' and differs from person to person, which possibly has not significantly changed

in meaning for centuries. There are aspects of adventure that are new (knowledge, transport modes, equipment and access to destinations) but for each generation the sociological aspects of adventure and risk still have the same tenets and traits, with each subsequent generation undertaking adventure experiences.

Old adventure might be seen as images of expeditions to conquer particular physical features or locations of the globe, but even repeating the same challenge could still be a new adventure for the current generation of adventurers. The Alpine Club and the climbing of the Alps might be seen within this context, but the Matterhorn and Mont Blanc still represent adventures for many current climbers, with similar objective risks and the likelihood of fatalities. New adventure may then be relative to a generation, related to the types of activities and destinations or landscapes that have not been explored or approaching expeditions in new ways (e.g. climbing without oxygen).

Ultimately adventure is a personal experience and new for the individual, even though it might have been achieved before. High-profile explorers and hard adventurers still 'push the envelope', by increasing the challenge or actually pursuing what is a new adventure – never performed before.

Slow Adventure

Slow adventure is a relatively new development in the adventure market and there have been a number of discourses concerning it (Box 8.1). As the name implies, it is seen as the antithesis of fast or hard adventure, taken to mean adrenalin-pumping outdoor sports, connected with speed, exhilaration and high risk. High-risk and fast-moving sports have been the driving forces of adventure tourism,

Box 8.1. A Case for Slow Adventure.

The 2015–2018 SAINT (Slow Adventure in Northern Territories) project was a Northern Periphery and Arctic (NPA) coordinated research and development scheme evaluating and developing new types of slow tourism. The main focus was on SMEs, encouraging these companies to make the most of the opportunities that this new form of adventure was offering.

The principal objectives were as follows (SAINT, 2017):

- To make SMEs more aware of new, lucrative markets which promote slow adventure activities.
- To increase SME awareness of how to effectively target these markets, through the use of new technology-oriented marketing models and clustering approaches, both local/regional and transnational.
- To develop SMEs' awareness of how to develop engaging, insightful and meaningful consumer experiences in a slow adventure context.

The countries involved in this research were primarily far northern hemisphere ones such as Norway, Finland, Sweden, Iceland and Scotland, with Ireland also being present.

The types of tourism to be encouraged would typically include elements of the following (SAINT, 2017):

- wild food;
- wildlife;
- comfort in the outdoors;
- creating and enhancing people's understanding;
- human- or nature-powered travel; and
- an enhanced engagement with place.

Clearly the idea of speed or stimuli which produce an adrenalin response was missing. It seems that many of the activities were related to aspects of cultural and ecotourism, once more creating a blurring at the margins of different tourist products.

---

perhaps reflective of aspects of the hyperreality and hypermodernity of a postmodern society. Since the 1990s this has been reflected in media sources such as the Extreme Sports channel and YouTube videos, which document the growth of adrenalin sports such as surfing, wingsuits, base jumping, free climbing, cave diving and other similar high-risk activities.

It could be assumed that 'slow adventure' is a misnomer not linked to adventure tourism and outdoor activities, but new adventure products do not have to be connected to high-risk activities, and adventure can be relatively safe. As noted throughout this book, adventure is a common theme in all cultures and reflected in the cultural stories that can be found in narratives for both adults and children. Within the Western tradition, classics such as *Robinson Crusoe* and *Moby Dick* are still read as adventure stories together with the more simplistic tales of Enid Blyton's 'Famous Five' (a form of micro adventures). Perhaps some of these can be associated with slow adventure, especially those involving journeys through dangerous places such as forests, jungles, deserts and oceans while confronting wild (wilderness) animals. In many ways slow adventure is a return to a less frenetic form of tourism (juxtaposition to hyperreality related to adrenalin sports).

Slow adventure tourism is the reduction of pace towards a more leisurely experience of the surroundings and an appreciation of the activity rather than the experience of the natural highs of the activity. However, being slow does not mean that customers cannot have a feeling of adventure. An aphorism related to this aspect is the importance of the journey, not just the arrival at the destination; what is tourism if it does not involve a journey? In many respects past explorers were exemplars of slow adventure. Transport systems were extremely slow and to reach the adventure destinations, such as the South Pole or Mount Everest, the journey often took more time than the expedition. Today's global transport system has increased the velocity of travel and journey speeds, to the extent that the journey becomes a chore rather than part of the adventure, perhaps creating a desire to return to slower forms of travel experience.

The destination can be experienced by slow adventure in a different way. For instance, being in one location for some time and developing skills, such as watching and listening, reveals the landscape often missed by fast adventurists whose focus is on the activity rather than the landscape. The Northern Lights experience (Fig. 8.1) is a slow adventure for many people and a number of destinations are developing similar products, including Greenland, Iceland, Norway and Scotland. Tourist boards have recognized the potential for these products and a review of some of their holidays shows a move towards slow adventure (Fig. 8.2) (Box 8.2).

Fig. 8.1. Northern Lights, Iceland. Source: Þorvarður Árnason, University of Iceland.

Fig. 8.2. Whale watching, Iceland. (Source: Ian Jenkins)

One of the possible reasons for this is that the largest tourism markets are those of an older age group, which has been identified as having the time and money to go on slower adventures. Also the inevitability of ageing reduces the propensity for hard adventure and the need to take part in softer and slower adventure products (Adventure Travel News, 2017).

The current array of 'slow' products is quite varied and seems to blur into other forms of tourism.

Whale watching is a part of slow adventure and it fits nicely into the development of this type of adventure tourism. It could also be considered a part of nature tourism. Watching whales usually involves a journey to some remote locations which could be considered 'wild-ness'. It can be seen as the need to see and feel real life and actually gaze on these animals through one's own eyes rather than the lens of a camera (hyperreality). There are no guarantees of success and some of the boat trips can be very disappointing and sometimes have no sightings. There are seasonal aspects to whale watching due to the migratory nature of these mammals.

Some of the top locations are Alaska, South Africa, Iceland, Scotland, Caribbean, Maldives and Mexico (Carwardine, 2017). The journey out to the whales' location is part of the experience and in many cases the passengers have to be dressed in protective clothing and safety gear to protect them from the elements. This all seems part of the package. But the sightings are sometimes only fleeting. Much of the time narratives are used to entertain the tourists and this is very much part of the experience too.

In Wales activities such as stargazing, walking the Brecon Beacons, canoeing on the River Wye and wildlife watching are marketed as slow adventure tourism (VisitWales, 2017). There also appears to be a move to encouraging family holidays towards this product. Slow tourism in France emulates these experiences, through the 'gaze' of the French cultural landscape, including French cuisine as part of the experience (Guzman, 2017).

There are many further examples of slow adventure tourism expanding at many destinations and it clearly seems to be an emerging market. Yet closer examination of slow adventure finds blurring with other defined markets, such as food and drink tourism, ecotourism, festival tourism, etc. It seems unclear where the boundary is drawn when it comes to adventure.

Exploration and Introspection

Exploration is a key attribute of all human beings as a means of learning. The unknown is something that needs to be known and this thirst for knowledge seems to have been energizing humans for eons. Classic historical expeditions are the pinnacle of this desire for humans to know; however, most individuals have some desire to explore, even if it is only within their spatial and cultural comfort zones.

Within adventure tourism and outdoor activities, there has been a strong educational link to learning and developing and current evidence has substantiated that being outdoors and being in the countryside helps the psychological mood and wellbeing of participants. Likewise, being active and participating in sports enhances mood receptors (serotonin) (BBC, 2017). Combining outdoor adventure with an activity therefore seems a common sense way to help people to improve their wellbeing and health. Moreover, the development of slow tourism is linked to the notion of taking time to reflect and meditate upon many aspects of one's lifestyle.

A future challenge for adventure companies will be to motivate the new consumers on the market: the 'iGeneration' and 'Generation Z', often seemingly caged in their bedrooms and only experiencing a virtual reality of the world of AT and ODA. Yet the hyperreality of adventure and outdoor activities may have a great potential to motivate the iGeneration to participate in the real world of adventure through utilizing media access points that they currently source (social media, virtual reality games and programmes) (Schneider, 2015). These will be the new adventurers, but how they will use adventure is still not fully understood. They probably have the best access to adventure products of all past generations, yet their lifestyles are increasingly sedentary.

The growth of adventure tourism is associated with the development of new markets, including the family unit spending time together. Many successful AT companies now have family adventure programmes, focused on activities such as rafting and glacier walking.

Adventurers can also have a desire for more introspective and spiritual experiences than physical adventures at a destination. Adventure tourists, e.g. surfers (Fig. 8.3), speak of spiritual experiences while riding waves and being 'in the eye of god'. This seems to imply that the activity and destination are affecting the internal processes of cognition

Fig. 8.3. Surfing. (Source: Ian Jenkins)

and the emotions of the adventure tourist. Adventure tourism is not just about physical attributes, but also the effects on the soul, mind and mood. Even hard adventurers have associations with spiritual introspection; playing with 'death' brings one closer to self and self-awareness and may be one of the reasons that adrenalin junkies need the experience to feel completely alive. That said, there is evidence to challenge the over-generalization of the adrenalin junkie; there are complex reasons for participating in extreme sports, which are never based on singularity of motive but multi-factorial composites (Kerr and Mackenzie, 2012).

Evidence is also found of paratelic (playful) behaviour of some extreme sport adventurers and may explain why these individuals pursue such sports to the limits (Pain and Kerr, 2004). The thrill of facing death and cheating it is saturated with introspection and elation. Fear is a key element and controlling it (or the illusion of controlling it) is part of the sport (Pain and Kerr, 2004). These adventurers are not the mainstay of the AT and ODA market, but tend to be clichéd as described in the media narratives of adventurers. Paratelic personalities can be linked to delinquent behaviour, as depicted in the original film *Point Break* (1991); the film narrative suggests an association between adventure sports and criminal behaviour, with bank robbery and surfing both providing highs,

through fear and thrills. The remake *Point Break* film (2015) exemplified the top end of the extreme sports of today and in some cases used the best extreme sport athletes (The Extreme Stunts of *Point Break*) (Murphy, 2015).

Mini Adventures

Mini adventures are a new phenomenon in the evolution of adventure tourism. Adventure does not have to be a long journey or necessarily made outside your own locale. Recently there have been adventure developments in day and short-time adventures similar to the growth of the short break market. The one-day adventure experience (incidental adventure) is quite common for many tourists who travel to destinations. Many adventure tourism companies that are domestically based rely upon the day or half-day market for what can be regarded as mini adventures. Bungee jumping is in this category and also the growth of coasteering and canyoning (Fig. 8.4). Both have increased in popularity having received extensive media coverage. Short breaks and mini adventures have also featured on media devices, helping to increase the demand for mini adventures.

Mini and micro adventures also lay the foundations for bigger, longer, more exciting adventures. They provide the adventurer with the skills and knowledge for undertaking more extensive adventure journeys.

Fig. 8.4. (a–d). Waterfall jumping, Neath Valley, Wales. (Source: Ian Jenkins)

The classic types of activities for micro adventure might include:

> … sleeping on a hill under the stars, wild swimming in a local lake, a cycling day out without forward planning, swimming in the local river, making a shelter in the woods and spending a night there …
>
> (Humphreys, 2014)

In many respects these seem to be linked to the frenetic pace of hypermodernity and the time famine that many people find they have. Quick one-hour adventures are compensations to fit into the hectic schedules of many jobs; they are 'doable', but do they create demand for a longer adventure holiday?

Some adventure tourism companies have recognized the idea of mini adventures and are running these as successful products. As a result, it is suggested that many mini adventures have developed into 'grand' adventures which are far ranging in destinations and the activities undertaken. Mini and grand adventures reflect a postmodern society with splintered activities and pastiches of the adventure genre all rolled into one.

Grand Adventures

Grand adventures are new forms of adventure tourism but not in the conventional sense. They are departures from the commercialized and cosseted products offered by many on the market. They are a form of disintermediation (see Chapter 2) and more akin to the wandering hippies of the 1960s (Independent, 2011). They seem to be characterized by spontaneity, the unusual, life changing, not goal oriented, eclectic and inexpensive (relatively). As Humphreys (2016) states, ' it is the most life changing, career enhancing personality-forging fun adventure of your life'. These adventures are about doing something different from the crowd and unique in many senses. Many are not those that would normally be advertised on an adventure tourism company's website. Examples from Humphreys (2016) include:

- cycling round the world on a penny-farthing;
- cycling from the UK to Tokyo for £1000;
- walking the length of the Nile;
- living in a treehouse for 6 months;

- driving around the world in a London black cab;
- first women to wild-camp solo at all the extreme points of mainland Britain;
- crossing Europe on a pizza-delivery bike;
- rowing the Pacific; and
- swimming 1000 miles down the Mississippi.

Expeditions such as these have made little commercial contribution to the tourist market or provided economic benefit to the destinations. They are inspirational, challenging the commercial products of adventure tourism. As grand adventures they are about personal development and the need to experience the reality of destinations and places without the control of commercialization. It is predicted that grand adventures will continue to grow and develop into even more unique quests.

Hyperreality in Adventure

A view held by some is that modernity has now transformed into postmodernism. Jean Baudrillard covered the idea in great depth with a number of treatises. One of the foundations of the philosophy was the subject of reality and hyperreality (Baudrillard, 1999). The feature of reality changing to hyperreality is part of the notion of postmodernism. Much of current reality is shaped by media experiences and written narratives, yet there is a clear divide between these and the actuality of the experience, such as wilderness (Box 8.3) or being adrift on an ocean. Watching YouTube, documentary films and Hollywood blockbusters like *Castaway* gives an impression of the reality of adventure, but to really know, one has to experience it. Furthermore, film is reality manipulated and therefore gives only a passing impression of reality and in one sense ensures a sense of 'hyperreality' (more than reality). Most films are designed not only to inform but also to entertain; they are not real, simply abstraction from reality. It is suggested that hyperreality is now a part of the adventure experience, where there is a notion of 'staged adventure' rather than actual adventure. This, it could be argued, is because reality is reflective of a form of authenticity. Being really true to an experience is as important as that of faked experiences and much of the debate on authenticity hinges around the subject of truth and actuality of experiences while on an adventure holiday.

Exploring this notion further raises questions such as: can an adventurer duplicate the exact experience of Scott's Expedition to the Antarctic or Shackleton's Expedition (Box 8.4)? The answer must be no: for exactness there would have to be a complete match in details including equipment, communication, food and transport (wooden sailing vessels). Furthermore, the remoteness of the Antarctic then is perceptively very different to now, and, perhaps the most important, the temporal element is lost and can never be retrieved. However, simulation or enactments of experiences are possible and in fact there are new adventure products that attempt to offer consumers just this. Sailing in a Viking boat is clearly an attempt to simulate what it must have been like for the early settlers in Iceland (Fig. 8.5).

Box 8.3. Wilderness in Adventure.

Wilderness is a key component of many adventure packages. It is a term much used and has, like tourism and adventure, changed over time. Where once the definition was thought to reflect landscapes or oceans untouched by human impact, the current image is somewhat different and in many cases inappropriate. Even the Poles and the highest mountains have some human impact through airborne pollution or access. There seems now to be a readjustment of this term away from the ideal of a landscape or seascape that has no human interaction at all. Much has been written and debated about what actually constitutes wilderness. Nature and wilderness can be seen as social constructs, even if they clearly have physical elements.

The last wildernesses on earth, the earth's Poles, have now yielded to human impacts and the adventure tourism industry is free to visit this ice-scape, mainly through slow adventure cruises. The marketing of these holidays seems to imply that the Poles are indeed wilderness landscapes.

The term wilderness currently seems to be identified by adventure markets as employing the notion of 'wild' rather than a simple landscape untouched by humans. Remoteness from human civilization is also a perspective that gives wilderness a timbre of adventure. There are still large spaces on earth that have little or no human settlement or visitors, ensuring a degree of 'wildness'.

Box 8.4. Footsteps of Scott, Amundsen and Shackleton – Hyperreality?

The Antarctic is no longer the remote wilderness it once was. Tourism has ventured to this part of earth and with it the development of different tourism products. Adventure is still linked to this locale, and with it the artificial simulation or idea of following the great explorers of the Antarctic. There are many examples of tours being offered around the exploits of the three most famous Antarctic explorers. Cruise liners now provide a white Christmas:

> Bing Crosby's recurring dream of a white Christmas was played incessantly and fulfilled at dawn. We awoke to the sight of the El Brujo glacier, a wodge of grubby ice inlaid among mountains scribbled with hieroglyphs of snow. Father Christmas, who arrived in an inflatable dinghy driven by an elf, wore a life jacket beneath his beard and shinned up the pilot's ladder. The Queen's broadcast was transmitted live. We sang carols in The Club lounge, next to the casino, summoning not only All Ye Faithful, but waiters with champagne.
>
> (Hughes, 2016)

The attempt is to emulate Scott's Christmas on the ice in 1911 but, as can be seen from the narrative above, Scott's Christmas was very different to this one. The commercialization of the adventure has given a hyperreality lift to what Scott and his fellow explorers might have felt or experienced before his departure to the South Pole.

The celebrations of Amundsen and Scott's centenary provided a platform to commercialize their achievements and this quote seems to summarize the blurring between reality and hyperreality:

> 'South Pole Champagne Flights'. What we would on the other hand like to highlight, while waiting for the 'Northerners' of the Arctic to get to the area (in approximately one month's time), is this somewhat obsolete not to say ridiculous fashion that raises energies and rakes as widely as possible so that the average tourist can come to ski for a few days on the Antarctic polar icecap and can if not compare, at least get closer to the exploits of two of the pioneers of the great period.
>
> (ExtraPoles, 2017)

Fig. 8.5. Sail Like A Viking. (Source: Ian Jenkins)

Likewise, the mountaineers of today who climb the old Alpine routes are not dressed in the clothes worn during the first ascents of the Alps in the 18 and 19th centuries. Worsted woollen suits and ties, fixed crampons and leather boots with nails in their soles and sash ropes without pliability are certainly not used by climbers today. But do these differences in equipment affect the experience? Well, yes, as clothing items like worsted suits and sash ropes give a whole other experience to how these mountains were scaled and certainly to aspects of increased risks.

Consequently, adventure experiences are to be found within these two realms of hyperreality and reality. The move to slow adventure is a move towards reality and seems to reflect a desire to experience aspects of reality seldom felt by developed societies, providing the opposite landscapes of where most adventure tourist live (i.e. large conurbations). On the other hand, the adrenalin-pumped extreme adventurers emulating past explorers are a form of hyperreality as espoused by Baudrillard's postmodernist world, and yet soft slow adventure expeditions also seem to challenge the notion of reality.

Space Tourism

Much has been written about this adventure product, yet little real adventure has happened for the majority of adventure tourists. The future of adventure tourism will embrace this development and if we learn anything from history it is that it repeats itself; the Grand Adventures of the 20th century will be repeated but on different frontiers. Space has all the elements related to pure adventure. It is unexplored, has high risks and few have experienced it. These are all the elements required to fuel the adventure market. Virgin Galactica has recognized the potential and it is now only a matter of time before the first commercial flight will take adventurers into space (Hall, 2013), although the projected launch dates are constantly being revised. Space walking and weightlessness will be the new sports, competing with the extreme edge adventures of today. For the majority of adventurers the availability of this product will be some time in the future, perhaps into the next century, and as with the initial exploration of the Poles it will be experienced only by a few.

Real Adventure Tourism versus Fake Adventure Tourism

The notion of hyperreality challenges the understanding of real adventure. Much could be discussed here, but the debate really rests with the individual and what they regard as an adventure. The essence of adventure appears to be linked to how it is perceived and the idea of what is actually being risked, if anything.

What are unreal or fake adventures? An insight into the development of fake adventures and post-truths might refer us to Instagram or Facebook, where posts are made by 'friends' who allegedly have been on an adventure such as climbing Kilimanjaro or trekking in the Antarctic. Verification of truth is somewhat difficult, as we are reliant on outside sources for information. Historically, there are many questions relating to explorers achieving their aims. For example, did George Mallory get to the top of Everest? It is possible but how do we know for sure?

Recently there has been a spate of alleged achievements that may be fake. The following excerpt illustrates how it can be done.

> Dutch graphic design student Zilla van den Born proved just how easy it is to manipulate people through social media when she spent five weeks hiding in her apartment while pretending to the world she was backpacking around south-east Asia … 'We live in a visual culture in which mediated information and reality are intertwined,' she said in a statement. 'What is reality?'
>
> (Coldwell, 2016)

An Indian couple in 2016 were banned from climbing Nepalese mountains after they are alleged to have faked their ascent of Everest. A number of complaints were made by fellow climbers that the couple did not actually reach the summit of Everest (Safi, 2016). It is not just amateur adventurers who fake adventure. In 2010 it was noted that an Austrian mountaineer alleged he had climbed K2, but his claim was later found to be untrue (Griffin, 2010).

Faking adventure is not a new phenomenon: historically there are instances. The Dr Cook expedition to Mt McKinley is an example of this, together with his claim to have reached the North Pole. Both assertions are shrouded in controversy, especially the climbing of Mt McKinley. The first person to reach the North Pole has been attributed to Robert Peary in 1909 even though Frederick Cook claimed to have reached this in 1908 (Tierney, 1998).

What is intriguing is: why fake it? For many adventurers this would be an anathema of the very essence of adventure – the experience. Certainly during periods of exploration in the 19th and 20th centuries there would have been quite high rewards from a monetary and social perspective. Yet adventure is really an individual achievement and one that is supposed to have emotional and cognitive effects on the individual, changing their perspectives on life.

Ethics of High-risk Adventure and High Customer Fees

The new phenomenon of cosseted high-risk high-cost adventures is fairly new, even though the 19th and 20th centuries had their fair share of armchair adventurers with lots of money. High-risk adventure has now become commodified into a tourist product and can be considered a phenomenon of postmodern societies linked to the axioms and discussions above. Fundamental to adventure is risk and whether the tourist really understands the concept of risk is contentious. There are many theories of risk perception and objective risks that illustrate the difficulty consumers have in understanding objective risks (Piekarz *et al.*, 2015).

Objective risks are those that can be measured and are likely to affect a certain category of individuals or activities. But these are not necessarily linked to the subjective risks that tourists usually perceive and will vary depending upon the personality of the tourist (Cater, 2006; Piekarz *et al.*, 2015).

Many hard adventure trips being offered do seem to venture into the higher objective risk category. As identified in Chapter 5, Everest has a mortality rate of one in ten ascents which, compared with other activities, is considered to be extremely high risk. There are ethical decisions to be made by companies as to whether or not the customer or adventurer fully understands the risks and to what extent the company conveys the objective risks to the customer.

Risk, then, is part of the adventure package and of many outdoor activities. It is important to the product and the way that individuals understand it. High-cost adventure holidays are not always linked with high risk but many are. Additionally, many high-cost destinations seem to be in wilderness or remote locations that have high objective risks. It is therefore incumbent upon companies to ensure that adventurers are able to cope with extremes of conditions and are fully cognate of exposure to high objective risks.

A review of companies advertising camping in the Antarctic seems to be at dissonance with this maxim, and some websites imply that no experience is required and that virtually anyone can undertake the trip. Inevitably there needs to be a balance between realistic information relating to objective risk and information that can deter the customer from purchasing a product. There is a delicate balance between advertising extreme adventure and commercial gains. Clearly, there is a need for adventurers to know the objective risks, and it seems that companies make consumers aware of this by ensuring that they sign waivers as a way of alerting them to the possible risks. It appears that the focus of bearing risk is on the customer and not the company. Nevertheless, an individual's assessment of risk is usually poor (especially inexperienced adventurers) without some valid objective data available. Under these extreme adventure conditions, UK law (and many other countries' health and safety legislation) would consider a higher 'duty of care' by companies, especially if the risks are considered high.

This ethical discussion is exemplified by 'Everesters' (tourist climbers of Everest) and the dying or dead climbers found en route to the summit. Should summiteers help dying climbers? In most normal circumstances this would happen but on many occasions climbers are just left to die, the bodies left *in situ* by companies. It seems once more that the hyperreality of adventure tourism kicks in and climbers are more focused on achieving their expensive adventure than helping fellow climbers. This quote seems to crystallize the debate:

> But can it ever be right, in the words of mountain leaders Chris and Simon Holloway, for climbers to 'carry on to the summit, while there are living people dying behind them'? Ben Yehuda, a former soldier, described his decision to stop as 'automatic'. For others, it plainly isn't. In an era when climbing Everest has become a form of extreme tourism open to anyone with $10,000, has human life come to count for less than the fulfilment of a personal ambition?
>
> (Henley, 2012)

It appears evident that the hyperreality of extreme adventure is causing a change in attitudes towards morality as well as challenging ethical conflicts.

The drive for adventure seems to be at variance with social norms and values. Yet if adventurers choose to enter what can be termed the death zone of wildernesses, then where does the responsibility lie to behave ethically, especially if the hyperreality adventure companies and adventurers have one goal: to reach the summit?

Conclusion

Adventure is a human trait and innate in all of us. The cosseted service world of the northern hemisphere countries has triggered a demand to experience risk, which has all but been removed from current developed societies. There have been a number of new developments, one of which, slow adventure, is juxtaposed with hard adventure. With an ageing population but a continuing desire for adventure, this less risky type of product has grown significantly, though it does blur the boundary with other categories of tourism such as ecotourism. It also seems that for many national tourist boards, the family market, regarded as demanding low-risk adventure products including soft and slow adventure, is extremely beneficial to a destination.

The advancement of technology and the need for profits has engendered a global adventure tourism market that has made inroads into every 'wild-ness' destination on earth. Adventure tourist demand has also grown in these adventure markets and with it the development of hyperreality adventure tourism, which dislocates social norms, encouraging risk taking that, for all intents and purposes, is sold as being 'relatively' safe. Furthermore, there has been a growth in adventurers wanting to emulate the illustrious explorers of the 19th and 20th centuries. What has changed is the illusion of protective packaging of adventure to wilderness locations, with high objective risks. It is suggested that the consumer society of Buadrillard's postmodernism has embraced hyperreality whereby consumers have little cognition of the effects of high risks (death zones). Death on Everest seems to be an acceptable part of the package for many Everesters. These new adventure products challenge management to question the ethics of providing adventure tourists with an opportunity to experience and participate in activities that have high mortality rates. Certainly, there has been a sterilization of ethical and moral principles by adventurers and companies, illustrated by the exemplar that reaching the summit is more important than saving a human life.

Questions

- What factors have affected the development of slow adventure tourism?
- Is there such a thing as fake adventure tourism?

References

Adventure in You (2017) 20 most inspiring quotes of all time. Available at: https://www.adventureinyou.com/travel-inspiration/20-most-inspiring-adventure-quotes-of-all-time/ (accessed 23 October 2017).

Adventure Travel News (2017) Adventure Travel Trends Revealed in 2017 Study (includes Albania). Available at: http://www.regproject.net/reg-news/2017/3/22/adventure-travel-trends-revealed-in-2017-study-includes-albania (accessed 10 December 2018).

Baudrillard, J. (1999) *The Consumer Society, Myths and Structures*. Sage, London.

BBC (2017) Exercise 'keeps the mind sharp' in over-50s, study finds. Available at: https://www.bbc.co.uk/news/health-39693462 (accessed 28 August 2018).

Carwardine, M. (2017) 10 of the best whale watching destinations. Available at: https://www.telegraph.co.uk/travel/safaris-and-wildlife/10-of-the-best-whale-watching-destinations/ (accessed 7 April 2018).

Cater, C. (2006) Playing with risk? Participant perceptions of risk and management implications in adventure tourism. *Tourism Management* 27, 317–325.

Coldwell, W. (2016) Fake-ations: when holiday adventures aren't what they seem. Available at: https://www.theguardian.com/travel/2016/jul/01/fake-ations-when-holiday-adventures-arent-what-they-seem (accessed 12 August 2016).

ExtraPoles (2017) In the footsteps of Scott and Amundsen? Available at: http://www.explorapoles.org/news/detail/in_the_footsteps_of_scott_and_amundsen (accessed 24 October 2017).

Griffin, L. (2010) Unfortunate deception on K2. Available at: https://www.thebmc.co.uk/unfortunate-deception-on-k2 (accessed 12 August 2017).

Guzman, P. (2017) Be a slow tourist in Gascony, France. Available at: https://www.cntraveler.com/story/be-a-slow-tourist-in-gascony-france (accessed 23 October 2017).

Hall, T. (2013) The future of space tourism. Available at: http://www.bbc.com/travel/story/20121025-the-future-of-space-tourism (accessed 23 October 2017).

Henley, J. (2012) Mount Everest: the ethical dilemma facing climbers. Available at: https://www.theguardian.com/world/shortcuts/2012/may/28/mount-everest-ethical-dilemma (accessed 12 August 2017).

Hughes, P. (2016) The ultimate white Christmas. Available at: http://www.telegraph.co.uk/travel/destinations/antarctica/articles/antarctica-cruise-footsteps-of-scott/ (accessed 24 October 2017).

Humphreys, A. (2014) *Micro Adventures, Local Discoveries for Great Escapes*. Williams Collins, London.

Humphreys, A. (2016) *Grand Adventures*. William Collins, London.

Independent (2011) Tune in to a spiritual highway. Available at: http://www.independent.co.uk/travel/europe/the-lonely-planet-journey-the-hippie-trail-6257275.html (accessed 23 October 2017).

Kerr, J.H. and Mackenzie, S.H. (2012) Multiple motives for participating in adventure sports, Available at: http://www.sciencedirect.com/science/article/pii/S1469029212000490 (accessed 23 October 2017).

Murphy, M. (2015) The extreme stunts of 'Point Break'. Available at: https://www.nytimes.com/interactive/2015/12/22/movies/point-break-extreme-sports.html (accessed 23 October 2018).

Pain, M. and Kerr, J.H. (2004) Extreme risk taker who wants to continue taking part in high risk sports after serious injury. *British Journal of Sports Medicine* 38, 337–339. Available at: http://bjsm.bmj.com/content/bjsports/38/3/337.full.pdf (accessed 23 October 2017).

Piekarz, P., Jenkins, I. and Mills, P. (2015) *Risk and Safety Management in the Leisure, Events, Tourism and Sports Industries*. CABI, Wallingford, UK.

SAINT (2017) The Project. Available at: http://saintproject.eu/projects/ (accessed 23 October 2017).

Schneider, J. (2015) How to Market to the iGeneration. Available at: https://hbr.org/2015/05/how-to-market-to-the-igeneration (accessed 23 October 2017).

Tierney, J. (1998) Author says photo confirms Mt McKinley hoax in 1908. Available at: http://www.nytimes.com/1998/11/26/nyregion/author-says-photo-confirms-mt-mckinley-hoax-in-1908.html (accessed 10 December 2018).

VisitWales (2017) Get active in the Brecon Beacons National Park. Available at: https://www.visitwales.com/explore/mid-wales/brecon-beacons/active-adventures (accessed 10 December 2018).

9 Cultural Perspectives on Adventure Tourism

Of all noxious animals, too, the most noxious is a tourist. And of all tourists the most vulgar, ill-bred, offensive and loathsome is the British tourist.

Rev. Francis Kilvert, 5 April 1870 (Plomer, 1938–1940)

Learning Objectives

At the end of this chapter the reader will be able to:

- contrast the key elements of cultural aspects of adventure tourism and their effects on adventure tourism; and
- fully examine the complexity and relationship of a country's cultural value and its relation with how adventure tourism operates at a destination.

Chapter Overview

Culture is what makes a destination appealing to many adventure tourists, sometimes in preference to its landscapes. Many of today's adventurers appear to wander aimlessly into tourist locales and wildernesses, apparently unaware of cultural traditions and mores and lacking the cultural skills to interact acquiescently with these communities. Although exotic destinations appear exciting and thrilling, in many wilderness areas can be found elements that are considered sacred and sensitive to indigenous peoples.

For thousands of years, the indigenous peoples of Australia regarded the wilderness as their homeland, maintaining a cultural connection to the landscape. Uluru (Ayres Rock) (Fig. 9.1) epitomizes this, but it has been seen by many tourists as simply a tourist attraction and an iconic symbol of the Australian landscape devoid of any connection to the first nation people. Today there has been a sea-change in how Uluru is viewed, used and recognized, ensuring that it has retained its historical significance as a sacred monument. Ascending Uluru is now discouraged due to its significance for first nation culture.

Likewise, New Zealand has many landscapes regarded as sacred and there has been much debate relating to the designation of a national park connected to the first nation peoples of North Island. Tongariro National Park was selected, primarily on the basis of its cultural status and sacred significance to the Maori, who use and continue to use it for religious purposes (100% Pure New Zealand, 2017).

Both of these examples engender debate on the ethical use and access to landscapes for adventure and tourist purposes. Furthermore, what types of activities should be allowed in such culturally sensitive locations and spaces? This chapter tries to illuminate some of the contentious issues of how adventure tourism and outdoor activities can be managed and made sustainable for indigenous cultures and adventure tourists. It also discusses how culture is now a part of adventure, even though most adventurers do not identify directly with it.

Adventure Tourism and its Connection to Religious Paradigms

Cultural destinations clearly have an important place in developing tourism, but how these places and spaces fit into adventure tourism is really a challenging debate. There are incidents of tourists creating religious anger by their ignorance or perhaps by blatant provocative acts; ranging from females exposing their breasts or bodies in photographs (Holmes and Weaver, 2015) to tourists wearing inappropriate clothing while visiting religious buildings such as mosques. It was even suggested that a recent incident on Mount Kinabalu, Malaysia, actually angered the gods and consequently caused an earthquake (Ng, 2015). These incidents illustrate that in some cultures religious beliefs are very powerful and go beyond those of more secular societies from which many Western adventure tourists now emanate. It is important

Fig. 9.1. Uluru (photo: Dr Jenny Evans).

that the social mores of a country are respected but for many tourists this is sometimes ignored because of the need to have an exciting experience. For the more commercial and commodified destinations this is less important, but even in Thailand, with its sexualized images, there are things that are not allowed such as exposing body parts while driving through Phuket, which might seem actually in keeping with the destination (Sherwell, 2016).

These incidents may seem distant from the activities of adventure tourism, but the Mount Kinabalu case was in a Malaysian National Park and had sacred significance for the locals and the wider Malaysian population. These locations clearly have cultural importance, which requires a greater need for respect by visiting tourists. An analogy might be the idea of climbing cathedrals and mosques just for the fun of it in the UK.

Culture can be part of adventure tourism and there are certain adventure tourism activities that are in themselves linked to religion and religious experiences. Surfing is one of those that has some spiritual framing and much of the language and expressions used relate to a type of spirituality akin to a religious experience (Norton, 2014). For example, the phrase 'eye of god' is used by surfers to explain the feeling of surfing a wave's tube, which is seen by many as the ultimate experience. Others state that they have religious or spiritual experiences whilst engaged in surfing (Serong, 2013; Blumberg, 2014). Participants often use terms such as 'brotherhood' and 'sisterhood', together with a kind of tribal language of their own, designed to describe the experience of surfing. The Hawaiians also saw connections to religious experience and much of their cultural background recognizes the sea and waves as connected to religion. Surfing, as we know it today, has its roots in Hawaiian culture and the lifestyle aspects of surfing can be linked to religious rites of the Hawaiians (Blumberg, 2014).

There are other adventure sports related to this aspect of religious commitment and obtaining the ultimate experience. Mountaineering, perhaps, has a drive towards an experiential spiritual high and, like surfing, has many adventurers who have made a lifestyle choice. Scaling a mountain, in some cultures, means to converse with the gods who were to be found beyond the clouds of the mountain top. Like the sea, mountains have religious and spiritual connotations (Taylor, 2005). There are examples of mountains being part of pilgrimages, principally in the Buddhist religion (Wood, 1992). Buddhist mountains have to be visited in the same way as pilgrims journey to Mecca and Rome. Furthermore, the motives for climbing mountains are argued to be akin to those of surfing and perhaps many other adventure sports. The experiential aspect of the climb/ascent could be likened to the ritual of attendance at a religious site, with all the preparation and expectation that goes into any trip of this nature. Mountaineering may also have connections with religious objects, such as the spire of a cathedral or church being similar to 'Alpine aiguilles' (rock needles) around Mont Blanc (Parker, 2008). The spiritual experience in adventure seems to be similar to many religions, with rituals and written instructions and 'pilgrimage' destinations (once-in-a-lifetime sites), and it can be argued that what mountaineers and surfers experience at their most extreme is that of a spiritual high.

Perhaps with the demise of organized religion in developed countries there has been transference to activities that duplicate or substitute the notion of a religious experience, which might explain the growing numbers of adventurers. Aspects of finding oneself have always been part of a religion and certainly that is what surfing and mountaineering provide for participants for some of the time.

Mountaineering and surfing are perhaps the adventure activities that are most cited as being possibly linked with religion and spiritual experiences. The literature has less emphasis on those taking part in other activities behaving in the same way, yet the simple act of walking in the wilderness does affect some individuals and provides profound changes in understanding and experiencing themselves. The current popularization of the concept of slow adventure fits nicely into this aspect, as the concept is that it is the journey (pilgrimage), not necessarily the activity, which is more important to the experience (Smith, 2017).

Destination Management and Cultural Integrity

National parks and landscape impacts

National parks are conceivably the most popular and notable places/spaces for tourists when visiting non-urban areas. They were purposely developed to provide access for tourists even though many of the primary aims relate to conservation. Consequently, it would seem perhaps a 'truism' that adventure tourism activities are commonly found within these park boundaries, given their wild landscapes and popularity for adventure activities. Certainly the appeal of national parks varies and also some forms of access. Switzerland has only one national park, Zernez, and this seems to have been used as an experiment in restoring habitats back to their natural state. It was designated in 1914 with public access restricted to the summer months, and no overnight camping or stopping is permitted within the park (Fig. 9.2). As a result, adventure tourism is restricted and little, if any, adventure is to be found within the park boundaries (SNP, 2014).

The Swiss National Park seems somewhat different from the majority of international models of national park, in particular those in the USA. The USA is attributed as being the first country to designate a national park, the aim of which was to allow public access, including many adventure tourism sports. 'The key concept of a public park open to all for benefit and enjoyment became the cornerstone of national park establishments worldwide' (Eagles and McCool, 2004, p. 30). An example is Yosemite National Park, which has some of the best climbing faces in the USA and was one of the first US national parks to be designated. In fact, one of the founding principles of the US national parks was to encourage tourism as a source of income to fund the conservation of the park (Eagles and McCool, 2004). Yet even within the USA there are conflicts between adventure tourism (climbing) and religious beliefs, a notable instance being the Devils Tower National Monument (Sink, 1996) (Box 9.1).

Among national parks that have been designated because of religious and cultural significance for the locale and the nation, there is Tongariro National Park:

… a dual World Heritage site recognized for its great natural and cultural value. The park has three volcanoes – Tongariro, Ngauruhoe, and Ruapehu, which boasts the world's only ski field within 500 m of an active volcanic crater.

(New Zealand Tourism, 2016)

It is interesting to note that this was gifted to the nation by the Māori because of the important sacred significance for New Zealand. The Māori also see much of the North Island as being sacred and

Fig. 9.2. Zernez National Park. (Source: Ian Jenkins)

Box 9.1. Devils Tower, Wyoming.

This physical feature has been featured in the film *Close Encounters of the Third Kind* and is a National Monument, but has also been used by climbers as it has some extremely challenging routes: 'Hundreds of parallel cracks divide Devils Tower into large hexagonal columns. These features make it one of the finest traditional crack climbing areas in North America' (NPA, 2018). However, the first peoples of America see this landform as a sacred symbol of their culture and still use it for religious purposes. Consequently, there has been a conflict between climbers and American Indians for some time.

This has presented the National Park authorities with some challenging management decisions in order to accommodate the two groups of users. The Park authority's note: 'American Indians have regarded the Tower as a sacred site long before climbers found their way to the area. As visitation increased and climbing became more popular, American Indian people have expressed concerns about recreational climbing at the Tower. Some perceive climbing on the Tower as a desecration to their sacred site' (NPA, 2018). In order to manage this situation the tower is considered closed in June of each year for climbers, when the American Indians use it for religious purposes, but this is voluntary and not mandatory for climbers.

---

spiritual and this presents a number of challenges for tourism and management of these resources. For example, what is an acceptable adventure tourist activity in a national park having sacred significance for first nation people? Undoubtedly, there are ethical concerns relating to accessibility and types of activities. As mentioned earlier in this chapter, in Malaysia taking one's clothes off and exposing the body in a sacred place is considered profane: would

these tourists have done the same at their own cultural icons?

As well as nudity, adventure activities present many different impacts. Many of these sacred landscapes are natural formations and using them for adventure tourism or outdoor activities must challenge management's approach. A consistent management policy to access and use national parks seems to be missing when faced with landscapes that have sacred or religious significance. That said, there has been a movement to recognize that nature and its accompanying landscapes are not devoid of cultural significance, implying that management needs to recognize, manage and protect these areas from over-tourism. Adventure tourism companies need to address the imperative of cultural impacts, especially as it is now considered an integral part of sustainable management (GSTC, 2017). Acculturation has been connected with tourist impacts for a long time (Murphy, 1991), but is a new impact in relation to sporting and adventure activities affecting local people.

The cultural mix and the physiognomy of a destination can combine to attract adventure tourists to a destination and may be a significant motive. The cultural attributes of a destination essentially add to the adventure tourism atmosphere, giving a new dimension to what the adventurer actually experiences from the activity. Whether it is climbing or surfing, there is nearly always a link with the locale and its culture, thereby imparting local cultural tenets to the adventure experience. Vice versa, there is an exchange of the tourist's culture on the destination, resulting in a two-dimensional cultural interaction. Hence adventure tourism can be a cultural experience as well as a physical one, depending upon the proximity and involvement of the local community. As with all cultural exchanges, they are usually unequal and the visiting culture has a tendency to be hegemonic or even effect major changes

to the indigenous culture (Box 9.2). Clearly this is the case of adventure tourism in the Himalayas:

> [Adventure tourism] has robbed and undermined the social and cultural values which have preserved the natural and social settings of the region for centuries. Now there is a growing disgruntled feeling in the minds of the new generation about the lifestyle and cultural values.
>
> (Farooquee *et al.*, 2008, p. 110)

Conversely, adventure tourism can assist the tourist industry in providing a balanced cultural exchange and equity between cultures and the UNWTO has recently seen the potential for adventure tourism to do this (GSTC, 2017). Given the discussion above on Māori landscapes, consideration must be given to how to manage the adventure tourism product, in particular the balance between adventure activities and their integration on and with indigenous peoples. For example, how many of the adventure guides in New Zealand are Māori and what is the effect of the cultural exchange between the tourists and the guides? Moreover, who benefits from tourism and what are the cultural gains (depending upon how this is defined) to the guides and indigenous people? The importance of culture and cultural exchange has been recognized by the United Nations and this has led to the construction of sustainability criteria that now include the effects of tourism on culture (GSTC, 2017).

GSTC and the importance of adventure tourism and cultural impacts

The Global Sustainability Tourism Council (GSTC) was launched in 2009 and has tried to establish a global system for measuring the sustainability of tourist destinations and companies. The GSTC index has a number of important criteria that it uses to evaluate a destination or company, including culture (GSTC, 2017). An exploratory research project by the author (Jenkins *et al.*, 2011) adapted the use of these criteria to evaluate companies and it was found that even the most sustainable companies managed a score of only 50% on the adapted index of GSTC (Jenkins *et al.*, 2011). The low scores were the result of ignoring cultural impacts and policies. Many companies had not considered culture as part of sustainability and this is where nearly all companies scored zero. It illustrates the point that culture has only recently become an important item for sustainability and therefore it is not unusual for many tourism companies, let alone adventure tourism companies, to disregard their impacts on the local culture.

Perhaps the arguments relating to cultural impacts are best explained when consideration is given to cultures that are very different from that of the tourist, though it could be said that adventure and adventure tourism are ubiquitous concepts and not solely limited to the Western hegemony of tourism, i.e. indigenous populations have adventure experiences and forms of tourism too.

All adventure tourism companies need to manage the cultural impacts of their operations and in particular their adventure tourist activities having an immediate effect on the culture of a destination. However, this is conditional upon interaction of tourists with locals and the importance of the destination's culture to the locale.

The Culture of Adventure Tourism

Adventure tourism and outdoor activities have their own cultures. As with most activities, humans create social bonding and rites of passage and adventure tourism certainly exhibits such characteristics. The narratives and argots relating to adventure sports provide the cultural base for adventurers even to the extent of types of equipment used. As shown in the section on religious paradigms above, both mountaineering and surfing have links to a spiritual experience and they can also be attributed to different types of clans, gangs or tribal aspects of the sport. Most adventure sports will have a separation and division between participants, which may be based on various criteria and gazes of the sport from novice to professionals and even to regional variations of these sports, giving rise to local cultural axioms.

The culture of surfing

The sport of surfing has grown exponentially from its inception in the 1950s and 1960s. Its history and culture are based in Hawaii, from where it was exported to the USA and then Australia. Originally it was an amateur sport, but very quickly in the late 1960s to early 1970s it started to become semi-professional, with moves to make it into a professional sport. The world surfing circuit known as the Association of Surf Professionals (ASP) was founded in 1976 and became fully operational in 1983; and in 2015 it changed its name to World Surf League (WSL) (WSL, 2017).

Surfing has now become a global brand and lifestyle, with icons such as Kelly Slater and Laird Hamilton epitomizing the success and popularity of the sport. Kelly Slater is perhaps the best-known star of the professional surfing circuit, but there have been many world champions prior to him. Female surfers too are to be seen on the circuit, but as with other professional areas it is much harder for them to become successful, as described in Chapter 16 (Fig. 9.3). Even at this level of surfing, there are tribal divisions, reflecting cultural differences in surfing. There are different competitions for shortboards and longboards and surfers who have taken another direction, riding Big Waves, such as Laird Hamilton rejecting professional competitions in favour of developing new ways to surf.

Surfing has also developed many cultural traits and cultural elements, such as clothes, narratives, language and territoriality. Many of the words in use are not common to normal language: 'stoked', 'over the falls', 'sick' and 'grommets' are common words heard by most surfers. Stories of the 'bad lands' in the West Country of England refer to certain surf breaks, where local surfers do not welcome anyone from outside surfing 'their' waves. This is more or less common knowledge to most regular surfers in the UK and similar examples are found in many other surfing destinations.

Laird Hamilton can be considered to be the Big Wave tribal leader (high priest) and he has attracted

Fig. 9.3. Jo Dennison, Welsh Surfer, Portugal (photo: Chris Vaughan).

worldwide support, developing the adventure sport of surfing into new directions, even featuring in one of the James Bond films (Surfer Today, 2012).

There are those who can be regarded as surf junkies, following the world's waves rather like the fictional charters in *Point Break* (1991). The film *Endless Summer* is a narrative of these types of surfers, always travelling and looking for different waves throughout the world. Today there are few places in the globe that have not been surfed and this has led to 'local surf crews' who frequent their surf breaks with a very protective attitude towards outsiders.

The type of board ridden by surfers also defines the tribal group. There is no longer one type of board, but a multitude of variants, such as short-boards, longboards, fish, fun boards, hybrid, gun and sup (Surfedukators, 2017). Some surfers will mix and match these boards, but many stick to what works best for them and there is now quite an ageing population of surfers (baby boomers), who grew up in the 1970s and 1980s, who are being replaced by 'young guns' on the waves.

The success of surfing and its cultural tenets have now been mirrored by the fashion industry. Surfing branding evokes an alliance of cultural identity with the surfing lifestyle, further exposing its culture to a wider market. With surfers the brand gives an indication of the tribe or clan you belong to. Surfers have their preferences for brands and now tend to reject more popular products, looking for niche and selective surfing images to represent their tribe. Surfing has become more or less mainstream and its 'vanilla' status is reflected in the large number of surf schools proliferating at most of the world's surfing beaches and surf destinations (Fig. 9.4).

Mountaineering culture

The culture of mountaineering reflects many of the cultural doctrines of surfing and from a Western cultural perspective perhaps has a much longer history connected to modern day adventure (Box 9.3). Mountains have a spiritual and cultural significance for many civilizations and the need to explore and climb them is probably a primeval urge. As with surfing, there is a clear ontology relating to the grouping of mountaineers and climbers, which has splintered into different sub-tribal groups, linked to differences in climbing philosophy and creating different epitomes and motivations within the sport. There has been a proliferation of films eulogizing

Fig. 9.4. Array of boards to hire at a local surf school, Wales. (Source: Ian Jenkins)

mountains and climbers, with supporting literature written about climbers and climbing exploits. Films like *Touching the Void* and *The Beckoning Silence* are tributes to some of the mountaineering feats and the culture of mountaineer.

There has also been a professionalization of the sport, with mountaineers earning their living from this activity through sponsorship and sometimes competitions, though these tend to be more related to climbing than to mountaineering.

As with surfing, the evolution of mountaineering has given rise to different philosophies. Over the past 30 years, free climbing has become popular and proponents such as Reinhart Messner, Alex Honnold, Tommy Caldwell and others have perfected this sport. Their feats have led to the climbing of the North Face of the Eiger in speeds that would have been unthinkable a century or even a half century ago. Climbing the mountain in 2 hours plus (Ueli Steck, 2 h 22 min; Dani Arnold, 2 h 28 min) seems incredible and is more like running than climbing. This tribal group of free climbers are seen as the elite and regarded as the extreme end of the mountaineering adventure sport. The push to be like the elite mountaineers has now engendered the commercialization of adventure climbing, selling holidays or climbing adventures to tourists, especially those wanting to climb the world's highest peaks. This commercialization has affected what elite climbers now consider to be elite peaks (DeFranza, 2008) rather than commercial peaks. There seems to have been a move away from the iconic tourist draw of mountains such as Everest to more technically difficult climbs, e.g. Nanga Parbat,

Kangchenjunga, the Matterhorn. Furthermore, there has been a growth in climbing walls and bouldering culture which is different from, if not supportive of, climbing per se. But all are linked to the cultural aspects of what it is to climb.

In addition, there has also been an extensive commercialization of mountaineering, with an expansion of product lines relating to equipment, particularly the branding of clothes, which are also worn as fashion items. Clothing sales in mountaineering gear, similar to those of surfing brands, are recognized as fashion icons for many non-mountaineers. The feats of elite climbers have engendered sponsorship of brands that are subsequently advertised to both mountaineers and non-mountaineers. By wearing the branded clothing, consumers are associated or show their allegiance with mountaineering; this cultural link even extends to TV presenters of news programmes and popular programmes such as the BBC's *Nature Watch*. Cultural brands (for example, Mammoth, Rab, North Face and Osprey) are frequently shown on these programmes, advertising mountaineering cultural emblems to a wider audience.

Gender Issues in the Culture of Adventure Tourism

History, it is said, is written by men. Consequently, many historical accounts of climbing are written by men. Likewise, adventure tourism seems to have had a male focus, especially activities that seek adrenalin experiences. Likewise, many sportswomen have been excluded from historic adventures and exploration, reducing greatly the number of well known heroines. Some sports do still have their female adventurers (climbing) and there were prominent female mountaineers during the Alpinism phase of mountaineering (Douglas, 2015). The emancipation of women and the current move towards greater gender equality have changed adventure tourism and more jobs and activities now have women participants. However, total gender equality is still some way off and currently the proportion of adventure tourist participants still favours men rather than women, especially in hard adventure.

The past couple of decades have seen many successful female adventurers but if one were to ask some pertinent questions relating to women's achievements, how many of the public would be able to name female adventurers and their achievements over the past 30 years? For example, who was the first woman to climb Everest, or to sail nonstop by circumnavigating the global, or who was the first woman to reach the North and South Poles? It is suggested that the names are elusive, reinforcing the hegemony of male culture in adventure.

Furthermore, the data relating to risk taking seems to support the premise that men are greater risk takers, which might explain why it is that men are the historical explorers rather than women. Or does this simply relate to the social constraints of women by men in order to control them?

There are and were women adventurers, and historical sources demonstrate that some women were able to throw off the shackles of a male-dominated society to take part in adventure activities. The following are some of the more notable female adventurers. Amelia Earhart should be a name instantly recognized by the general public. She was the first woman to fly solo across the Atlantic Ocean. She broke the women's world altitude record of 14,000 ft, but died while trying to set a record for flying solo round the globe. There were also several famous female mountaineers who achieved success. Although in an activity dominated by males, female mountaineers do exist, such as Maria Paradis and Henriette d'Angeville, who during the 19th century were the first women to reach the summit of Mont Blanc (see Box 9.3). They were separated by some 30 years and by their social standing, but 'in their different ways, Paradis and d'Angeville had blazed a trail for women climbers, and then by showing they could climb

competently without assistance from men' (Douglas, 2015, p. 101). Yet these women were excluded from the famous adventure clubs such as the Royal Society and the Alpine Club.

Nevertheless, there are growing numbers of female adventurers who have been heralded by the press, alongside male adventurers. For example, many people in the UK would be able to name Ellen MacArthur as an adventurer. As described in *Yachting & Boating World*, MacArthur

> … sailed single handedly around the world with the fastest solo circumnavigation of the globe, completing the 27,354 nautical mile trip in 71 days, 14 hours, 18 minutes and 33 seconds. She beat the previous record by one day, eight hours, 35 minutes and 49 seconds.

(Y&BW, 2016)

There were other female sailors who had achieved this feat but Ellen MacArthur is the latest to beat the record.

Many more females are establishing adventure records, such as Jade Hameister who, at the age of 16, skied to the South Pole in –50°C temperatures, demonstrating the resilience of women in adventure. She is the youngest person to have completed traversing the North and South Poles, plus the Greenland Ice sheet (National Geographic, 2018). Recently (2015–2017) Alienor Le Gouvello, in searing heat, travelled 5000 km along Australia's longest trekking route. These are just a few of the female adventurers who are pushing the limits (Guardian, 2018).

Clearly, there has been a sea-change in society's attitude towards women being exposed to risk. Adventure tourism has been fully embraced by females as a way to experience thrill and risk, signifying that in adventure they are just as capable as men.

Following increased participation by women in adventure, the market for female adventure tourism has expanded. There are also some emerging female heroes who are now well known, such as Surfer Bethany Hamilton, who lost an arm in a shark attack. She is a classic example of women now being more visible while participating in adventure sports, and being regarded as just as steely and as competent as men (Barney, 2016). While men have always been allowed and encouraged to be adventurers, historically women have not been encouraged to participate and although much has changed there is still more that can be done to reach adventure parity of females, especially in the elite aspects of adventure tourism. Top female surfers are not as well known as males and similarly in the adrenalin sports, including mountaineering. Women are there, but their successes are less eulogized.

Aspects of segregation in adventure also still seem to exist, which may or may not help with equality of gender. Currently, there are numerous companies offering adventure solely for women. Is this another separation of women within adventure and why is this the case? There is clearly a demand for these types of adventure tourism holidays by women, which seems to strengthen the trope that women still find it problematic to engage in adventure tourism alongside men. This suggests that equality of status still has some way to go in adventure.

Conclusion

Culture and adventure tourism are associated, but not necessarily in an obvious way. Adventure tourism and outdoor activities do have cultural traits and also the potential to affect local cultures in as many ways as conventional tourism products; in particular the exchange of views and ideas when adventurers and indigenous people meet. The consequences can be both negative and positive, depending upon how the exchanges are managed. Also landscapes are not neutral cultural locations but in many circumstances have cultural meanings and identity for both the indigenous populations and adventure tourists. Many companies fail to recognize that management of cultural exchange is part of sustainable development.

Many adventure tourism sports have a lifestyle culture to which participants adhere. The sport forms an identity and even provides a purpose in life which can be akin to a religious affiliation. Furthermore, some adventure activities provide a physiological stimulus that is similar to religious experiences resulting in a psychological/spiritual high. It is suggested that the move towards a more secular society in many developed countries may have created an internal need for a spiritual experience which adventure tourism may well provide for some participants.

It is also evident that within adventure and outdoor activities there is still discrimination between genders and cultural/social expectations, so much so that women are still not regarded as being on a par with male adventurers. This is changing and some parity is being achieved, but there is still much to be done to erase the discrimination and gender bias within adventure tourism.

The AT and ODA industry must address the aspect of cultural impacts and ensure that their activities at a destination create a balanced cultural exchange together with respect for the cultural landscape. Additionally, the adventure industry must tackle the cultural aspects of gender inequality and recognize that women have an equal part to play in management, participation and guiding the cultural future of adventure and outdoor activities.

Questions

- Why is culture now considered an important element at adventure tourism destinations?
- How can a company ensure that adventure tourism does not negatively impact on culturally sensitive destinations?

References

100% Pure New Zealand (2017) Tongariro National Park. Available at: https://www.newzealand.com/uk/feature/national-parks-tongariro/ (accessed 02 October 2017).

Barney, L. (2016) Bethany Hamilton: surfing with only one arm isn't as hard as beating the stigma. Available at: https://www.theguardian.com/sport/2016/aug/25/bethany-hamilton-surfing-espy-award (accessed 10 December 2018).

Blumberg, A. (2014) The spirituality of surfing: finding religion riding waves. Available at: http://www.huffingtonpost.com/2014/08/03/religion-of-surfing_n_5617472.html (accessed 29 August 2016).

DeFranza, D. (2008) 11 most dangerous mountains in the world for climbers. Available at: https://matadornetwork.com/trips/11-most-dangerous-mountains-in-the-world-for-climbers/ (accessed 27 October 2017).

Douglas, B. (2015) *Mountaineers, Great Tales of Bravery and Conquest*. Dorling Kindersley, London.

Eagles, P.F.J. and McCool, S.F. (2004) *Tourism in National Parks and Protected Areas, Planning and Management*. CABI, Wallingford, UK.

Farooquee, N.A., Budal, T.K. and Makhuri, R.K. (2008) Cultural and social impact analysis of adventure tourism in Himalayan River Ganga in India. *Indian Journal of Youth Affairs* 12(2), 104–111. Available at: http://environmentportal.in/files/Cultural%20and%20social%20impact.pdf (accessed 25 October 2017).

GSTC (2017) GSTC Criteria Overview. Available at: https://www.gstcouncil.org/gstc-criteria/ (accessed 2 October 2017).

Guardian (2018) The woman who rode Australia's longest trekking route – a photo essay. Available at: https://www.theguardian.com/artanddesign/2018/mar/11/the-woman-who-rode-australias-longest-trekking-route-a-photo-essay (accessed 10 December 2018).

Holmes, O. and Weaver, M. (2015) Malaysia to free British tourist over naked mountain pose. Available at: https://www.theguardian.com/world/2015/jun/12/british-tourist-eleanor-hawkins-three-day-jail-naked-malaysian-mountain-pose (accessed 26 August 2016).

Jenkins, I.S., Rios Morales, R. and Cevera, R. (2011) *Sustainability of websites using GSTC.* IGT Conference, Martinique.

MOCTCA (2013) *Nepal Tourism Statistics – 2012.* Government of Nepal, Ministry of Culture, Tourism & Civil Aviation, Planning & Evaluation Division Statistical Section, Singha Durbar, Nepal.

Murphy, P.E. (1991) *Tourism: a Community Approach.* Routledge, London.

National Geographic (2018) Teen skier completes gruelling 'Polar Hat Trick,' breaking world record. Available at: https://www.nationalgeographic.co.uk/travel-and-adventure/2018/01/teen-skier-completes-grueling-polar-hat-trick-breaking-world-record (accessed 10 December 2018).

New Zealand Tourism (2016) New Zealand's sacred mountains. Available at: https://media.newzealand.com/en/story-ideas/new-zealands-sacred-mountains/ (accessed 10 December 2018).

Ng, K. (2015) Malaysia shouldn't scapegoat the naked volcano tourists. Available at: https://www.theguardian.com/commentisfree/2015/jun/11/malaysia-scapegoat-volcano-tourists (accessed 26 August 2016).

Norton, A. (2014) Could surfing be the world's next religion? No, honestly it might be … Available at: https://mpora.com/surfing/surfing-religion (accessed 29 August 2016).

NPA (2018) Devils Tower. Available at: https://www.nps.gov/deto/planyourvisit/climbing.htm#CP_JUMP_5320585 (accessed 8 April 2018).

Parker, P. (2008) *Mountains and Mountaineering: their Spiritual Significance.* Farmington Institute, Harris Manchester College, Oxford, UK. Available at: http://www.farmington.ac.uk/index.php/ps57-mountains-and-mountaineering-their-spiritual-significance/ (accessed 10 December 2018).

Plomer, W. (ed.) (1938–1940) *Kilvert's Diary 1870–1879. Selections from the Diary of the Rev. Francis Kilvert.* Jonathan Cape, London.

Rai, D.B. (2017) Tourism development and economic and socio-cultural consequences in Everest Region. *The Geographical Journal of Nepal* 10, 89–104.

Serong, J. (2013) There is a god – and she wants us to surf. Available at: https://www.theguardian.com/commentisfree/2013/dec/04/surfing-spirituality (accessed 16 August 2017).

Sherwell, P. (2016) Western tourists fined for flashing their breasts on Thai island of Phuket. Available at: http://www.telegraph.co.uk/news/worldnews/asia/thailand/12080723/Western-tourists-fined-for-flashing-their-breasts-on-Thai-island-of-Phuket.html (accessed 26 August 2016).

Sink, M. (1996) Religion and recreation clash at park. Available at: https://www.nytimes.com/1996/07/01/us/religion-and-recreation-clash-at-park.html (accessed 5 March 2018).

Smith, R.S. (2017) 6 spiritual adventures to challenge the mind and body. Available at: http://www.nationalgeographic.com/adventure/lists/hiking-backpacking/spiritual-pilgrimage-hikes-adventures/#close (accessed 16 August 2017).

SNP (2014) Swiss National Park leaflet, Available at: http://www.nationalpark.ch/tasks/sites/en/assets/File/2014_01_23_Basis_E_k(1).pdf (accessed 17 August 2017).

Surfedukators (2017) Common types of surfboards. Available at: http://www.surfedukators.com/common-types-of-surfboards/ (accessed 26 October 2017).

Surfer Today (2012) The famous James Bond surfing scenes in '007 – Die Another Day'. Available at: https://www.surfertoday.com/surfing/7928-the-famous-james-bond-surfing-scenes-in-007-die-another-day (accessed 2 October 2017).

Taylor, B. (ed.) (2005) *Encyclopaedia of Religion and Nature.* Continuum, London.

Wood, F. (1992) Around Buddha's Magic Mountains. Available at: http://www.independent.co.uk/travel/round-buddhas-magic-mountains-chinas-buddhist-pilgrims-have-four-peaks-to-aim-for-frances-wood-goes-1533898.html (accessed 16 August 2017).

WSL (2017) History. Available at: http://www.worldsurfleague.com/pages/history (accessed 2 October 2017).

Y&BW (2016) 11 Top Females. Available at: http://www.ybw.com/features/eight-top-female-sailors-1410 (accessed 31 August 2016).

10 Adventure Lifestyles

Twenty years from now you will be more disappointed by the things that you didn't do than by the ones you did do. So throw off the bowlines. Sail away from the safe harbor. Catch the trade winds in your sails. Explore. Dream. Discover.

H. Jackson-Brown (1990)

Learning Objectives

At the end of this chapter the reader will be able to:

- distinguish between the competing genres of adventure tourism and their markets; and
- differentiate the categories of adventure tourism and the conceptual frameworks underpinning them.

Chapter Overview

Lifestyles are the way that we as individuals function in our societies. This is not a new concept but has evolved from the 1970s as part of societal changes and clever marketing, mirroring the 'VALS' system representing Values and Lifestyles. Lifestyle theory has been evaluated and discussed by many academics (Glyptis, 1981; Roberts, 2006) illustrating our understanding of how individuals adapt to society. Lifestyle is usually related to personality traits and leisure behaviours and is a useful method for profiling individuals. It differs from past concepts of profiling that reflected more structural aspects of society related to demographic profiles such as gender, age and employment. This is now regarded as somewhat outdated and has evolved into a more multifaceted lens, analysing our daily actions and the way we interact with our leisure and work environments. Adventure lifestyles are a development of lifestyle research and with the growth and development of a postmodernist society, sports and outdoor activities reflect many traits and aspects of adventure (Wheaton, 2004). Nonetheless the growth of tourism and, concomitantly, adventure products has been engendered by widening access to an increasing palette of outdoor activities.

Adventure lifestyles can be considered as just one of the many lifestyle choices that individuals make in a postmodern society. They reflect an individual's adventure gaze of the world and also dictate choices that are mostly adventure and outdoor focused. These are not necessarily large actions or decisions but rather small choices and changes that accumulate into bigger actions, such as a full-on expedition or adventure holiday. This chapter explores the influences that have affected and effected these incremental changes in society, allowing increased participation in adventure lifestyles.

Postmodernism Effects: The Firm and Adventure Tourists

Most operators in the adventure tourism market are SMEs or sole traders who have seen an opportunity to develop commercial products from a growing demand in this sector of tourism. The way that firms operate is different to that of 50 or even 30 years ago, as the sector has changed significantly in terms of customer demand and developments in technology. Postmodern and post-industrial economies have very different social and economic structures, eliciting new demands from customers, though some authors have suggested that many companies are still using antiquated marketing methods to reach consumers who have new lifestyles and want alternative products (Berner and Van Tonder, 2003; Williams, 2006).

Quality of delivery has also changed, with higher expectations in terms of service value and aspirations. Quality is a relative concept closely linked to monetary payment, but quality is not always price dependent, as poor-quality products can often be expensive and overpriced. As with all tourism services, it is difficult for consumers to evaluate quality before purchasing the product. This is one of the main challenges of the tourism industry and service sector; there is usually no realistic way to experience the product before purchase.

The proliferation of tourism customer review sites such as Trip Advisor has allowed consumers some insights into products, including those of adventure tourism. But this is 'post purchase' and is of no benefit to those customers who have purchased a poor product. It really only informs prospective customers about the service and the company's approach to delivery.

The adventure tourism market reflects changes in society and in particular the need for risk, excitement and stimulation. However, within the AT market, there are many variants of excitement and stimulation depending on whether the customer purchases hard or soft adventure. Matching customer expectation of the product is key to management achieving success in an adventure tourism organization and it is interesting to note that some companies market their activities related to customer ability. In Iceland, for example, a number of companies, when marketing mountaineering trips, identify the difficulty of the climbs and conditions, with their websites clearly stating what level of fitness and experience is crucial for the activity (IMG, 2016). This is mirrored by many other companies who provide customers with an idea of the skills and experience needed (Table 10.1).

With changes in customer expectation has come increased demand for more qualified adventure tourism staff to ensure peak experience for customers. Currently, many customers have experience of different types of adventure activities and there is an increasing need to ensure that staff have the appropriate

Table 10.1. Types of customer skill and experience (Arctic Adventures, 2017; Explore, 2017).

Company	Adventure	Difficulty	Suitability
Arctic Adventures	3 Day South Coast - Golden Circle, Jokulsarlon Glacier Lagoon & Ice Cave Golden Circle, Glacier Lagoon, Northern Lights, Ice Cave & Reynisfjara	Easy	Suitable for most people in fair condition. You have to be able to walk on uneven surfaces and hike for at least 2–3 hours at a slow pace with breaks. Trails are generally of good quality and glacier travel at a relatively low angle
Arctic Adventures	Grand Laugavegur Trek – 8 Day Hike Best Of The Highlands	Moderate	Suitable for those in good condition who are able to walk 4 hours at a low and moderate pace. Trails are generally of good quality and glacier travel at a relatively low angle
Arctic Adventures	Vatnajökull Wilderness, Djupa To Skaftafell Trek 6 Day Backpacking Expedition	Demanding	For someone in very good hiking condition. Trails generally in fair conditions but large sections of the tour might be off track. Glacier/snow travel on uneven ground with some challenging sections. Increased distance. We recommend the guests have the ability to cover 20 km a day on uneven trails and snow. A significant increase in elevation and some technical difficulty should be expected
Explore	Walking in New Zealand 20 days	Easy	Suitable for most people in good health, these easy walks are predominately on good paths, at low altitude and on undemanding terrain. Previous walking and trekking experience is not necessary
Explore	Self-Guided Cycling Canal de la Garonne 7 days	Easy to Moderate	This is ideal if you want to enjoy both easy and moderate rides on the same tour. You'll be cycling through flat or gently undulating terrain with occasional more energetic ascent
Explore	Annapurna Sanctuary 15 days	Challenging	You need to have a good level of fitness and trekking experience is recommended. Trekking days are generally longer, challenging and at higher altitudes. Terrain may be difficult and ascents and descents are often demanding

qualifications and experience to ensure a minimum risk environment whilst also allowing the customer to engage in risky activities (see Chapter 7). There has been a corresponding expansion in the number of educational courses linked to adventure tourism and outdoor activities, supplying adventure tourism companies with staff. Following a number of tragedies in the AT and ODA sector, there is also renewed pressure on the industry to ensure that staff have appropriate first aid qualifications and risk assessment skills.

Furthermore, green adventure and sustainable adventure are growing markets creating supplementary pressures on AT and ODA companies to deliver sustainable products as well as those that are safe and exciting. Although the evidence showing why clients choose 'green' adventure products is still not fully explored, ethical aspects (safety and sustainability) of AT products are becoming more important for companies.

Lifestyle Shift: Adventure Tourism

Earlier chapters of the book have discussed the expansion of adventure tourism, due to a number of economic and societal factors. Clearly, there has been a move towards more specialized types of leisure activities, sports and working practices (French, 2015). There has also been a rise in the professionalization of sport, mirrored in activities in the outdoors or adventure. Burgeoning tourism markets have assisted in these developments, with mass tourism markets becoming more fragmented and specialized, which is linked to increased demand for more adventure holidays and types of activities. The trope of the 1960s holiday of simply lying in the sun, recovering from manual work, is now somewhat clichéd and not reflective of the 21st century tourist (Bramwell, 2004).

There has been an emergence of new lifestyles imbued with leisure activities (Wheaton, 2004). The 1960s saw the development of new sports such as surfing, which began fashioning and creating the ideal of a surfing lifestyle. This has now become a lifestyle sport (Fordham, 2008; Veale, 2015) reflected in the many seasonal jobs within the sporting industry, including adventure tourism (Fig. 10.1).

Other activities such as hiking and mountain guiding now offer employment too. The mountain guide or adventure guide is another example of lifestyle development, where employment is also part of leisure activities, very much like the current upsurge in surf schools.

With this lifestyle shift has come the supporting superstructure of the industry seen in the growth of outdoor adventure equipment shops, some focused on very specialised markets; surfing again being a good example of this. Surfing has evolved from the 'surf bum' image to a mainstream adventure sport, embraced by the popularist 'vanilla' tourism market.

Fig. 10.1. Surf School, Wales. (Source: Ian Jenkins)

The proliferation of marketing and advertising, has assisted in making surfing more popular and mainstream. The magazine *Surfer Today* lists some 16 advertisements featuring surfing as the marketing image and agent to sell products. The most iconic and perhaps the most famous, and at the time most expensive, was the Guinness advert of 1998 (Surfer Today, 2017). Even the Ford Motor company's Volvo cars feature surfing adverts (Volvo XC60 'Seek Feeling' campaign of 2014) (Gianatasio, 2014), which, given the imagery of Volvo being known for its conservative mainstream characteristics (Grey, 2014), seems to support the argument of surfing now becoming mainstream.

The fashion and clothing industry has also helped the image of adventure by supporting adventure clothing brands and turning them into fashion statements (see Chapters 8 and 9). Marketing and the purchase of branded clothes have become forms of social marking displaying an image of adventure lifestyles. Brands such as North Face, Rab, Mammoth, Heli Hansen and 66° North (Fig. 10.2) are seen as expressions of lifestyle choices as well as being essential equipment for adventure participation.

Furthermore, adventure tourism and outdoor activities are significant products for most tourist destination markets, demonstrating the inherent and latent demand of AT and ODA. There also seems to be a growing demand for riskier 'wild adventure' destinations such as Iceland, South America and trips to the Poles (ATTA, 2017). Hot and tropical climates still attract mass markets but colder macroclimates seem to be in the ascendancy for adventure products, which might explain the substantial growth of tourists to Antarctica and the Arctic.

Adventure lifestyles have commercial and marketing potential, as seen with surf adverts and others such as the Pepsi Max adventure adverts of 1993 (Byrne 2005). One of the most iconic exemplars of this is the Volkswagen (VW) Camper Van, which for many symbolizes the spirit of adventure. The most recent example of this is the new BMW Sports vehicle which is being marketed with an adventure lifestyle label:

> BMW is touring climbing centres across the UK to target adventurous people with its X2 sports model … Emily Latham, experiential and sports marketing executive at BMW UK, said: 'The new BMW X2 is designed to allow people to go beyond the everyday commute and get adventurous.'
>
> (Degan, 2018)

Fig. 10.2. Advertisement for 66° North. (Source: Ian Jenkins)

The VW van (Fig. 10.3) can be associated with older adventure tourists (baby boomer generation, 1950s and 1960s) but also seems to support the image of current adventure lifestyles.

Hollywood films also seem to reflect the need for adventure. The film *The Beach* can be regarded as a seminal portrayal of a quest for this, characterizing the need to escape from the more commercial aspects of mass tourism. In many respects it is a throwback to the hippy lifestyle of the 1960s (Wainwright, 2013).

A review of Twitter, Facebook and other social media sites also supports the growth of an adventure lifestyle. The number of global tourists who are exploring as a 'way of life' has increased, many working their way around the globe. In many respects it has become an industry in itself, one of those 'musts' on the bucket list such as diving off coral reefs. The 'gap year' has also helped to foster

Fig. 10.3. Volkswagen Camper Van. (Source: Ian Jenkins)

an adventure lifestyle, energizing demand and creating appetites for further exploration, especially once students have obtained their initial qualifications. The sustainable development charity Raleigh International, the variously sponsored 'Tall Ships' races and similar organizations and events have added to an expansion in opportunities for adventure, providing a stimulus for further adventures and fostering opportunities for an adventure lifestyle (Neeves and Brignall, 2010; Raleigh International, 2018).

Professional Adventure Tourists

The professionalization of extreme sports has added to the demand profile for staff in the AT and ODA industry. Professional climbers and surfers did not really exist 50 years ago and the sponsorship of adventure by large corporations and companies has fuelled both the images and activities related to adventure. It is now possible to make a living out of adventure by living an 'adventure

lifestyle'. As with more mainstream sports (football and ice hockey, for example) adventure tourism has begun to emulate the employment structures and job opportunities provided by more commodified and professionalized adventure products. Climbing the highest mountains, exploration to the Poles and sailing around the world single handed, have now become commercial ventures.

The development of qualifications has allowed the professionalization of adventure sports too (Boxes 10.1, 10.2 and 10.3). With the growth in litigation there has been a need to provide competence in a market where validation of qualifications is important; thus the rise in specific certificates for adventure and outdoor activities has helped to foster greater professionalization in these adventure sports.

The types of employment that are on offer for adventure professionals can be far ranging, with a global reach. Certain qualifications are country specific but others have a more global validity, such as PADI diving qualifications. Most developed

Box 10.1. Professionalization of mountaineering.

The requirement for guides has always been an imperative within the adventure industry. Even on the historical expeditions of the past two centuries, guides were an important asset for the success of any expedition. Likewise, today, there is an overriding need to ensure that companies offering mountaineering expeditions have experienced and well qualified guides. For France and the UK, the International Mountain Leaders (IML) qualification is seen as a mandatory requirement for leading groups on mountains of higher altitudes, providing clear guidance on aspects of risk assessment and customer safety. IML is seen as the professional qualification that should be acquired if working in the mountaineering sector and guiding groups on a more global scale. The USA has an equivalent: the American Mountain Guides Award (AMGA).

Sherpas were perhaps some of the first professional guides for Western expeditions to the Himalayas.

Without the Sherpa many expeditions and perhaps the 1953 Hillary and Tensing expedition would never have succeeded. The modern professional focus is on gaining qualifications and evidence of competence.

There is clearly a proliferation of qualifications for adventure sports and also a need for more specific locational authentication of competence on specific mountains. Most countries have specific facilities and locations where these professional qualifications can be taken and validated . For example, in the UK, Glenmore Lodge Scotland and Plas y Brenin and the National Mountain Centre in Wales all offer qualifications for UK mountain guides. Most countries will have their own specific qualifications, such as in France and Spain, who run specialist centres where qualifications are obtained.

Box 10.2. Meru: the professional mountain.

Meru may be termed the 'Anti-Everest'. The Disneyfication of climbing has pushed expert and professional climbers to discover new locations and mountains, where commodification of climbing is very limited or the routes just impossible for mountaineering tourists.

It seems evident, as with aspects of adventure lifestyles, that serious climbers have a very different lifestyle to adventure tourists. The summiting of Meru, a 20,000 ft peak in the Himalayas, is an exemplar of both the extreme elements of climbing and the climbing lifestyle that accompanies this type of adventure sport. It is the professional's mountain and one that no tourist climber could ever attempt successfully.

This peak had not been climbed before and many attempts had failed to reach the summit. Its technical challenges were an incorporation of many different types of climbing abilities and it could be confirmed to be at the extreme edge of current climbing

performances. The mountain was eventually summited in 2011 by three professional climbers, whose lifestyle typifies the professional climber.

It was symbolized by living in vans, participating in many high-risk expeditions and climbing peaks that were technically difficult. The climbers who summited Meru were Conrad Anker, Jimmy Chin and Renan Ozturk, all well seasoned climbers who were evidently at the 'peak' of their climbing careers (clocking many difficult climbs and expeditions). Their narratives of the climb affirm a climber's lifestyle as being very different to that of an adventure tourist, as their whole life was focused on climbing (McCarthy, 2015; Bailey, 2016).

These climbers and their decision to climb Meru illustrate the growing divide in many aspects of the adventure market between professional climbers and tourist climbers. Both follow aspects of adventure lifestyles, but with one group really living it and the other dipping in and out.

---

countries now have infrastructure and education systems offering many types of adventure tourism jobs. For example, the New Zealand adventure tourism industry is one of the most advanced in the world, with a variety of adventure courses for prospective employees. By way of illustration, after

taking a Certificate in Adventure Tourism Level 5 (NMIT, 2018), the likely possible careers for students might include:

- sea kayak guide;
- whitewater raft guide;

Box 10.3. Rab sponsorship.

Rab® is a well known UK mountaineering brand established in the 1980s which has become a renowned equipment and clothing company for mountaineers. Sponsorship can be a useful indication of the growth of professional development within a product area and it is evident that many mountaineering expeditions, which are creative and journey to challenging destinations, attract sponsorship.

Rab is a useful company to examine in order to understand how sponsorship operates for adventure tourism and professional and aspiring climbers too. As with most companies, it is overwhelmed with requests for sponsorship and much sorting and editing has to be undertaken. Each request is looked at, with casual requests of regular or unexciting events usually not considered. The focus now is upon creative, novel expeditions and those with aspects of daring. However, extreme risk taking and foolhardy expeditions are excluded.

The overriding principles seem to be focused on mountaineering and new aspects or innovative ideas of climbing. Rab has a number of 'Ambassadors' whom it considers to be representative of the product and also competent through proven abilities in successful climbing. Richard Parks is a good example of one of these (Rab, 2017); he was already sponsored by other companies and his completion of seven summits and both Poles in 7 months was an example of an exciting, creative and daring expedition.

Rab offers a variety of different sponsorship packages depending upon the request and the impact this will have on sales. A key element is access to social media and the corresponding hits on RAB's sites. These can then be linked to sales of goods though developing accurate metrics is difficult. It appears that closeness to the industry and its climbers is a key element in deciding sponsorship deals of climbers and expeditions.

Association with the brand is important and there appear to be connections with the general customer who wants to be seen wearing the RAB brand but not actually undertaking climbing. However, association with a brand no doubt does have some effect on the choice of adventure holidays and activities.

Rab has clearly decided to keep within its specialized niche of mountaineering and has not been tempted to expand into other adventure markets, unlike bigger brands such as North Face and Billabong.

- snowboard/ski instructor;
- hiking/tramping guide;
- glacier guide;
- rock climber;
- whitewater kayaker; and
- adventure tourism operator.

Adventure Tourism Narratives

Books are a means of entertainment through relaxation, information and imagination, all of which help to create demand and shape attitudes in an area or topic on which the narrative is based. Electronic media is now advancing quickly, with visual and aural stories being used for information and entertainment, yet a book or tome maintains popularity and book sales remain buoyant.

Books on tourism, and certainly adventure, have always had a market – maybe not as popular in terms of sales as other topics, but certainly the adventure genre has sold well and enabled many armchair adventurers to become active, galvanizing them into becoming real adventurers. Evaluating the number of books on adventure is a near-impossible task. One of the problems relates to the changing definition of adventure tourism. The definition of adventure has widened and now encompasses new adventure activities, such as volunteer tourism and aspects of cultural tourism. There have been attempts to classify the top adventure tourism publications but these tend to be subjective evaluations (Table 10.2).

The growth of adventure tourism is reflected in increasing publication of adventure tourism narratives and books. Explorers and adventurers are now often expected to write a book after returning from their expeditions or adventures, boosting publications even more.

Travel books of a general nature could also be seen as helping to fuel the adventure tourism market. Many destinations are commendable adventure tourism locations and descriptions in travel books must also help the development of markets by highlighting new destinations around the globe. Many travel books were written in the 18th and 19th centuries, especially the 19th century; the

Table 10.2. Top ten adventure tourism publications.

Position	Top 10 real-life adventure books nominated by professional adventurers (Hersey, 2017)	Top 10 greatest adventure books of all time (*National Geographic*) (Brandt, 2001)
1	*The Kon-Tiki Expedition* (1950) by Thor Heyerdahl. (Nominated by *To the End of the Earth* author Tom Avery)	*The Worst Journey in the World* (1922) by Apsley Cherry-Garrard
2	*The Long Walk* (1955) by Slavomir Rawicz. (Nominated by British explorer and *Into the Abyss* author Benedict Allen)	*Journals* (1814) by Meriwether Lewis and William Clark
3	*The Worst Journey in the World* (1922) by Apsley Cherry-Garrard. (Nominated by Polar explorer Ben Saunders)	*Wind, Sand & Stars* (1940) by Antoine De Saint-Exupéry
4	*Mawson's Will* (1999) by Lennard Bickel. (Nominated by *Between A Rock And A Hard Place* author Aron Ralston)	*Exploration of the Colorado River* (1875) by John Wesley Powell
5	*Lost in the Jungle* (2005) by Yossi Ghinsberg (Nominated by *Touching the Void* author Joe Simpson)	*Arabian Sands* (1959) by Wilfred Thesiger
6	*In The Heart of the Sea* (2001) by Nathaniel Philbrick. (Nominated by climber and Esquire contributor David Pickford)	*Annapurna* (1952) by Maurice Herzog
7	*No Picnic on Mount Kenya* (1974) by Felice Benuzzi. (Nominated by mountaineer and *Learning to Breathe* author Andy Cave)	*Desert Solitaire* (1968) by Edward Abbey
8	*Touching the Void* (1988) by Joe Simpson. (Nominated by Polar explorer and mountaineer Adrian Hayes)	*West With the Night* (1942) by Beryl Markham
9	*The Dig Tree* (2002) by Sarah Murgatroyd. (Nominated by adventurer Ben Fogle)	*Into Thin Air* (1997) by Jon Krakauer
10	*Into the Heart of Borneo* (1987) by Redmond O'Hanlon. (Nominated by American explorer Todd Carmichael)	*Travels* (1298) by Marco Polo

Victorian era was a time of Western empires with their agents sent on adventures exploring new territories. Exploration of such territories was reflected in these publications although only one of the top travel books are indeed from this time period, as can be seen from Table 10.2. Additionally, it was a significant period for Alpine mountaineering adventures, and many publications are related to the Alpine Club, which produced regular narratives describing new routes and summiting:

[t]he Alpine Club, the world's first mountaineering club, has members from around the world. Since it was founded in 1857 Alpine Club members have been at the leading edge of worldwide mountaineering development and exploration.

(Alpine Club, 2016)

The Club was a source of adventure narratives that heavily influenced the purview of the climbing community; at the time it played a noteworthy part in the development of mountaineering as we know it today.

The 19th century also saw a number of travel books and writers who were able to encourage tourism development (Tickle, 2009). In many cases these could be seen as all-purpose tourism destinations, but more specific publications were related to aspects of adventure, giving the public a vicarious experience of destinations and adventure:

At the beginning of the 19th century, a revolution in travel took place. 'The Grand Tour' as a sort of aristocratic institution was brought to an end, and traveling became a more common endeavour: new transportation – in particular, the steamboat – the publishing of Baedeker guides, and the birth of the tourist agency Thomas Cook & Son, which organized group trips, were unequivocal signs of that transformation.

Di Nepi and Marzano (2013)

The current growth of adventure tourism and outdoor activities is also reflected in the growth of adventure magazines. A review of magazine racks will identify an array of publications dedicated to specific adventure activities and also more general aspects of adventure. In the English language world, these must run to a 100 plus, depending on the definition of adventure. Even *National Geographic* has acknowledged this growth in adventure by publishing the *National Geographic Adventure Magazine* as well as books such as *World's Best Travel Experiences: 400 Extraordinary Places* and *Destinations of a Lifetime: 225 of the World's Most Amazing*

Places, which seems to echo the travel writers of the 19th century.

The internet has further fuelled demand, especially the development of social media forums and the growth of travel writing through blogs. This can be seen in the same context as Victorian 'bloggers', who would have had travel diaries and reports and other similar approaches to record their exploits and adventures (Di Nepi and Marzano, 2013). Social media travel blogs provide an immediate but second-hand experience of adventure destinations. When this is added to video and pictorial forms of documentation the impact is significant, though their accuracy and validity could be challenged. Nonetheless it could be argued this is no different from 19th century travel writers who would also have voiced their opinions on favourite destinations, influencing travel guides of the time.

In terms of market impact, it is difficult to gauge to what extent social media has increased sales in adventure tourism and outdoor activities. Certainly when considering Twitter, Facebook, Instagram etc. there is little doubt that they stimulate immediate consumer responses, especially where to visit and what activities to participate in. The rise of Iceland as a tourist destination can be linked to this phenomenon (other factors too have been significant):

> … here thus from what had seemed to be a bankrupt nation [Iceland] of 320,000 people, a total of 700 million ISK (3.7 million GBP) could be whipped up at short notice for marketing purposes. The campaign used extensive viral marketing, through Facebook, Twitter and other social media … Web pages were launched through which people could access web cameras, providing a direct view to the main tourist attractions.
>
> (Benediktsson *et al.*, 2011, p. 80)

The travel diary, like the travel blog, is a means of conveying in words the reality of adventure. Indeed many diaries have been used as sources of information, illustrating the trials and tribulations of exploration and adventure as well as describing the physical and psychological elements of adventure sports. They also give a great insight into the personalities of adventurers and aspects of endurance. Current diaries are usually digital and able to be released immediately, though many are retained and then published as a document (text or virtual) at a later stage.

Newspapers, albeit now in decline, have made significant contributions to travel, often printing specific reports and in-depth coverage on adventure tourism products. They remain a source of inspiration for 'lifestyle' ideas of where to travel and what to do and feature many new developments in tourism. In the UK, *The Guardian*, *The Times* and *The Telegraph* have reputable travel sections often covering adventure tourism narratives.

The book *1000 Ultimate Adventures* noted:

> Hankering to tackle a long-distance trek, or an icy mountain peak? 1000 Ultimate Adventures brings together activities and challenges to captivate and inspire gung-ho adventurers and armchair travellers alike. From the epic to the local, on land, sea or even in mid-air, the offerings here will encourage you to dream, plan and set off on your own adventure.
>
> (Lonely Planet, 2016)

Clearly the adventure tourism market has widened to include, as mentioned here, 'armchair' adventurers. This further illustrates the assertion that 'soft' forms of adventure are now being sold to tourists, encouraging them to engage in the adventure market.

Films on Adventure Tourism

The proliferation of texts on adventure tourism is often mirrored through film and reflects the adventure lifestyle. This is not unexpected, given that digital media tends to document and provide entertainment on aspects of travel and adventure. There are currently numerous documentaries focused on adventure tourism professionals or semi-professionals and social media has also produced a plethora of lesser-known adventurers featuring in adventure expeditions. A perusal of the number of videos on YouTube confirms this. A classic example, which set the standard for others, is possibly that of Thor Heyerdahl's 1947 *Kon-Tiki* expedition, the subject of his own documentary film (1950, subsequently dramatized in 2012) as well as his book. Heyerdahl's aim was to try to support his theory that it was possible to cross the Pacific on a papyrus raft, thus providing a potential explanation for the migration of peoples across the Pacific.

Jacques Cousteau's underwater exploits also helped to transform the diving and water sports elements of exploration and adventure. His pioneering feats aided in the widening of water adventure for many and for the children of the 1960s and 1970s he inspired future aquatic explorers. Films such as *The Silent World*, *The Golden Fish* and *World Without Sun* (Nath, 2009) are notable examples of Cousteau's influence.

Many current adventure documentaries seem to be within this genre of exploration and adventure. The current adventure tourism market is littered with a plethora of adventure films such as *Seven Years in Tibet* (1997), *Touching the Void* (2003), *The Beckoning Silence* (2007), *Meru* (2011) and the most recent, *Everest* (2015), which leave a lasting impression of adventure. Supporting these films are the 'docusoaps' such as that celebrating the anniversary of Ernest Shackleton's Antarctic Expedition (1911–1914). This helped to engage consumer interest in wanting to explore Antarctica, perhaps leading to the development of more Antarctic cruises such as the 'Spirit of Shackleton' (G Adventure, 2017).

The current breadth of adventure and the splintering of products is reflected in many films. Cult surfing films have been a staple of most lifestyle surfers and are often used for motivational as well as relaxation purposes; it is suggested that surfers often gain inspiration from them to explore other countries and waves. The surfing community has an abundance of such films (some of which have become legendary), often made by semi-professional film makers who are frequently surfers themselves. For example, IMDb (Internet Movie Database) lists 25 of the best surfing films, some mainstream, others less well known, but many will be familiar not only to surfers, but to a wider, more general audience. *The Endless Summer*, *Riding Giants* and *Single Yellow Fin* are those familiar to surfers, while also on the film list are 'Hollywoodesque' blockbusters including *Point Break* (1991), *Big Wednesday* and *Blue Crush*, which are generally heard of or seen by non-surfers (Zlotnick, 2011). Perhaps one of the latest that identifies the expansion of surfing to extremes is *Under the Arctic Sky* (2017), a film about surfing in Iceland in Arctic conditions under the Northern Lights.

Mountaineering has a number of seminal and lifestyle films similar to those of surfing. Films about mountaineering and climbing are equally diverse, with a long history of recording adventures and exploits (Sinsanati, 2012).

Mainstream adventure films are supported by amateur films such as those found on YouTube, which are excellent sources of free adventure material and stimulation. YouTube offers many extreme types of adventure tourism films, often providing a grittier, more realistic source for adventure tourism. The BBC has its own adventure slots, such as the BBC 2 *Adventure Show*, and if this is connected to the *Travel Show* (shown also on BBC World) then adventure tourism is prominently covered for a mainstream audience.

Recently there have been a number of centenary and half-century celebrations of great exploits such as the climbing of Everest in 1953, Shackleton's Antarctic expedition and Amundsen's successful journey to the South Pole in 1911 together with Scott's attempt. All of these anniversaries have provided excellent material for adventure films which may well have further engaged the public in wanting to experience adventure and outdoor lifestyles.

Then there has been the development of specialist channels for adventure tourism. In terms of more mainstream films and documentaries there is a focus on personalities such as Bear Grylls and Ray Mears, who are both classic adventure personalities on UK television. Bear Grylls has been involved in a number of survival and adventure programmes, the most recent being *Running Wild with Bear Grylls*, which is a US programme. He has had a number of programmes on mainstream television in the UK, such as *Mission Survive* (2015) and *The Island* (2014). The reach of such programmes is increasing and it is suggested that they are creating a new genre of adventure and widening access by exposing more of the public to adventure lifestyles. The programme that launched Bear Grylls as a TV personality was the series *Born Survivor/Man vs Wild*, which was also shown on networks in Australia, New Zealand, Canada, India and the USA. In terms of audience reach and as an indication of his popularity, he regularly obtains figures of more than 3 million viewers for some of his latest programmes.

As well as more general adventure programmes, there has been the development of those dedicated to specific areas of adventure tourism. The Extreme Sports Channel (ESC) makes an interesting case, associated with the growth of adventure tourism. It was never mainstream and had a variety of different adventure sports featured on it, including surfing, snowboarding, motocross, wakeboarding, BMX and FMX. Not only were sports featured but also the lifestyles accompanying them:

> Extreme Sports Channel is the only 24-7 channel bringing you skate, surf, snow and bike action and attitude direct to your TV in over 50 countries around the world. We are dedicated to showcasing the best programmes, events, riders, films, competitions and behind-the-scenes exclusives from the grassroots groms to the pro star talent.
>
> (ESC, 2016)

In 2015 the UK version of the Channel closed, though one would have expected it to be growing and developing alongside the expansion of adventure tourism. But even the idea of an Extreme channel seems to be in decline and some pundits are forecasting its possible demise. It is also interesting to note that some of the extreme sports featured on the channel have been transformed from minority into more mainstream sports.

Conclusion

The past 50 years have seen significant changes for consumers, one of the most notable being that of lifestyle. This first started to be more fully recognized by marketers in the 1970s and 1980s with the idea of the VALS (Values and Lifestyles) system of profiling customers. It reflected the fact that people had more money and leisure time, which engendered increased access to leisure activities, including adventure sports such as surfing and mountaineering. The professionalization of adventure sports has also helped to foster adventure lifestyle which, in parallel, has developed more extreme aspects of these sports. Likewise, participation rates for adventure tourism and outdoor activities have grown, requiring an increasing supply of professional instructors and guides. A consequence of these factors has been the development of new courses in higher educational establishments furthering opportunities for employment and hence allowing many adventurers to live and work the adventure lifestyle.

Furthermore, expansion of the internet and digital and social media platforms have helped in the proliferation of the adventure tourism lifestyle gaze. Also books and films have engaged more of the public with notions of adventure and fostering participation, to the extent that even extreme environments such as the earth's Poles are now accessible to adventure tourists. It seems inexorable that the adventure lifestyle will continue to grow in popularity as more and more adventurers are attracted to living and working the adventure lifestyle dream.

Questions

- To what extent are changes in lifestyle affecting the adventure tourism market?
- Can the theory of postmodernism be considered to fully explain changes in adventure tourism?
- To what extent do films and book have an effect on the development of the adventure lifestyle?

References

Alpine Club (2016) Home page. Available at: http://www.alpine-club.org.uk/ac2/index.php (accessed 11 April 2016).

Arctic Adventures (2017) Arctic Adventures – Iceland Tours & Adventure Holidays, your adventure tour operator in Iceland since 1983. Available at: https://adventures.is/?gclid=Cj0KCQiA3dTQBRDnARIsAGKSfInt2ys1TWx-oFjcLJmHayY29BtJHXopWQmrol-X-Q6lr630tnjcoOoaAquGEALw_wcB (accessed 22 November 2017).

ATTA (2017) 2017 Adventure Travel Trends Snapshot. Available at: https://www.adventuretravel.biz/research/2017-adventure-travel-trends-snapshot/ (accessed 16 March 2018). Adventure Travel Trade Association, Seattle.

Bailey, M. (2016) Jimmy Chin: why climbing Meru Peak is tougher than Everest. Available at: https://www.telegraph.co.uk/health-fitness/body/jimmy-chin-why-climbing-meru-peak-is-tougher-than-everest/ (accessed 10 December 2018).

Benediktsson, K., Lund, K.A. and Huijbens, E. (2011) Inspired by eruptions? Eyjafjallajökull and Icelandic tourism. *Mobilities* 6(1), 77–84.

Berlingieri, G. (2014) Outsourcing and the shift from manufacturing to services. *CentrePiece* 18(3), 16–19. Available at: http://cep.lse.ac.uk/pubs/download/cp413.pdf (accessed 12 July 2017).

Berner, A. and Van Tonder, C.I. (2003) The postmodern consumer: implications of changing customer expectations for organisation development in service organisations. *SA Journal of Industrial Psychology* 29(3), 1–10.

Bramwell, B. (2004) *Coastal Mass Tourism Diversification and Sustainable Development in Southern Europe.* Channel Publications, Bristol, UK.

Brandt, A. (2001) The 100 Greatest Adventure Books of All Time. Available at: http://adventure.nationalgeographic.com/2001/07/adventure-books/anthony-brandt-text/1 (accessed 21 November 2017).

Byrne, C. (2005) A new front is opened up in the cola wars: diet-conscious men. Available at: http://www.independent.co.uk/news/a-new-front-is-opened-up-in-the-cola-wars-diet-conscious-men-5384904.html (accessed 7 November 2017).

Degan, G. (2018) BMW targets adventurous crowd with climbing centre activations. Available at: https://www.campaignlive.co.uk/article/bmw-targets-adventurous-crowd-climbing-centre-activations/1460261 (accessed 26 March 2018).

Di Nepi, S. and Marzano, A. (eds) (2013) Travels to the 'Holy Land': Perceptions, Representations and Narratives.

Quest: Issues in Contemporary Jewish History. Journal of Fondazione CDEC, no. 6 (December 2013). Available at: http://www.quest-cdecjournal.it/index.php?issue=6 (accessed 22 November 2017).

ESC (2016) About Extreme Sports Channel. Available at: http://extreme.com/tv/about (accessed 12 April 2016).

Explore (2017) Destinations. Available at: https://www.explore.co.uk/destinations (accessed 22 November 2017).

Fordham, M. (2008) Riding the wave to riches. Available at: https://www.theguardian.com/travel/2008/jun/16/surfing.adventure (accessed 12 July 2017).

French, L. (2015) Adventure tourism grows in popularity. Available at: https://www.businessdestinations.com/move/adventure-tourism-grows-in-popularity/ (accessed 12 July 2017).

G Adventure (2017) The Spirit of Shackleton. Available at: https://www.gadventures.co.uk/trips/spirit-of-shackleton/XVSHSX/ (accessed 22 November 2017).

Gianatasio, D. (2014) Volvo really takes the plunge in powerful ad that leaves the car on shore. Grey London's 'The Swell'. Adweek, September 29, 2014. Available at: https://www.adweek.com/creativity/volvo-really-takes-the-plunge-powerful-ad-leaves-car-shore-160453 (accessed 2 September 2018).

Glyptis, S.A. (1981) Leisure life-styles. *Regional Studies* 15, 311–326.

Grey (2014) The Swell. Available at: http://grey.com/london/work/key/the-swell/id/5020/ (accessed 7 November 2017).

Hersey, H. (2017) The 10 Greatest Real-Life Adventure Books. A panel of explorers nominate their favourite tales of suffering and survival. Available at: http://www.esquire.co.uk/culture/books/news/g5553/adventure-books/?slide=10 (accessed 21 November 2017).

IMG (2016) Hvannadalshnúkur – Iceland's Highest Summit – IMG25. Available at: http://www.mountainguides.is/day-tours/mountain-climbing/icelands-highest-summit/ (accessed 12 April 2016).

Jackson-Brown, H. (1990) *P.S. I Love You: When Mom Wrote, She Always Saved the Best for Last.* Rutledge Hill Press, Nashville, TN.

Lonely Planet (2016) Home. Lonely planet's 1000 Ultimate Adventures. Available at: http://shop.lonelyplanet.com/world/lonely-planets-1000-ultimate-adventures/ (accessed 12 April 2016).

McCarthy, E. (2015) 9 facts about climbing Mount Meru – and making a documentary out of it. Available at: http://mentalfloss.com/article/67362/9-facts-about-climbing-mount-meru-and-making-documentary-out-it (accessed 21 November 2017).

Nath, B. (2009) *Environmental Education and Awareness*. UNESCO, Oxford, UK. Available at: https://www.eolss.net/ebooklib/ebookcontents/E4-16-ThemeContents.pdf (accessed 26 August 2018).

Neeves, J. and Brignall, M. (2010) Paying the price for a gap year of adventure. Available at: https://www.theguardian.com/money/2010/jun/26/paying-price-gap-year-adventure (accessed 16 March 2018).

NGA (2001) The 100 Greatest Adventure Books of All Time. Available at: http://adventure.nationalgeographic.com/2001/07/adventure-books/anthony-brandt-text/1 (accessed 11 April 2016).

NMIT (2018) *Adventure Tourism and Guiding, LEVEL 5*. Nelson Marlborough Institute of Technology, Nelson, New Zealand. Available at: https://www.nmit.ac.nz/study/programmes/adventure-tourism-and-guiding-level-5/#drawer (accessed 28 August 2018).

Rab (2017) Richard Parks. Available at: https://rab.equipment/uk/people/richard-parks/ (accessed 10 December 2018).

Raleigh International (2018) An adventure worth sharing. Available at: https://raleighinternational.org/adventure-worth-sharing/ (accessed 16 March 2018).

Roberts, K. (2006) *Leisure in Contemporary Society*, 2nd edn. CABI, Wallingford, UK.

Sinsanati (2012) Best Climbing and Mountain Movies. Available at: http://www.imdb.com/list/ls050926084/ (accessed 12 April 2016).

Surfer Today (2017) The best surfing commercials ever. Available at: https://www.surfertoday.com/surfing/7744-the-best-surfing-commercials-ever (accessed 7 November 2017).

Tickle, L. (2009) Early adventures in travel writing. Available at: https://www.theguardian.com/education/2009/nov/03/18th-19th-century-travel-writing (accessed 22 November 2017.

Veale, R. (2015) Surfing a lifestyle. Available at: http://nutsandboltssports.com/surfing-lifestyle/ (accessed 12 July 2017).

Wainwright, O. (2013) VW camper van: farewell to the symbol of 60s freedom. Available at: https://www.theguardian.com/artanddesign/2013/dec/30/vw-camper-van-last-ever-farewell (accessed 7 November 2017).

Wheaton, B. (2004) *Understanding Lifestyle Sports: Consumption, Identity, and Difference*. Routledge, London.

Williams, A. (2006) Tourism and hospitality marketing: fantasy, feeling and fun. *International Journal of Contemporary Hospitality Management* 18(6), 482–495.

Zlotnick, J. (2011) 25 Best Surfing Films Available at: https://www.imdb.com/list/ls000294021/ (accessed 12 April 2016).

11 Sustainability in Adventure Tourism

Learning Objectives

At the end of this chapter the reader will be able to:

- understand the importance, links and requirements of sustainability for adventure tourism; and
- evaluate the need to incorporate sustainable development with adventure tourism.

Chapter Overview

Sustainability is clearly a concept that all tourism companies should embrace, including adventure tourism. Yet a quick review of websites and marketing material will usually identify that the concept of sustainability is given a lower status than other products offered by a company. There are a number of global criteria that give minimum standards of sustainability for any company in the tourism industry, but are these effective for the adventure tourism industry? These themes will be explored in this chapter to evaluate how effective company sustainability is.

Sustainability has evolved from a nascent concept to one that is universally acknowledged. It emerged from the green movements of the 1960s and 1970s when prominent texts such as 'Blue Print for Survival' acted as a presage of diminishing world resources, especially focusing on the resource issues of the developed industrial nations and the pressing need to change the systems of consumption (Goldsmith and Prescott-Allen, 1972). The 1960s and 1970s were also a time of change related to heavy industry and manufacturing: the increase of mechanization began to replace labour and thus a shift towards a tertiary (service) economy.

There emerged a refocus on nature and the realization of nature having economic value and the need to conserve and protect it. This period saw the advent of independent environmental organizations and lobby groups, such as Friends of the Earth and Greenpeace. These lobby groups were fundamental in energizing and changing society's attitude towards a more environmentally responsive future. During the 1970s a series of economic shocks, caused by a scarcity of resources such as oil, further highlighted the vulnerability of economies and people when reliant on naturally occurring resources.

The defining moment for sustainability as a political and economic ideology is cited as being the Brundtland Report of 1987, published by the United Nations (UN) as *Our Common Future* (UNCOSD, 2007). This was a significant moment in the importance of sustainability and enhanced the power of environmental campaigning groups and individuals to press for more measures to ensure protection of the environment.

> The Brundtland Commission's report defined sustainable development as 'development which meets the needs of current generations without compromising the ability of future generations to meet their own needs'. The concept supports strong economic and social development, in particular for people with low standards of living. At the same time it underlines the importance of protecting the natural resource base and the environment. Economic and social well-being cannot be improved with measures that destroy the environment. Intergenerational solidarity is also crucial: all development has to take into account its impact on the opportunities for future generations.
>
> (UNECE, 2016).

It can be argued that sustainability is a process reflected within the development of postmodernism. Postmodernism is referred to as a paradigm shift towards new concepts and ideas within society and the economy. Sustainability has also been developed in tandem with mass markets and globalization, where sustainability is now in essence on the global agenda, not limited simply to destinations and locales. Sustainability can be reflected in global companies and NGOs such as the UN's World Tourism Organization (UNWTO). In addition there has been a change in the tourism consumer, so that older concepts have been replaced by new ideas, from the 3Ss of tourism (Sun, Sea and Sand) towards the 3Ts (Travelling, Trekking and Trucking) (Mowforth and Munt, 2009). Many of these further emphasize a move towards more environmental issues and products.

Inevitably this paradigm shift (sustainability) has affected the ways that businesses operate and customer expectations, though the actual support that consumers have for sustainability is somewhat unclear (Cohen *et al.*, 2005). There are protagonists who argue that the public want more sustainable products, especially those associated with environmental groups, yet evidence from some operators in adventure tourism in the UK would refute this to some extent, noting that consumers are not actively engaged in choosing sustainable products. There is perhaps dissonance between what consumers think they should do and what they actually do.

The 1987 Brundtland Report set the agenda for the forthcoming years and continues to do so. Even the climate change agenda has roots in this report and it can be argued that in fact sustainability and climate change are immutable ideologies that are symbiotically linked to each other (Campagnolo *et al.*, 2016). The Green Movement of the 1960s and 1970s was seen by some as somewhat militant and, in terms of business, a threat to its ideology of nature being there to be exploited. Friends of the Earth and Greenpeace were founding members of a number of organizations that emerged from this period of environmental lobbying in the late 1960s.

Much has changed since then and today the integration of sustainable practices, such as corporate social responsibility (CSR) and climate change mitigation are clearly important themes for most global businesses and economic markets. However, the extent to which companies engage in sustainable measures is still questionable (Jenkins *et al.*, 2011). It is suggested that many companies are aware of sustainability but remain neutral or limited in the actions taken by them. Leading corporations and prominent businesses such as the UK company Marks and Spenser (M&S) (Smithers, 2012) and Patagonia (a leading adventure clothes company) are striving to endorse and action these sustainable principles while maintaining business viability.

A key element in any sustainability process is the maxim of businesses maintaining profitability. Profits are the modus operandi of the commercial world and protagonists have argued that sustainable principles have a cost which can impair competitive advantage. Therefore, if sustainability costs are not universally applied to businesses, this would render a company less competitive.

There now seems to have been a significant shift in approaches to sustainable principles and aspects of profitability. There is emerging a move towards embracing more of these principles within businesses while not jettisoning the raison d'être of a company: profits.

There are examples of companies incorporating cost reduction principles and reducing their overheads by considering more environmentally friendly strategies. M&S has embarked upon a sustainability development strategy and in many ways is leading the way in the UK (Smithers, 2012). This must have a ripple effect upon other sectors of the economy and companies, especially if M&S continues to maintain profitability. As can be seen, some adventure tourism-related companies have also started to develop sustainability strategies (Steynberg and Grundling, 2005). Some companies are actively engaged in sustainable measures, such as Twr y Felin (TYF) and Call of the Wild (COTW), both based in Wales. A visit to their websites clearly shows the sustainable measures that they are taking.

The climate change debate is focused upon the reduction of energy obtained from fossil fuels and there has been a move towards more climate-friendly energy and reduced carbon outputs. Some companies are heating buildings in more environmentally friendly ways. Natural sources of energy are being used to reduce carbon outputs. For example, thermal heating and solar power are sources of energy now being incorporated into reduction of costs. There are some initial capital outlays but the calculations show that in the longer term these can be recouped and costs reduced. Support from government sources has also aided in this and continues to be pursued by some governments.

More than the Triple Bottom Line

Since 1987 there have been a series of developments relating to sustainability and its relevance to tourism. For many in business the notion of a triple bottom line – Profits, People and Planet (Economist, 2009) – became fashionable and with that has emerged the development of CSR. These concepts and mantras have guided the economic development of corporations and businesses. These ethical changes in business approaches accompanied a change towards tourism and the aspect of not only sustainability but also 'responsible tourism'. Perhaps sustainable tourism and responsible tourism can be seen as semantics, as the goals are similar and the differential seems to lie in the word 'personal' responsibility. Responsible tourism focuses upon the individual rather than the corporate or the group in being responsible for the environment and social consequences of commercial activities.

There are companies that seem to have ethical principles and are enacting them, but it is difficult to differentiate 'green washing' and the actual delivery of environmental and social products offered to consumers. It is difficult to envisage petrochemical companies being green when their very products contribute to the current climate change angst (Gunther, 2015). Yet to simply jettison their products would devastate the global economy and so some move to mitigation and change to greener sources of energy by these companies is possibly a sensible route towards a sustainable future. What is heartening is that most businesses are now fully aware of the ethical consideration of sustainability and the actions they need to take (Balch 2016). That said, there are questions relating to enforcement of regulations for companies and governments. Just looking at the COP21 (Conference of the Parties) talks at the UN Climate Change Conference in Paris in 2015, it is evident that change is a very slow process given the outcomes of the 1992 UN Conference on Environment and Development (UNCED), often known as the Earth Summit or Rio Summit. But the agreement of COP21 was ratified in 2016 and agreed upon by 171 nations (McGrath, 2016), which seems to demonstrate some progress.

It is asserted that these changes to business practices must be seen as a normative response and especially beneficial for the environment and social development, though the evidence that consumers want environmentally sound products is somewhat tenuous, and issues of price sensitivity are still a market concern. It still seems evident that consumers remain economic animals and will purchase (all things being equal) along the lines of competitive prices rather than competitive ethics. The price elasticity of ethical and sustainable products is one that needs further research and development in the adventure tourism industry. Adventure consumers' ethical choices seem still to be governed by price and there is evidence that adventure tourism companies have to educate the consumer when they are participating in an activity, not before they arrive (Jenkins et al., 2011).

Another aspect is attempting to evaluate how sustainable businesses are; and what measures businesses are really engaging with to ensure that they operate in a responsible and sustainable manner. There is no universally accepted scheme or labelling system and there are many versions of global verifications. As with eco-labelling this creates a number of problems in terms of comparative standards. Trying to evaluate what is or is not sustainable has many problems for consumers and without any real standardization of labels the consumer is unable to understand the difference in sustainability of businesses. There have been attempts at standardization so that consumers are able to verify the sustainable characteristics of companies. One such global initiative is the Global Sustainability Tourism Council's criteria (GSTC, 2016) and the International Standards Institute has gone some way to try to address this problem by producing ISO 14001 as the International Standard for Environmental Management Systems and ISO 20121 for Event Sustainability Management Systems as global benchmarks for industry to follow (ISO, 2016). There has also been the emergence of more general criteria for companies such as B Corp, which is designed to assess the level of sustainability a company has reached, and there are other standards that have been developed such as One Planet Development (OPD) (B Corp, 2016).

In view of the above it can be said that the business maxim of 'triple bottom line' has certainly been changed from simply 'profits, people and planet', although it is asserted that these three elements are part of the sustainable development programme. That said, there is now far more emphasis on 'people' and 'the planet' and how these two entities interact and react. The current debate on climate change is an exemplar of this and all companies need to engender a sustainable future.

Adventure companies need to be thinking more than simply the triple bottom line and moving towards aspects of responsible tourism where the individual, consumer and employee function along sustainable guidelines (Fig. 11.1). This needs to be imbued into the company philosophy and encompassed in a company at every level. It is about transforming the sustainability agenda from policy to operational delivery. As with safety, the sustainability of a company should be assessed and viewed through the actions of its employees. They are the

Fig. 11.1. Red Sea reef damage by tourists walking on reef (photo: Ian Jenkins).

essence of where sustainability can be seen in action within a company.

With the advent of today's technology, immediate access to AT companies is possible through their websites and a review of company websites provides an indication of a company's approach to sustainability. Websites are windows to a company's profile and what they consider to be important. Research has identified that the website can be an indicator of a company's levels of sustainability: an evaluation of its website can give an indication of how a company operates using sustainable principles. Even a casual look at adventure tourism websites can indicate how engaged a company is in using sustainable principles and the sustainable actions that they take when dealing with customers and their suppliers. A study carried out by Jenkins *et al.* (2011) provided useful research. Using the GSTC criteria as an indicator for sustainability, the study found that most companies were falling short of full sustainable development, as defined by GSTC. The higher-scoring companies registered 40% according to the research's index. Many companies only scored 20%. Nevertheless, since this research the sustainable agenda has moved forward and it is speculated that these companies would now probably have much higher scores.

Sustainability in Adventure Tourism

Adventure tourism companies should now be enacting and operating sustainable principles. The premise should be focused upon the four principles of sustainability: economic, environmental, social and cultural (Fig. 11.2). It is also particularly relevant that most AT companies operate in environments that are not urban but are closely connected to nature, which engenders even more impetus for adventure tourism companies to ensure that their operations and customers have sustainable outcomes and that the goals of sustainable development are being met.

Most AT companies operate in natural surroundings and it is implicit that many of these destinations may have environmentally sensitive locations that can be affected by adventure tourism activities. Certainly, national parks are likely locations for AT companies to operate in and many of these landscapes have been designated national parks because of their unique natural environments, sometimes also having a cultural importance – for example, New Zealand's Tongariro National Park (UNESCO, 2016) and Thingvellir National Park in Iceland.

However, GSTC criteria are designed for destinations and hotels rather than general tourism companies and an evaluation of the criteria is not effortlessly transferred to adventure tourism. There are local initiatives relating to sustainable operations of AT companies. For example, the Green Dragon award in Wales was introduced to evaluate tourism companies' environmental impacts and it states that 'Green Dragon is an environmental standard that is awarded to organizations that are taking action to understand, monitor and control their impacts on the environment' (Ground Work Wales, 2016). This award has been adopted by AT operators and expanded to include a forum for furthering sustainable development. Sometimes these aims are also reflected in the policies of national parks in which AT companies operate; for example, the Brecon Beacon National Park in Wales has a policy on sustainability that encompasses activities, including adventure tourism, that take place within the park (Tourism Company, 2011).

Within the UK there are moves for AT companies to join federations or forums that allow sharing between members and discussions of sustainable operations and policies, which helps to disseminate good practice. There needs to be some standardization of sustainable operations within a company, which currently is lacking in the UK. The type of ownership – private, voluntary, or state – will determine the sustainable approaches to adventure tourism even though all three should be identical in terms of sustainability levels. All organizations should adhere to a universally accepted standard, whatever the ownership type of the organization.

Company Resources Areas for Sustainability

For a company, the main aspect is the operational perspective of how a company can be more sustainable. This can be categorized into certain areas that need action and development. It will also depend upon the resource location of company operations. For example, certain locations are not necessarily resource hungry for energy or water (e.g. Iceland), whereas others would need to be extremely cautious when using these resources (e.g. Africa). It is also not just about environmental aspects of operations, but this was the primary focus of sustainability and it is suggested that it is still perceived as the area of sustainability that most consumers understand.

Figure 11.3 shows the elements of significant areas for action that every AT company should be actively managing and delivering through their products. The following sections explore, in more detail, the expected actions in which an AT company should be responsibly engaged.

Resources

This element covers a wide range of different sustainable actions for a company. Carbon trading and mitigation are now standard practices sanctioned by many companies to try to reduce carbon emissions.

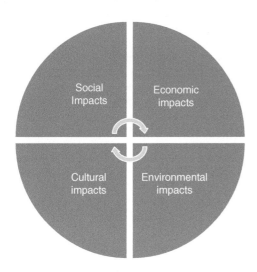

Fig. 11.2. GSTC '4 Pillars of Sustainability'.

Fig. 11.3. Areas of Sustainable Action for an adventure tourism company or organization.

For most AT companies this would be seen in the use of energy and types of energy that produce carbon emissions. The climate change debate is focused upon the reduction of energy made from fossil fuels and there are now many options to choose based on more climate-friendly energy (carbon free) and reduced carbon outputs (see Fig. 11.4, typical high carbon emissions vehicle used by tourists and tourist companies in Iceland). Certainly, aspects of heating buildings have changed significantly, towards more natural sources of energy with reduced carbon outputs. For example, thermal ground heating and solar power are sources of energy now being incorporated into reduction of costs. There are some initial capital outlays but the calculations show that in the longer run it is possible that within 2–10 years these costs be recouped (USDOE, 2016). Help from government sources has also aided in this transition and continues to be pursued by many governments.

The ultimate goal should be a 'carbon neutral' business, which would clearly demonstrate ethical actions towards sustainability. Carbon neutral means that a company's carbon release has been counterbalanced by buying carbon credits or using different fuels, which can be offset by carbon sequestration into carbon sinks.

There are other strategies that can be used, such as limiting transport of AT activities to the locale that a company operates in, thereby reducing carbon footprints of vehicles. Operating vehicles that have climate friendly emissions or no emissions (electric) are other alternatives used by some AT companies. With the rise of electric cars or hybrids there are now far more opportunities to select carbon-reducing fuels like hydrogen cells or reclaimed vegetable oil. Use of methane captured from waste tips or sewage plants is another sustainable approach to carbon reduction (Table 11.1).

In many countries water is a precious resource and needs conserving, so management of water is a key element in sustainable delivery. Even in countries with a plethora of water, reduction in use can reduce costs as many commercial firms are on water meters. In addition, disposal of water is a cost issue even if there are plentiful supplies. The use of grey water should be considered within a sustainable strategy.

Adventure activities need community involvement and access agreements to resources such as cliffs and mountains. Overuse or using environmentally sensitive areas needs to be evaluated carefully. Advice needs to be taken from environmental organizations and the local land management organizations such as national park authorities. Where a destination is suffering impacts from overuse, some form of capacity measures and cooperation of usage is needed. Development of AT forums can help to solve some of these issues at destinations and are an element of good practice (Box 11.1).

There are also issues relating to appropriate equipment use at destinations. In certain destinations there has been a growth in use of 4×4 vehicles to ensure navigation of difficult terrain. In Iceland, for example, these vehicles have moved to another level: they have become gigantic and are used for AT activities on glaciers (Fig. 11.4) (Box 11.2). Glacial adventures need to be considered within the realm of sustainability and raise ethical issues: where would such an activity fit in the evaluation of sustainable principles? So the resource management for an AT company is much wider than the main focus of energy and carbon footprinting; it must also include destination activities.

Employment

The 'triple bottom line' maxim means that people have become part of sustainability and sustainable employment practices focusing on equity as an important principle. Within this context of employment, the emphasis is on the Local, or Locale (defined by the *Oxford English Dictionary* as a place where something happens, or is set, or that has particular events associated with it). Employment practices that encourage employment of local labour are to be encouraged, the premise being that monies given to these employees are more likely to remain in a circular economy, multiplying the income of others who work and provide goods and services in the locale. This is perhaps more relevant to global or international (transnational) companies (TNCs) that operate in less developed countries, where local employment providing good wages would make a significant impact on the community.

The principle of sustainability is once again equity, relative to what a company earns from its consumers. Some companies might offer profit sharing as a means to provide equity for its employees. Employment is also about conditions and working hours and these too need to be evaluated to ensure that they are not being exploitative, especially for women or local employees. These are issues identified by some tourism organizations, such as Tourism Concern.

Table 11.1. Types of alternative fuels (Meyers, 2012).

Fuel	Description	Positive	Negative
Ethanol	An alcohol-based alternative fuel made by fermenting and distilling crops such as corn, barley or wheat. It can be blended with gasoline to increase octane levels and improve emissions quality.	Materials are renewable.	Ethanol subsidies have a negative impact on food prices and availability.
Natural gas	Natural gas is an alternative fuel that burns clean and is already widely available to people in many countries through utilities that provide natural gas to homes and businesses.	Cars and trucks with specially designed engines produce fewer harmful emissions than gasoline or diesel.	Natural gas production creates methane, a greenhouse gas that is 21 times worse for global warming than CO_2.
Electricity	Electricity can be used as a transportation alternative fuel for battery-powered electric and fuel-cell vehicles. Battery-powered electric vehicles store power in batteries that are recharged by plugging the vehicle into a standard electrical source. Fuel-cell vehicles run on electricity that is produced through an electrochemical reaction that occurs when hydrogen and oxygen are combined.	Electricity for transportation is highly efficient, and we already have an extensive electricity network. In the case of fuel cells, they produce electricity without combustion or pollution.	Much electricity is generated today from coal or natural gas, leaving a bad carbon footprint. (Nonetheless, electric vehicles are still the greenest option around when it comes to cars.)
Hydrogen	Hydrogen can be mixed with natural gas to create an alternative fuel for vehicles that use certain types of internal combustion engines. Hydrogen is also used in fuel-cell vehicles that run on electricity produced by the petrochemical reaction that occurs when hydrogen and oxygen are combined in the fuel 'stack'.	No bad emissions.	Cost. And also the lack of fuelling infrastructure and difficulty of putting it in place.
Propane	Propane – also called liquefied petroleum gas or LPG – is a by-product of natural gas processing and crude oil refining. Already widely used as a fuel for cooking and heating, propane is also a popular alternative fuel for vehicles.	Propane produces fewer emissions than gasoline, and there is also a highly developed infrastructure for propane transport, storage and distribution.	Natural gas production creates methane, a greenhouse gas that is 21 times worse for global warming than CO_2.
Biodiesel	Biodiesel is an alternative fuel based on vegetable oils or animal fats, even those recycled after restaurants have used them for cooking. Vehicle engines can be converted to burn biodiesel in its pure form, and biodiesel can also be blended with petroleum diesel and used in unmodified engines.	Biodiesel is safe, biodegradable, reduces air pollutants associated with vehicle emissions, such as particulate matter, carbon monoxide and hydrocarbons.	Limited production and distribution infrastructure.
Methanol	Methanol, also known as wood alcohol, can be used as an alternative fuel in flexible fuel vehicles that are designed to run on M85, a blend of 85% methanol and 15% gasoline, but automakers are no longer manufacturing methanol-powered vehicles.	Methanol could become an important alternative fuel in the future as a source of the hydrogen needed to power fuel-cell vehicles.	Automakers are no longer manufacturing methanol-powered vehicles.
P-series fuels	P-Series fuels are a blend of ethanol, natural gas liquids and methyltetrahydrofuran (MeTHF), a co-solvent derived from biomass. P-Series fuels are clear, high-octane alternative fuels that can be used in flexible fuel vehicles.	P-Series fuels can be used alone or mixed with gasoline in any ratio by simply adding it to the tank.	Manufacturers are not making flexible fuel vehicles.

Fig. 11.4. Super jeep Iceland, exemplar of off-road tourist vehicle, high carbon emissions (photo: Ian Jenkins).

Everest Sherpas are an excellent example of this principle and problems of equity of adventure companies and their contribution to the local economy as highlighted in the global media in 2014 (Box 11.3).

Education and training

This is seen within the context of both the stakeholders and the customers. Proper training and education are essential in allowing employees and customers to understand what sustainable principles of AT products are being purchased by tourists. Properly trained staff are in effect the policy of the company in action; their behaviour should be reflective of a sustainable company.

Development of energy-efficient policies needs to be imparted to employees and training is a means to do this. A policy of energy reduction or efficiency

Box 11.2. Use of gigantic vehicles in Iceland.

Iceland's extreme weather and climate have meant the development of specialized vehicles to navigate some of the more difficult terrain and also to drive on the glaciers. Many of these vehicles have been adapted from ordinary ones and have had their suspensions changed to give the appearance of gigantic vehicles. Sometimes these vehicles can be found in Reykjavik and they seem totally out of place given the size of normal cars. Many ordinary cars also have larger tyres so that they can navigate the gravelled roads that surround many of the country's access routes (Fig. 11.4).

That said, these vehicles also develop the perception that the terrain in Iceland is very different to many other locations. There is some truth in this; rental companies recommend that only 4×4 vehicles be used to access The Highlands and that vehicles travel in pairs as there are many obstacles which can make a vehicle become trapped, such as fording rivers and quicksands.

A quick review of the Icelandic Tourism Websites will identify a plethora of vehicle tours termed 'super jeep tours' which are reflective of these types of vehicles. There are also reports of tourists attempting to drive on glaciers using ordinary SUVs and this is somewhat reflective of tourists being unaware of the risks.

Box 11.3. Case Study of Sherpas.

Sherpas are an essential part of the Everest adventure product and without them it is likely that all commercial climbing would stop on Everest. It has become a multi-million pound business to climb Everest and is now a 'bucket list' destination. With all this money changing hands the employees who seem to get the least are those who actually take the most risks on this mountain.

In 2014–2015 the Sherpas had had enough of exploitation and risk and there was a withdrawal of labour from the mountain as a mark of respect for some 13 Sherpas who were killed and three others who went missing. The Sherpas felt that they were being exploited both by the Nepalese Government and by the companies that employed them to help adventurers climb Everest. In many respects this is a classic case of tourism 'unsustainability', with the local guides being exploited and paid much lower wages. However, counterarguments run as follows:

> Western guides, who lead and manage the expeditions, can make $50,000 to $100,000 guiding on Everest, so, at least on the surface, Sherpas seem to be severely underpaid. But this comparison fails to take into account the cost of living. Sherpas make five times the average

income in Nepal, which is about what mountain guides make in their profession at home.

> (Jenkins, 2014)

It is also noted (Jenkins, 2014) that the 'per capita income in Nepal is less than $800 a year, and a Sherpa will make on average $5,000 for two to three months of work'.

Many of the Sherpas are used to carrying heavy equipment and map out the routes up Everest, in particular the route over the Khumbu Icefall. The Icefall is one of the most dangerous areas and it is these Sherpas who are expected to verify the route and lay out the equipment. The Sherpas are an important case study of inequality in the tourism industry and some of the counterarguments are along the lines that the wages they earn are proportionally as much, if not more, than the Western guides in terms of what can be purchased in Nepal.

It is not only the Western AT companies who can be accused of being inequitable but also the Nepalese government, which takes a Permit Tax for summiting Everest but it is alleged that very little money ever gets back to the Sherpas who lead the expeditions. It is noted that, for Everest, 'every climber has already paid a $10,000 peak fee to Nepal's Ministry of Tourism' (Jenkins, 2014)

---

needs to be enacted through the employees. Instigating a system (similar to safety) of random testing and perhaps an online question-and-answer session are ways to try to ensure that the policy is being delivered.

Customers are not always aware of sustainable principles and a number of AT operators have commented that once out on an AT activity the guides or instructors have an opportunity to educate the customers on some of the more relevant sustainable issues relating to the location and the activities. As noted by hoteliers:

> ... to have a real positive impact they [hotels] also need to be educating and encouraging their guests to subscribe to the mind-set of responsible, authentic tourism.
>
> (Green Hotelier, 2014)

This should certainly relate to AT too. Customers are not necessarily seeking a company that operates along sustainable lines. It can be suggested that their primary motive for buying is the activity (often based on price and recommendations) and other factors that the company might be offering, which might include sustainable principles. This is an area of AT that would benefit from further research in order to ascertain what the attitudes of customers are to sustainable policies and how these can be imparted without appearing to be patronizing to the adventurer.

This perhaps raises the issue of tourist visas for special destinations that are environmentally sensitive. If there are visas for entry into certain countries (Bhutan restricted entry for some time), why not a tourist visa for sensitive destinations? This could be issued along the lines of the environmental criteria of the tourist and their knowledge of the destination they are visiting.

Waste

This component of sustainable management is probably the one most people would identify with and one in which many of the customers will themselves be engaged. As noted earlier, the environment was the first pillar of sustainability; it relates to the green movements of the 1960s and 1970s and much of the awareness of sustainability is seen through the lens of waste disposal and recycling. Maxims like the 3 Rs 'recycle, reuse, reduce' are commonly seen and heard and probably are recognized by many tourists in their understanding of sustainable principles (Anderson, 2016). Waste management has evolved exponentially over the past few decades and companies that do not have a recycling policy would probably be seen as archaic and irresponsible. Recycling waste is now, in most developed countries, a ubiquitous process and the location of recycle bins for various materials are common sights in most public or private organizations (EC, 2010).

It is an imperative that all AT companies have recycling policies and provide environmentally friendly waste management. In many respects the polemics have moved on to more specific aspects of recycling and the one that seems to garner most angst is that relating to plastic. This category of waste seems to produce heated debate and issues such as beach clean-ups and the growing problems of micro plastics are very high on the current environmental agendas (Fig. 11.5). Ocean pollution by plastic is the more visible and research looking at plastic waste globally identified this, stating that:

> [s]caling by the population living within 50 km of the coast (those likely to generate most of the waste becoming marine debris), we estimate that 99.5 million MT of plastic waste was generated in coastal regions in 2010.
>
> (Jambeck et al., 2015)

Therefore AT companies should be very active in this area, understand the implication of plastic waste and think about using other alternatives.

One of the main issues in the use of plastics relates to cost of transport. Using other materials such as paper, which like-for-like are heavier, means that transportation of goods increases the carbon footprint (Marsh, 2007). The counter-argument is the longevity of plastics over other degradable materials, which will cause long-term damage to the environment. However, the debate over packaging is not just simply about weight but has other important aspects, like protecting coastal areas.

Food waste is also a useful source for composting, though the decomposition does have greenhouse gas (GHG) emissions, producing gases such as methane as a by-product of the decomposition process. But this gas can be captured, using it for fuel and energy sources.

The commonly recycled materials are paper, metal and glass, all of which are now reprocessed

Fig. 11.5. Plastic waste on strandline (photo: Ian Jenkins).

in waste disposal plants in most developed countries. It would be incongruent to have an AT company that did not recycle or follow the principles of recycling.

A key to good waste management is monitoring volumes of waste and types of waste recycled. This is proactive management and indicates a commitment to sustainable waste disposal.

For those AT companies not connected to a mains sewage system, other opportunities arise relating to human waste disposal. It is interesting to note that this is managed on Everest expeditions, where most human waste is collected and removed from the destination. A number of approaches can be taken. Capturing methane gas and reusing in vehicles or a source for heating are possibilities (Kluger, 2015). Natural filter systems to decompose the waste through reed beds and other filtering sources can be used, together with applying the treated material as fertilizer if the AT company has its own vegetable/horticulture system on site (though precautions need to be taken relating to cross-infections from human waste, especially with the production of disease bacteria).

Supply chain

AT companies will be supplied with goods and services in order to deliver their own products. The evidence relating to how many ATs actually assess and examine the sustainability profile of their suppliers is limited. It is argued that most companies have enough to do just controlling and managing their own sustainability, but carbon footprints and employment rights are key to sustainability on a more global scale. Given that most companies operate in a global market, it is important to verify the profiles of the companies used to supply services and goods.

[i]ncreased global development and competition have pushed many industries to operate on a much more global level. Together with increased outsourcing, the number of companies involved in a typical supply chain has greatly increased. As a response to the above-mentioned pressures and incentives, a number of companies have introduced supplier evaluation schemes which integrate environmental and social criteria ... Related measures include supplier self-evaluation ... where suppliers have to declare how they deal with environmental and social issues.
(Seuring and Müller, 2008, p. 1705)

AT companies should try to verify key elements of sustainability in a supply chain company, which should include where the goods have been supplied from and in what conditions the employees in less developed countries work (Patagonia, 2016). Carbon footprint measurements and other resources would also be part of the assessments process. It is still extremely difficult to evaluate how sustainable a company is and more standards or codes of practice are needed to make the process of evaluation a lot easier (Hassinia *et al.*, 2012).

There are a number of categories within the supply chain that need to be considered. Most AT companies have to provide equipment for their customers and evaluating the ethical nature of equipment is an interesting and challenging area. Obtaining equipment that is environmentally friendly is still a challenge, especially when related to derivatives of plastic. Surfboards are not usually made from environmentally friendly material, but there are moves now towards ecologically cleaner materials such as bamboo and balsa wood, with some wetsuits even being made from recycled or natural material such as 'limestone-based polychloroprene' (Patagonia, 2015) and recycled polyester for the clothes linings.

Clothing is perhaps another area where green or sustainable choices should be a maxim for an AT company. Some suppliers have taken the lead in this area and Patagonia is certainly one. They are not the cheapest for clothes and equipment but their maxim is towards environmentally friendly behaviour based upon sustainable principles.

There are a number of evaluation systems that rank outdoor suppliers for their sustainability principles, such as Rankabrand (Rankabrand, 2016), and on their matrix Vaude is the highest ranked of the top outdoor suppliers (Fig. 11.6). However, it is suggested that Patagonia is probably the company that has led the way in developing sustainable outdoor clothes. Many of their goods are recycled and sourced from Fair Trade suppliers and equitable employment companies (Patagonia, 2015).

Some strategies for sustainable development are often overlooked by companies, such as renting equipment or sharing the costs with other companies or having a central rental company for equipment. If a company were to audit its equipment use, it would no doubt see that many items of equipment are used infrequently or irregularly. Sharing or renting would seem a sensible sustainable way forward.

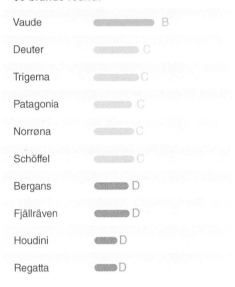

Fig. 11.6. Sustainable brands (Rankabrand, 2016).

Marketing

This element seems somewhat anomalous in a section on sustainability. Its aim is similar to education, communicating to the customer the intended experience of the activity together with providing a sustainable product. Information technology (IT) is a feature of the GSTC certification, which notes the following:

A5: Promotional materials are accurate and complete with regard to the organization and its products and services, including sustainability claims. They do not promise more than is being delivered.

A5.a: Marketing materials set realistic expectations and do not make false or misleading claims.

(GSTC, 2016)

A review of AT company websites by the author (Jenkins *et al.*, 2011) revealed a mix of different types of activities and products, with some emphasizing sustainable and environmental issues and others with little or no information at all on sustainability. Again there seems to be a need to standardize the website claims relating to sustainability and a universally recognized grading system is needed similar to Rankabrand (Fig. 11.6), which is able to evaluate the level of sustainability a company has obtained. Perhaps an agreed index score system similar to hotel ratings which provides the customer with an idea of the companies' ethical stance, such as that used for Fair Trade products, would give a degree of assurance to consumers of an AT company's sustainability.

Climate Change and its Effects on Adventure Tourism

It seems that there is a general consensus in the scientific community that climate is changing and with it will be new types of weather systems and risks. Adventure tourism is usually associated with destinations that have some elements of risk and certainly many of these can be related to climate and weather conditions (exposure, frostbite, heat exhaustion, dehydration, etc). It is not easy to envisage how climate changes will affect adventure tourism but there are indications that the risks to the adventurer will increase and, if the predictions hold true from the IPCC models (IPCC, 2007), more extreme weather conditions will create increased risks for certain activities. Due to the broad range of activities that AT provides, it is somewhat difficult to evaluate which specific activities will be affected and it is perhaps complicated by the predicted changes being incremental, not immediate. In general terms the changes will be more extreme weather patterns, which will create more intensity of rain, snow, wind and heat as the main sources of risk. Fig. 11.7 identifies the likely physical changes that will occur with climate change and these then have to be linked to the adventure activities that companies routinely manage in various geographical locales.

Everest fatalities and accidents over the past few years might be an indication of the likely effects of climate change, certainly in high mountain regions, where glaciers will be retreating and melting. These will present new hazards such as glacial melts and perhaps changes in avalanche dynamics at certain

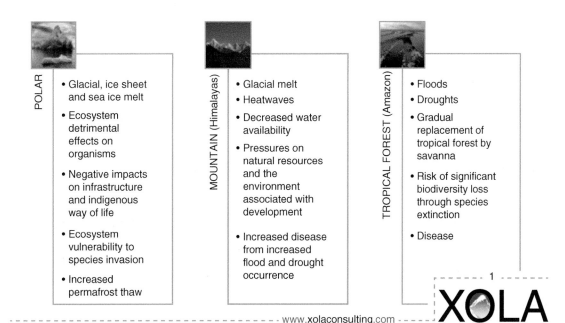

POLAR
- Glacial, ice sheet and sea ice melt
- Ecosystem detrimental effects on organisms
- Negative impacts on infrastructure and indigenous way of life
- Ecosystem vulnerability to species invasion
- Increased permafrost thaw

MOUNTAIN (Himalayas)
- Glacial melt
- Heatwaves
- Decreased water availability
- Pressures on natural resources and the environment associated with development
- Increased disease from increased flood and drought occurrence

TROPICAL FOREST (Amazon)
- Floods
- Droughts
- Gradual replacement of tropical forest by savanna
- Risk of significant biodiversity loss through species extinction
- Disease

1

XOLA

www.xolaconsulting.com

Fig. 11.7. Possible climate change effects of adventure tourism (Piotrowski and Xola Consulting, 2009).

times of year. Illustrating this point, a number of examples can be found. A lake at the base of Everest has been expanding due to higher temperatures resulting in increased glacial melt and it has become necessary to take immediate action to prevent serious flooding and possible risk of mortality if the glacial damn fractures (Khadka, 2016). New hazards and risks will be created at skiing zones; higher or less snowfall than usual as well as changes to melting and freezing conditions on the pistes will affect and change the times of year for safe skiing.

The main evidence related to climate change risks seems to be commercial and economic rather than personal adventure risks. AT will be affected in the same way as other tourism operators who are dependent upon the destination resource. There will be some mountain regions that will receive less snow and the snowfields will be higher up, which means that activities will have to move, increasing transport costs. This is also the case with activities such as glacier walking and lower ski resorts in the Alps. Retreating glaciers will change the way that ATs operate and may well increase the cost to companies.

In hotter regions there are predictions of water shortages, which will increase pressure on resources and AT operations are likely to incur increased costs in water supply and treatment. This may well be combined with intense heat, which will have higher risks for AT customers and will require new risk assessments and plans for adventure expeditions.

Adaptation and Mitigation

Adaptation and mitigation related to resilience are new agenda items in climate change and sustainability. Adaption in AT seems to be following many other businesses in the tourism sector: that of review rather than action. It is suggested that the challenge relates to the speed of climate change. Although the UN's Intergovernmental Panel on Climate Change (IPCC, 2007) is predicting rapid climate change, 'rapid' is a relative term for a company's business modus operandi: 50 years, for example, is a long time in the operation of a company and if the extreme weather predicted will be incremental, not immediate, what are the operational issues to plan for such an event? Evidence suggests that companies in AT are not taking immediate action to adapt but are considering what may need to be done. Also the polemic that AT will feel the effects of climate change before other areas is not being acted upon by these businesses (Piotrowski and Xola Consulting, 2009).

Mitigation on a global scale might actually reduce the impact of climate change but the processes and time to do this are in the long term. Certainly the COP 21 agreement seems to be actively trying to mitigate climate change (McGrath, 2016) and it would be difficult to find businesses that were not aware of their carbon emissions or were actively avoiding reducing their carbon footprint. There is much debate around how to mitigate climate change and the idea of sequestration by other companies or countries does raise some ethical issues relating to an AT company's sustainability principles. Mitigation incorporates some of the principles of sustainability and actions such as reducing energy, water usage and recycling are appropriate and expedient for reducing carbon footprints on a global scale. It is suggested that moving from a local approach to a global outlook is perceptively difficult, as a company sees only its locale. However, there now appears to be clear strategic change and many AT companies are embracing aspects of sustainability that are clearly interlinked with climate change.

Conclusion

This chapter has outlined and discussed the key elements of making an AT company sustainable. There is clearly a move towards more sustainable measures but without a standardized framework companies are limited in evaluating where they are as sustainable companies. GSTC can be a useful tool for reducing impacts and making a company more sustainable, but there are many other tools too such as those provided by ISO. It would be helpful and encouraging for the AT industry to standardize a global label for sustainability so that consumers are able to evaluate the level a company has reached. Furthermore, climate change is now seen as being integrated with sustainable development and AT companies need to be reducing their carbon footprint and ensuring that their impact on GHGs is of a low level or even carbon neutral. With the COP 21 Agreement signed, the future does seem more hopeful for sustainable development, but it also requires the consumer to be fully aware of sustainable products and to insist that these are embedded as part of the adventure tourism experience. The current research shows that this has not yet been achieved and there is some way to go before consumers insist on a sustainable adventure tourism product.

Questions

- Why is sustainability now an important element in adventure tourism products?
- Will climate change significantly affect adventure tourism?

References

Anderson, R. (2016) The firms planning on making less and recycling more. Available at: http://www.bbc.com/news/business-35755492 (accessed 6 December 2016).

B Corp (2016) What are B Corps? Available at: https://www.bcorporation.net/what-are-b-corps (accessed 8 December 2016).

Balch, O. (2016) P&G and Kraft Heinz criticised for recycling label failures. Available at: https://www.theguardian.com/sustainable-business/2016/dec/08/unilever-kraft-pg-heinz-recycling-failure?CMP=Share_iOSApp_Other (accessed 8 December 2016).

Campagnolo, L., Carraro, C., Davide, M., Eboli, F., Lanzi, E. and Parrado, R. (2016) Available at: https://link.springer.com/article/10.1007/s10584-016-1791-6 (accessed 28 August 2018).

Cohen, M.J., Comrov, A. and Hoffner, B. (2005) The new politics of consumption: promoting sustainability in the American marketplace. *Sustainability: Science, Practice, & Policy* 1(1), 58. Available at: http://ejournal.nbii.org

EC (European Commission) (2010) Being wise with waste: the EU's approach to waste management. European Union, Luxembourg. Available at: http://ec.europa.eu/environment/waste/pdf/WASTE%20BROCHURE.pdf (accessed 6 December 2016).

Economist (2009) Triple bottom line, it consists of three Ps: profit, people and planet. Available at: http://www.economist.com/node/14301663 (accessed 25 April 2016).

Goldsmith, E. and Prescott-Allen, R. (1972) A Blueprint for Survival. *Ecologist* 2(1), 136–139.

Green Hotelier (2014) Talking Point: Educating guests = more sustainable tourism. Available at: http://www.greenhotelier.org/our-themes/community-communication-engagement/talking-point-educating-guests-more-sustainable-tourism/ (accessed 26 April 2016).

Ground Work Wales (2016) Green Dragon, About Us, Programmes, Green Dragon Environmental Standard. Available at: http://www.groundwork.org.uk/Sites/wales/pages/green-dragon (accessed 25 April 2016).

GSTC (2016) Global Sustainable Tourism Council Criteria. Available at: https://www.gstcouncil.org/en/

gstc-criteria/sustainable-tourism-gstc-criteria.html (accessed 26 April 2016).

Gunther, M. (2015) Campaign aims to turn oil companies into climate allies. Available at: https://www.theguardian.com/sustainable-business/2015/apr/17/ceres-fossil-fuels-sec-carbon-chevron-exxonmobil-cnr (accessed 11 December 2016).

Hassinia, E., Surtib, C. and Searcy, C. (2012) A literature review and a case study of sustainable supply chains with a focus on metrics. *International Journal of Production Economics* 140(1), 69–82.

IPCC (2007) *Fourth Assessment Report: Climate Change 2007: Working Group I: The Physical Science Basis Projections of Future Changes in Climate*. Available at: https://www.ipcc.ch/publications_and_data/ar4/wg1/en/spmsspm-projections-of.html (accessed 8 December 2016).

ISO (International Organization for Standardization) (2016) *ISO 20121 Event Sustainability Management System*. Available at: http://www.iso20121.org/ (accessed 8 December 2016).

Jambeck, J.R., Geyer, R., Wilcox, C., Siegler, T.R., Perryman, M., Andrady, A., Narayan, R. and Law, K.L. (2015) Plastic waste inputs from land into the ocean. *Science* 347 (6223), 768–771. Available at: http://science.sciencemag.org/content/347/6223/768.full (accessed 6 December 2016).

Jenkins, I.S., Rios Morales, R. and Cevera, R. (2011) Sustainability of websites using GSTC. IGT Conference, Martinique.

Jenkins, M. (2014) Everest's Sherpas issue list of demands with climbing season in question, Sherpas want changes in working conditions. Available at: https://news.nationalgeographic.com/news/2014/04/140422-everest-sherpa-manifesto-avalanche-nepal-himalaya-base-camp-khumbu-icefall/ (accessed 11 December 2018).

Johnston, A. (2016) Getting to 100% renewable energy in the US. Available at: https://cleantechnica.com/2016/01/07/getting-100-renewable-energy-us/ (accessed 16 April 2018).

Khadka, N.S. (2016) Nepal drains dangerous Everest lake. Available at: http://www.bbc.com/news/world-asia-37797559 (accessed 15 December 2016).

Kluger, J. (2015) How poop can be worth $9.5 billion Nov. 3, Power plant: There's more going on here than you might think. Available at: http://time.com/4098127/human-waste-energy-recycling/ (accessed 7 December 2016).

Marsh, K. (2007) Food packaging and its environmental impact. (First published in *Food Technology* Magazine, April 2007). Available at: http://www.ift.org/knowledge-center/read-ift-publications/science-reports/scientific-status-summaries/editorial/food-packaging-and-its-environmental-impact.aspx (accessed 7 December 2016).

McGrath, M. (2016) Nations sign historic Paris climate deal. Available at: http://www.bbc.com/news/science-environment-36108194 (accessed 8 December 2016).

Meyers, G. (2012) Gasoline and diesel are still fossil fuel kings of the fuel supply chain but alternative fuels are now swinging the scale more toward green. Available at: (accessed 16 April 2018).

Mowforth, M. and Munt, I. (2009) *Tourism and Sustainability: Development, Globalisation and New Tourism in the Third World*, 3rd edn. Routledge, London.

Patagonia (2015) Environmental + Social initiatives. Available at: http://www.patagonia.com/on/demandware.static/Sites-patagonia-us-Site/Library-Sites-PatagoniaShared/en_US/PDF-US/patagonia-enviro-initiatives-2015.pdf (accessed 8 December 2016).

Patagonia (2016) Stories from our Supply Chain. Available at: http://www.patagonia.com/eu/enSE/footprint (accessed 27 April 2016).

PCF (Pembrokeshire Coastal Forum) (2016) Pembrokeshire Outdoor Charter Group. Available at: http://www.pembrokeshirecoastalforum.org.uk/ (accessed 11 December 2018).

Piotrowski, R. and Xola Consulting (2009) Adventure tourism companies and climate change: observations from the Himalaya, Amazon, and Polar Regions spark adaptation strategies for business. Available at: https://cdn.adventuretravel.biz/wp-content/uploads/2010/04/ClimateFull.pdf (accessed 11 December 2018).

Rankabrand (2016) Sustainability: sport and outdoor clothing. Available at: http://rankabrand.org/sustainable-outdoor-clothing (accessed 27 April 2016).

Seuring, S. and Müller, M. (2008) From a literature review to a conceptual framework for sustainable supply chain management. *Journal of Cleaner Production* 16, 1699–1710.

Smithers, R. (2012) M&S becomes 'carbon neutral'. Available at: https://www.theguardian.com/environment/2012/jun/07/marks-spencer-carbon-neutral-sustainability (accessed 7 December 2016).

Steynberg, L. and Grundling, J.P. (2005) Sustainability of adventure tourism: the economic highway. In: Kungolos, A.G., Brebbia, C.A. and Beriatos, E. (eds) *Sustainable Development and Planning II*. WIT Press, Southampton, Vol. 2, pp. 1419–1428. Available at: https://www.witpress.com/elibrary/wit-transactions-on-economy-and-the-environment/84 (accessed 27 August 2018).

Tourism Company (2011) *A Strategy and Action Plan for Sustainable Tourism in the Brecon Beacons 2012–2016 Final Draft*. Available at: http://www.beacons-npa.gov.uk/wp-content/uploads/tourism-strategy-2011.pdf (accessed 8 December 2016).

UNCOSD (United Nations Commission on Sustainable Development) (2007) *Framing Sustainable Development. The Brundtland Report – 20 Years On. Sustainable Development in Action*. Available at:

www.un.org/esa/sustdev/csd/csd15/media/
backgrounder_brundtland.pdf (accessed 7 December
2016).

UNECE (United Nations Economic Commission for Europe)
(2016) Sustainable development – concept and action.
Available at: https://www.unece.org/fileadmin/DAM/oes/
nutshell/2004-2005/focus_sustainable_development.
htm (accessed 11 December 2018).

UNESCO (2016) Tongariro National Park World Heritage
Centre. Available at: http://whc.unesco.org/en/list/421
(accessed 8 December 2016).

USDOE (US Department of Energy) (2016) Choosing and
installing geothermal heat pumps. Available at: https://
energy.gov/energysaver/choosing-and-installing-
geothermal-heat-pumps (accessed 11 December
2018).

PART II: CASE STUDIES

The concept for the book was to provide information and discourses on adventure tourism that would be both practical in terms of its functions and helpful in understanding how it has developed. When I first began teaching adventure tourism, there were limited texts available, with few expedient or relevant to my particular adventure tourism course. Consequently, I developed a stock of material which I felt best suited the requisites of students and future managers, of which this book is the culmination. It contains case studies which I have always found a useful vehicle for helping students make sense of the theory they are taught. It also provides managers and practitioners, within the industry, with sound examples of good practice that can be imitated or adapted. I considered that such a series of case studies from different actors and past students would help clarify and support some of the key aspects of the adventure tourism industry.

I have included seven cases which I think provide a detailed overview of the adventure industry and also provide an insight into the motivations and requirements necessary to work within the sector. The cases reflect my personal experience and research, both relating to the adventure tourism industry. Additionally I have incorporated leitmotifs which I consider to be useful for future adventure

students and managers. For me one of the cornerstones of transforming students into competent adventure tourism employees is the practical experience they gain whilst pursuing their educational courses. Without this I believe the student experience would be somewhat incomplete and would almost certainly constrain their employability.

Some of the cases in the book deal with current adventure tourism topics and challenges, whilst others illustrate the essential elements of running a successful adventure tourism company. Companies are essential for providing students with vital experience before they launch themselves onto the adventure industry. Furthermore, it is very pleasing to see that some of the students that I taught, are now 'doing it', not just talking about it. It is therefore implicit that universities and educationalists can and must help the industry to help shape future employees. It was often the academic course they studied, especially the vocational aspects of the programme, which provided them with the knowledge and skills necessary to be employed in the industry. As a lecturer I sometimes wonder what effect academics have on students and what career path such students take once they have qualified. I hope these case studies illustrate the positive effects education can have on adventure tourism employees and concomitantly the industry we, and they, work in.

12 Altruistic Adventure Voluntourism: Help Manage the Park You Visit

Robert S. Bristow, PhD

Westfield State University, Massachusetts

Introduction

Adventure tourists are engaged in a variety of activities around the world in parks and protected areas. For these tourists, one of the more popular interests is hiking. Research found that hiking is the most popular single backcountry activity, with 33% adult participation in 2008 and is expected to increase by about 3% by 2030 in the USA (White *et al.*, 2016). Hiking may involve a short walk in the local park or an extended long-distance experience found during the pilgrimage on the Camino de Santiago or America's long-distance giant, the Appalachian Trail.

In order to optimize the benefit for the adventure tourist, the planning and management of long-distance trails is necessary. The bulk of parks and protected areas are undeveloped even though a network of trails may be found winding through the area. The adventure tourist may not be directly aware of these off-trail resources, yet management is still essential to protect the park's ecological, historical and aesthetic environments from natural and anthropogenic encroachments.

For this chapter, a new form of adventure tourism is suggested, one that combines the skills needed for non-motorized trekking and backcountry experiences with that of orienteering and wayfinding to promote the new adventure volunteer tourism necessary to protect our parks and protected areas. Volunteer tourism, sometimes called voluntourism, reflects the evolving importance of tourists in giving something back to the resource through some altruistic behaviour (Wearing, 2001; Callanan and Thomas, 2005). Adventure tourism has a similar motivation, since sustainable practices are encouraged. Adventure tourists desire pristine natural environments and meaningful cultural experiences and the protection of these resources is vital (WTO, 2014).

The combined interest here provides the adventure experience for the tourist while at the same time helping to protect our natural areas. As this chapter is written, the US National Park Service just celebrated its 100th-year anniversary. This history is made possible due to the overwhelming public support for these national treasures and builds on decades of public–private cooperation between the adventure tourist and a volunteer work ethic.

One such partnership that exemplifies cooperation to the fullest potential is the working relationship between the Appalachian Trail Conservancy (ATC) and the National Park Service (Burch, 1979). The Appalachian National Scenic Trail (or AT, as it is commonly known) is one of the longest continuously maintained foot trails in the world. It stretches along the Appalachian Mountains nearly 3500 km (2200 miles) between Springer Mountain in Georgia and Mt Katahdin in Maine. To date, nearly 18,000 adventure tourists have hiked the entire trail (ATC, 2017).

Parks and Protected Areas Management

Adventure tourists travel the world seeking outdoor environments to participate in their favourite experience. Parks and protected areas are valuable choices for these adventure tourists. As these lands experience increased visitors, resource protection is vital and a better understanding of the resource management is needed.

Most research on the management of the parks and protected areas to date has dealt with visitor impact studies (Cole *et al.*, 1987; Anderson *et al.*, 1998; Eagles and McCool, 2002; Ervin *et al.*, 2007; Hammitt *et al.*, 2015) and resource protection including soil, habitats, invasive species, encroachments, air, water and sound pollution (Manning,

1979; Benninger-Truax *et al.*, 1992; Collinge, 1996; Brown and Harris, 2005; Davis and Hansen, 2011). Manning (1979) suggested concentrating research efforts in areas receiving the high visitor use, like travel routes and the destination areas found at a campsite or a fishing spot. For trails, Birchard and Proudman (1981) prepared specific guidelines for trail design, construction and maintenance. Subsequently, additional research by Cole *et al.* (1987) provided a comprehensive guide to identify, document and mitigate trail impacts in wildlands. Since trails are an important attraction in many parks and protected areas, it makes sense that there would be so much attention to the management of these necessary elements.

But trails are not the only recreation resource that needs management. Other impacts in parks and protected areas include waste, soil erosion, ecological habitats, vegetation, invasive species and the many social impacts such as crowding, noise, visual and pollution. To address these broad-reaching influences, a more holistic approach to resource changes in parks and protected areas is found in Hammitt *et al.* (2015), where the impacts are not just confined to the specific resource impacts, i.e. trails and campsites so popular with adventure tourists, but a more ecological approach that includes the entirety of the natural resources throughout the park. The landscape surrounding these high-impact areas serves as a buffer and this is the environment in which the adventure voluntourist can help.

Case Study: The US National Park Service

The US National Park Service (NPS) has just celebrated a centennial benchmark in the planning and management of the nation's parks and protected areas (NPS, 2016). A hundred years may be short to some, but the legacy of the nation's parks and protected areas has matured to match the changing demographics of visitors (Sellars, 2009). Like most parks and protected areas, these resources are managed for a multitude of reasons, including biological and geological reserves, and are constantly being challenged by humans and their desired uses (Wright, 1996). Thus these parks and protected areas are attractive options for the adventure tourist.

Under the US Department of Interior, the NPS managed 34,243,490 ha (84,617,507 acres) in 2015 (NPS, 2017). There are not simply National Parks; the managed units include National Battlefields, Historic Sites, Monuments, Preserves, Rivers, Seashores and Scenic Trails, among many other designations. For the 372 units managed by the NPS, a total of 307,247,252 recreation visitors were recorded in 2015, representing potentially every citizen in the country.

Shortly after the formation of the NPS, a regional planner named Benton MacKaye penned 'The Appalachian Trail: A Project in Regional Planning' in the *Journal of the American Institute of Architects* (MacKaye, 1921). This paper proposed a land management strategy for the eastern mountain range of North America. Building on this enthusiasm, the Appalachian Trail Conference was founded in 1925 by MacKaye and like-minded outdoor enthusiasts. A national not-for-profit corporation that linked volunteers from the region to help plan and manage the Appalachian Trail was now established (ATC, 1981).

The management viewpoint of the trail was further reinforced in MacKaye's work, *The New Exploration: A Philosophy of Regional Planning* (MacKaye, 1990) and sought to build a 'dam' to the encroaching urban sprawl. Managing the trail expanded into something that would need more than just trail maintenance (e.g. water bars and such); it required a whole new strategy to meet the growing needs of adventure tourists desiring outdoor experiences, be it a day hike or an extended end-to-end adventure. This attention to detail led Charles Little (Little, 1995) to proclaim that MacKaye's vision may be the major impetus into today's greenway movement. It is certainly clear that the foresight of MacKaye was instrumental in the establishment of the trail (Anderson, 2002).

The 20th century is an important era that saw the birth of adventure tourism. In the USA, for example, the American hiking community evolved from the exclusive membership of 19th century urban elites to the mass participation fuelled by an increased environmental awareness in the 1970s (Chamberlin, 2016). Societal changes meant that a middle class had not only free time but also the income for leisure pursuits. Trails grew out of this demand and tourists quickly found this resource for their adventures.

The Appalachian Trail was built in the early part of the 20th century and completed in 1937. As a non-motorized and non-mechanized trail system, foot travel is the main use. The Trail is a good example of how to emphasize existing natural features. The general path has followed ridgelines along the Appalachian Mountains. The area is rich with scenic landscapes of both cultural and natural features (Flink *et al.*, 2001). It has evolved over time, changing the route and even the southern terminus (Fisher and Durrance, 1972; Foster, 1987).

Figure 12.1 shows the general route of the Trail. Frequent relocations and landowner disputes riddled the route. Increased interest in adventure tourism during the post Second World War era and a burgeoning population meant the informal 'handshake' agreements on which the Trail depended began to disappear. These concerns meant the future of the Trail was threatened.

National Trails System Act

Growing interest in adventure tourism led to the nationwide expansion of public resources to meet the increased demand. American President Lynden B. Johnson even proclaimed in his Special Message to the Congress on Conservation and Restoration of Natural Beauty speech, 'In the back country we need to copy the great Appalachian Trail in all parts of America, and to make full use of rights of way and other public paths' (Johnson, 1965).

Shortly after, in 1968, the National Trails System Act (NTSA Public Law 90-543) (GPO, 1968) recognized the importance of the Trail and, through an amendment of the Act in 1978, provided the necessary funds to secure a permanent right-of-way

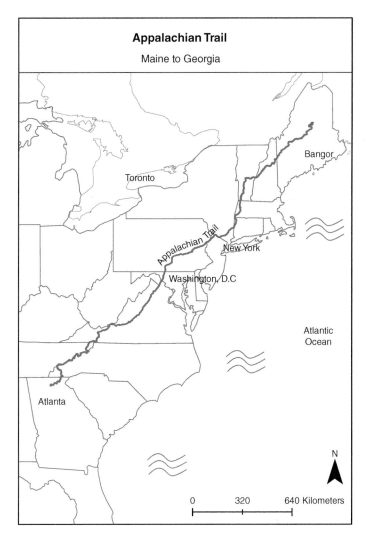

Fig. 12.1. Appalachian Trail.

that would preserve not only the route but also the character of the AT corridor. Fuelled by the NTSA, the NPS began acquiring lands on both sides of the Trail and exterior corridor boundary surveys were conducted between 1979 and 2005 as part of the NPS land protection programme.

The law enhanced the working relationship between the Appalachian Trail Conference (now Conservancy) and federal land management agencies, principally the NPS. The Appalachian Trail shifted from being an informally managed trail park to being part of the National Park system (Mittlefehldt, 2010). During the period of trail corridor acquisition, in 1984 the NPS took a historic step by delegating the ATC and its member trail-maintaining clubs with the responsibility for managing the newly acquired AT lands. This was the first time that the federal government had delegated a group of citizens with the responsibility of managing a national park. The management of the trail system began to be a true partnership between the federal, state and local agencies through whose land the Trail passed and the volunteer trail-maintaining groups. It formalized a long-term relationship that has made the Appalachian Trail one of the premier hiking experiences available to the public and a model for other long-distance trails (Burch, 1979; Bristow, 2004).

There are many recognized benefits in a protective corridor in parks (Shafer, 1999). These corridors provide some connectivity to facilitate movement of ecological processes such as animals and plant species (Benninger-Truax et al., 1992; Ahern, 1995; Harris et al., 1996; Collinge, 1996; Brown and Harris, 2005). Encroachments on national parks can be mitigated when the park corridor protects the ecological resources found within the environs (Davis and Hansen, 2011). The AT corridor also acts as a buffer to protect the Trail from neighbouring land use (Yahner et al., 1995).

Despite the benefits, pieces of irregular-shaped parcels of land define this corridor and act as a fragile buffer against the neighbouring land owners. This planned jigsaw puzzle of land acquisition was an expensive yet necessary planning tool needed to protect the nation's premier scenic foot trail. Figure 12.2 maps the NPS corridor in western Massachusetts and the intertwining of public and private land ownership. Even a narrow greenway encompasses many natural and social factors that must be deliberated (Leonard, 1979). Each parcel in the map has a unique identifier (e.g. '246-12') that records the historic ownership of the land.

For example, in 2006, the Berkshire Group of the Appalachian Mountain Club prepared a comprehensive management plan for the Trail in Massachusetts (AMC, DCR and ATC, 2006). This cooperative agreement between the maintaining trail club and the federal government delegated that 'volunteers organized by the Massachusetts AT Management Committee may assist in maintaining these boundaries'.

Today, the Appalachian Trail encompasses 236,739.33 acres (95,805 ha), where the majority (180,000 acres) (72,843 ha) are federal lands, 50,000 acres (20,234 ha) are other public areas and some 8000 acres (3238 ha) are under private ownership (NPS, 2017). In Massachusetts alone, some 5069 acres (2051 ha) of national park are defined by 79.82 miles of boundary (Pirog, 2017).

Adventure Voluntourism

For those hikers seeking an adventure in the backcountry, often away from trails and development, boundary monitoring is needed to protect the parks and protected areas. As an important component of any planning process, monitoring recreation resources is necessary since conditions change over time and, as a result of these changes, managers must adapt to meet administrative mandates. For example, the Limits of Acceptable Change (LAC) is a planning model utilized by the US Forest Service (Stankey et al., 1984). Monitoring is a part of the LAC planning process and provides management with the data necessary to adapt strategies as conditions change. Other recreation models are possible, but most address the direct impacts of the adventure tourists and not the holistic needs of parks and protected areas.

This method is inherently dependent on paid personnel, something becoming scarce on public recreation lands. A more sustainable arrangement is the long-term partnership that has already been in place along the Appalachian Trail for decades where volunteers aid in the management of the park resources. This is where the adventure voluntourist can help, by providing regular field inspections of corridor lands and becoming the eyes and ears for the ATC and NPS. Like any land manager, the main concern is protection of the land against unwanted uses, including timber theft, motorized vehicles, dumping, overuse and misuse (ATC, 2011). Further, there is a need to be aware of natural changes in the landscape such as insect deforestation, storm damage or accelerated

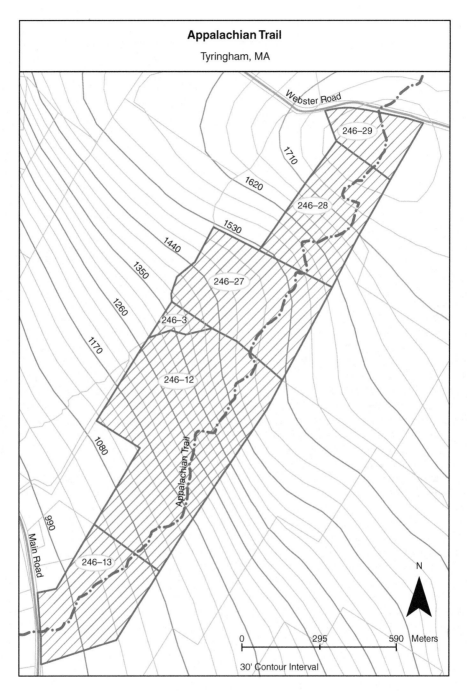

Appalachian Trail

Tyringham, MA

246–29
246–28
246–27
246–3
246–12
246–13

1710
1620
1530
1440
1350
1260
1170
1080
990

Webster Road

Appalachian Trail

Main Road

N

0   295   590 Meters

30' Contour Interval

Fig. 12.2. Appalachian Trail Corridor in Tyringham, Massachusetts.

erosion. Beyond these natural resource concerns are the threats from a neighbouring and growing urban population (Yahner *et al.* 1995; Wade and Theobold, 2010). Off-road vehicles, including snow mobiles, continue to be a major threat to the natural environment provided by the foot trail.

The ATC has identified some of the problems that may be encountered on corridor lands. The characteristics of human-caused encroachments facing the NPS lands are as follows.

- Minor problems:
  - Dumping of yard waste inside the corridor by adjacent landowners
  - A vehicle parked on the corridor
  - Adjacent landowner extending use into corridor for personal gain
- Moderate problems:
  - Unauthorized ATV, horse or mountain bike trail into the corridor
  - Deer-tree stand for hunting built inside corridor
  - Junked cars or equipment storage inside the corridor
- Severe problems:
  - Timber theft
  - Large-scale or hazardous material dumping
  - New road access across corridor
  - Repeated and escalating encroachments.

The adventure voluntourist can bushwhack off-track and at the same time document vital information needed to protect the national park. Given that much of the NPS corridor lands are away from the daily visitor experiences, regular site visits are required so that severe encroachments are not likely to occur. Corridor boundaries on steep or other inaccessible areas can be thought as having a low priority, since access is typically limited for most casual visitors, yet must still be monitored because the lands are NPS properties (Naser and Gass, 2008). A minimum level of monitoring should be established depending on the historic trends, impacts and use patterns.

Depending on the presence of known or suspected problems and the priority of need, monitors can determine what type of inspection is appropriate. More often than not, a combination of methods may be necessary. For instance, a boundary bushwhack is the most comprehensive type of inspection and is required for initial inspections. It is important to walk the entire boundary of the corridor during one visit, if possible, in order to get the 'big picture'. Furthermore, this is the time to take a comprehensive inventory of boundary monuments (Fig. 12.3). These monuments are found along the boundary at approximately 150 m (500 ft) intervals and are official boundary markers for the National Park. Becoming familiar with this backcountry area will aid in subsequent inspections, especially if a problem is discovered, and will need constant monitoring. Extensive note taking and

Fig. 12.3. Appalachian Trail Boundary Monument Tract 246-MA-22 (note AT symbol points north).

photography (Kim *et al.*, 2003) will support and document the findings.

During the site survey, care should be taken by being appropriately dressed and equipped for the off-trail experience. The adventure voluntourist must be comfortable with map and compass since they will be bushwhacking property lines away from the trail and other well travelled ways. The use of GPS is an option to corridor monitors, although one should not depend on it since the varied mountainous topography may mean that a GPS signal is poor or unreliable. Similarly cellphones are not dependable in the backcountry. Prudent preparation is necessary for the adventure voluntourist.

Many AT corridor lands have been surveyed and blazed to provide monitors with up-to-date and accurate information about the properties (Fig. 12.4). One must then visit the property with the AT Exterior Corridor Boundary Survey Map and compass. A US Geological Survey topographic map is useful as well. Under ideal conditions, the monitor can follow the survey blazes fairly easily, but survey blazes fade over time. Maintaining the boundary with fresh coats of paint will be necessary every few years.

However, some sections of the Appalachian Trail remain unsurveyed and the adventure voluntourist has only the deed information to follow in conducting the inspection. This requires a little more skill and patience; subsequently the corridor boundary is not as clearly marked. Fortunately, for some segments, old landmarks may still exist and make the job easier, or at least possible. An old stone wall may line a boundary, or even the edge between a field and the woods. In either case, the adventure voluntourist must have the requisite skills for the trip.

The preparation of documents from each survey is important. It is vital for tracking the history of

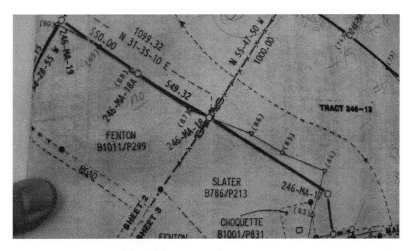

Fig. 12.4. Exterior Corridor Boundary Survey Map (ECBS).

problem areas and getting this information into the hands of professional land managers and if necessary the NPS Rangers. The documentation may also become legal information in the prosecution of crimes committed on corridor lands. The necessary forms can be downloaded from the ATC website. The monitor may wish to create sketch maps, photographs, video logs and other supporting evidence that will document the status of the park. While designed specifically for NPS lands, the toolkit can easily be adapted by the adventure voluntourist for similar backcountry surveys.

Discussion

As adventure tourism grows in popularity, there has been a likewise growth in commercial outdoor equipment suppliers catering for the demand (Tomazos, 2009). While the World Tourism Organization stresses the need to be sustainable in practice, for those adventure voluntourists seeking to return to a more altruistic experience, the scenario presented here can fill that need. By establishing citizen partnerships, the ties between the adventure tourist and those who want to give something back to the parks and protected areas can be expected to strengthen. These 'Friends of the Parks' become advocates to ensure the continued protection of areas such as the Appalachian Trail. Volunteering is big. Almost 63 million people in the US volunteered at least once between September 2014 and September 2015 (BLS, 2016). This represents about 25% of the people in the country.

Like many outdoor settings, the Appalachian Trail is more than just the trail. The Bureau of Outdoor Recreation (1966) noted early that the Trail helps to sustain a high-quality environment and makes neighbouring communities more attractive places in which to live and work, deserving of protection. Over 9000 hours of volunteer efforts to manage the Trail in Massachusetts were tallied in 2016. Of this figure, 206.25 hours were devoted to boundary monitoring, a small price to pay to protect this National Park (Massachusetts AT Committee, 2017).

Periodic and regular field inspections can be fun and provide excellent exercise for the adventure voluntourist. The best time of the year to undertake the monitoring is between the fall and spring, when the leaves are off the trees and visibility is maximized. Late spring may be muddy and since the monitor may be bushwhacking through the woods, there is a need to be careful about trampling on young plants. However, the best about this season is the lack of insects, cooler temperatures and the private experience one finds walking in the Appalachian Mountains.

There are tremendous opportunities for adventure voluntourism to continue in the future. As additional lands become protected for open space, traditional land management agencies will become financially burdened to oversee these properties properly. Creative partnerships are needed, since multiple levels of government are involved in parks and protected area management (Flink *et al.*, 2001). And adventure voluntourists fit that bill.

The partnership described in this chapter is one way that adventure voluntourists can become involved in the management of public lands. Besides the obvious savings of tax dollars from the free labour, there are three distinct advantages to this partnership.

First, it strengthens the bond between local public agencies and private citizens and provides an opportunity for all parties to better understand the needs and issues related to protecting our natural resources. MacKaye (1921) had suggested that each section of the trail should be managed by local people. Research by Propst *et al.* (2003) found that volunteers as an engaged team want to be able to influence decisions.

Secondly, there is the satisfaction from bushwhacking in the mountains, knowing that they can have fun, exercise and yet still help to manage the Appalachian Trail. The likelihood that adventure voluntourists exhibit place attachment behaviour in parks and protected areas will mean that their civic engagement is reinforced (Payton *et al.*, 2005). Success stories are found in Europe, where many fine examples of adventure voluntourism opportunities can be found by checking Thomson (2013) and Mitrofanenko *et al.* (2015).

Finally, as voluntourists, there is knowing that they are providing a protected park for adventure tourists to visit today and in the future.

Acknowledgement

I am grateful to Ms Chelsey Pousland, Class of 2017, Westfield State University, for the trail maps.

References

Ahern, J. (1995) Greenways as a planning strategy. *Landscape and Urban Planning* 33(1), 131–155.

AMC, DCR and ATC 2006. *Massachusetts Local Management Plan for the Appalachian Trail in Massachusetts.* Appalachian Mountain Club, Massachusetts Department of Conservation and Recreation and the Appalachian Trail Conservancy. Available at: http://www.appalachiantrail.org/docs/local-management-plans/2006-amc-berkshire-local-management-plan.pdf

Anderson, D.H., Lime, D.W. and Wang, T.L. (1998) *Maintaining the Quality of Park Resources and Visitor Experiences. A Handbook for Managers.* University of Minnesota, Minneapolis, Minnesota.

Anderson, L., 2002. *Benton MacKaye: Conservationist, Planner, and Creator of the Appalachian Trail.* JHU Press, John Hopkins University, Baltimore, Maryland.

ATC (1981) *Comprehensive Plan for the Protection, Management, Development and Use of the Appalachian National Scenic Trail.* Appalachian Trail Conservancy, Harpers Ferry, West Virginia. Available at: http://atfiles.org/files/pdf/ATCompPlan.pdf.

ATC (2011) *A.T. Corridor Stewardship Field: A Guide to Corridor Monitoring and Boundary Maintenance for Volunteers.* Appalachian Trail Conservancy, Harpers Ferry, West Virginia. Available at: https://www.appalachiantrail.org/home/volunteer/toolkit-for-trail-clubs/boundary-resources.

ATC (2017) *Two Thousand Miler Listing.* Appalachian Trail Conservancy, Harpers Ferry, West Virginia. Available at: http://www.appalachiantrail.org/home/community/2000-milers.

Benninger-Truax, M., Vankat, J.L. and Schaefer, R.L. (1992) Trail corridors as habitat and conduits for movement of plant species in Rocky Mountain National Park, Colorado, USA. *Landscape Ecology* 6(4), 269–278.

Birchard, W. and Proudman, R.D. (1981) *Trail Design, Construction, and Maintenance.* Appalachian Trail Conference, Harpers Ferry, West Virginia.

BLS (Bureau of Labor Statistics) (2016) Volunteering in the United States 2015. Available at: http://www.bls.gov/news.release/pdf/volun.pdf (accessed 11 October 2016).

Bristow, R.S. (2004) Volunteer-based recreation land management: the eyes and ears for the Appalachian Trail. In: Camarda, I. (ed.) *Global Challenges of Parks and Protected Area Management: Proceedings of the 9th ISSRM: October 10–13, 2002.* Carlo Delfino, La Maddalena, Sardinia, Italy.

Brown, R. and Harris, G. (2005) Co-management of wildlife corridors: the case for citizen participation in the Algonquin to Adirondack proposal. *Journal of Environmental Management* 74(2), 97–106.

Burch, W.R. Jr (ed.) (1979) *Long Distance Trails: The Appalachian Trail as a Guide to Future Research and Management.* Yale University, New Haven, Connecticut.

Bureau of Outdoor Recreation (1966) *Trails for America: Report on the Nationwide Trails Study.* United States Department of Interior, Washington, DC.

Callanan, M. and Thomas, S. (2005) Volunteer tourism. In: Novelli, M. (ed.) *Niche Tourism: Contemporary Issues, Trends and Cases.* Elsevier Butterworth-Heinemann, Oxford, UK, pp.183–200.

Chamberlin, S. (2016) *On the Trail: a History of American Hiking.* Yale University Press, New Haven, Connecticut.

Cole, D.N., Petersen, M. and Lucas, R.C. (1987) *Managing Wilderness Recreation Use: Common Problems and Potential Solutions.* US Department of Agriculture, Forest Service, Intermountain Research Station, Ogden, Utah.

Collinge, S.K. (1996) Ecological consequences of habitat fragmentation: implications for landscape architecture and planning. *Landscape and Urban Planning* 36(1), 59–77.

Davis, C.R. and Hansen, A.J. (2011) Trajectories in land use change around US National Parks and challenges and opportunities for management. *Ecological Applications* 21(8), 3299–3316.

Eagles, P.F. and McCool, S.F. (2002) *Tourism in National Parks and Protected Areas: Planning and Management*. CABI, Wallingford, UK.

Ervin, J., Spensley, J., Hayman, A., Lopez, C., Blyther, R. and Bryne, J. (2007) *Capacity Action Planning for Protected Areas: A Quick Guide for Practitioners*. Quick Guide Series (ed. J. Ervin). The Nature Conservancy, Arlington, Virginia.

Fisher, R.M. and Durrance, D. (1972) *The Appalachian Trail*. National Geographic Society, Washington, DC.

Flink, C., Olka, K. and Searns, R. (2001) *Trails for the Twenty-first Century: Planning, Design, and Management Manual for Multi-use Trails*. Island Press, Washington, DC.

Foster, C.H. (1987) *The Appalachian National Scenic Trail: A Time to Be Bold*. Appalachian Trail Conference, Harpers Ferry, West Virginia.

GPO (1968) The National Trail Systems Act (NTSA P.L. 90-543) US Government Publishing Office, Washington, DC. Available at: https://www.gpo.gov/fdsys/pkg/STATUTE-82/pdf/STATUTE-82-Pg919.pdf (accessed 3 September 2018).

Hammitt, W.E., Cole, D.N. and Monz, C.A. (2015) *Wildland Recreation: Ecology and Management*. John Wiley & Sons, Chichester, UK.

Harris, L.D., Hoctor, T., Maehr, D. and Sanderson, J. (1996) The role of networks and corridors in enhancing the value and protection of parks and equivalent areas. In: *National Parks and Protected Areas: Their Role in Environmental Areas*. Blackwell Science, Cambridge, Massachusetts, pp.173–198.

Johnson, L. (1965) *Special Message to the Congress on Conservation and Restoration of Natural Beauty*. Available at: http://www.presidency.ucsb.edu/ws/?pid=27285.

Kim, S.O., Lee, C.H. and Shelby, B. (2003) Utilization of photographs for determining impact indicators for trail management. *Environmental Management* 32(2), 282–289.

Leonard, R. (1979) Protecting the Long Trail resource: A Problem Analysis. In: Burch, W.R. Jr (ed.) (1979) *Long Distance Trails: The Appalachian Trail as a Guide to Future Research and Management*. Symposium on the Appalachian Trail, 11–13 October, 1977. Yale University, New Haven, Connecticut.

Little, C.E. (1995) *Greenways for America*. JHU Press, John Hopkins University, Baltimore, Maryland.

MacKaye, B. (1921) An Appalachian trail: a project in regional planning. *Journal of the American Institute of Architects* 9, 325–330.

MacKaye, B. (1990) *The New Exploration: a Philosophy of Regional Planning* (reprint). University of Illinois Press, Champaign, Illinois.

Manning, R.E. (1979) Impacts of recreation on riparian soils and vegetation. *Journal of the American Water Resources Association* 15, 30–43.

Massachusetts AT Committee (2017) *Report at the 2017 Mass AT Volunteer Gathering*. MATC, Dalton, Massachusetts.

Mitrofanenko, T., Muhar, A. and Penker, M. (2015) Potential for applying intergenerational practice to protected area management in mountainous regions. *Mountain Research and Development* 35(1), 27–38.

Mittlefehldt, S. (2010) The People's Path: conflict and cooperation in the acquisition of the Appalachian Trail. *Environmental History* 15(4), 643–669.

Naser, S. and Gass, E. (2008) *A.T. Journeys*. ATC, Harpers Ferry, West Virginia.

NPS (2016) *National Park Service Centennial*. National Park Service, Washington, DC. Available at: https://www.nps.gov/index.htm

NPS (2017) *NPS Statistics*. National Park Service, Washington, DC. Available at: https://irma.nps.gov/Stats/Reports/National

Payton, M., Fulton, D. and Anderson, D. (2005) Influence of place attachment and trust on civic action: a study at Sherburne National Wildlife Refuge. *Society and Natural Resources* 18(6), 511–528.

Pirog, D. (2017) *Corridor Summary Report for CY 2016*. Report to the Massachusetts Appalachian Trail Corridor Management Program, Dalton, Massachusetts.

Propst, D.B., Jackson, D.L. and McDonough, M.H. (2003) Public participation, volunteerism and resource-based recreation management in the US: what do citizens expect? *Loisir et Société/Society and Leisure* 26(2), 389–415.

Sellars, R.W. (2009) *Preserving Nature in the National Parks: a History*. Yale University Press, New Haven, Connecticut.

Shafer, C.L. (1999) US national park buffer zones: historical, scientific, social, and legal aspects. *Environmental Management* 23(1), 49–73.

Stankey, G.H., McCool, S.F. and Stokes, G.L. (1984) Limits of acceptable change: a new framework for managing the Bob Marshall Wilderness complex. *Western Wildlands* 10(3), 33–37.

Thomson, J. (2013) *Volunteer Management in European Parks: Research on Impact of Volunteering in European Protected Areas*. EUROPARC Consulting, Regensburg, Germany. Available at: http://www.europarc.org/wp-content/uploads/2015/05/2013-Volunteer-Management-EU-Grundtvig-project.pdf

Tomazos, K. (2009) *Volunteer Tourism, an Ambiguous Phenomenon: an Analysis of the Demand and Supply for the Volunteer Tourism Market*. University of Strathclyde, Glasgow.

Wade, A.A. and Theobald, D.M. (2010) Residential development encroachment on US protected areas. *Conservation Biology* 24(1), 151–161.

Wearing, S. (2001) *Volunteer Tourism: Experiences that Make a Difference*. CABI, Wallingford, UK.

White, E.M., Bowker, J.M., Askew, A.E., Langner, L.L., Arnold, J.R. and English, D.B.K. (2016) *Federal Outdoor Recreation Trends: Effects on Economic Opportunities*. Gen. Tech. Rep. PNW-GTR-945. US Department of Agriculture, Forest Service, Pacific Northwest Station, Portland, Oregon.

WTO (2014) *Global Report on Adventure Tourism*. UN World Tourism Association, Madrid.

Wright, R.G. (1996) *National Parks and Protected Areas: Their Role in Environmental Protection*. Blackwell Science, Cambridge, Massachusetts.

Yahner, T.G., Korostoff, N., Johnson, T.P., Battaglia, A.M. and Jones, D.R. (1995) Cultural landscapes and landscape ecology in contemporary greenway planning, design and management: a case study. *Landscape and Urban Planning* 33(1–3), 295–316.

Szabo, E.A., Lawrence, A., Iusan, C. and Canney, S. (2008) Participatory protected area management. A case study from Rodna Mountains National Park, Romania. *The International Journal of Biodiversity Science and Management* 4(4), 187–199.

Thomas, L. and Middleton, J. (2003) *Guidelines for Management Planning of Protected Areas*. Series No. 10. IUCN, Gland, Switzerland and Cambridge, UK.

Worah, S. (2008) *Participatory Management of Forests & Protected Areas: A Trainer's Manual*. Regional Community Forestry Training Center for Asia and the Pacific (RECOFTC), Bangkok, Thailand.

Further reading

Bristow, R.S. (1998) Volunteer-based recreation land management. *Parks and Recreation* 33, 70–77. National Recreation and Park Association, Ashburn, Virginia.

Eagles, P.F.J., McCool, S.F. and Haynes, C.D. (2002) *Sustainable Tourism in Protected Areas: Guidelines for Planning and Management. Best Practice Protected Area Guidelines*. Series No. 8. IUCN, Gland, Switzerland and Cambridge, UK.

Getzner, M., Jungmeier, M. and Lange, S. (2010) *People, Parks and Money: stakeholder involvement and regional development; a manual for protected areas*. NATREG training manual for partners. Heyn, Klagenfurt, Germany.

González, A.M., and Martin, A.S. (2007) *Park Guards in the Conservation of Protected Areas*. Innovations in Conservation Series. Parks in Peril Program. The Nature Conservancy, Arlington, Virginia: Available at: https://www.cbd.int/

Pimbert, M.P. and Pretty, J.N. (1997) Parks, people and professionals: putting 'participation' into protected area management. *Social Change and Conservation* 16, 297–330.

Toolkit websites and additional resources

Appalachian Trail Corridor Stewardship Field Book. https://www.appalachiantrail.org/docs/boundary-program-resources/2011/04/14/a-t-corridor-stewardship-field-book.pdf?sfvrsn=1

Appalachian Trail Toolkit for Trail Clubs. http://www.appalachiantrail.org/home/volunteer/toolkit-for-trail-clubs

Friends of Parks. http://www.europarc.org/

Global Parks, Expert Volunteers strengthening the Management of Natural Resources Worldwide. http://globalparks.org/index.html

Iceland Conservation Volunteers. https://www.facebook.com/ICV.is/ and http://www.ust.is/the-environment-agency-of-iceland/volunteers

National Geographic, Basic Map and GPS Skills. http://maps.nationalgeographic.com/downloads/Map_Skills_Booklet.pdf

Ordnance Survey Ireland, How to Use a Map and Compass. https://www.osi.ie/education/map-reading/how-to-use-a-map-and-compass/

Service Leader, Guide to Volunteering Outdoors in Parks and Wilderness Areas. https://www.serviceleader.org/volunteers/parks

USGS, How to Use a Compass with a USGS Topographic Map. https://education.usgs.gov/lessons/compass.html

13 Adventure Tourism in the Four Different Worlds of Ecuador

Maximo Ortega

Co-owner, Blue Walkers Adventure Travels, Quito, Ecuador

Introduction

The intention of this chapter is to show how adventure tourism is now a thriving industry in South America, using Ecuador as an example and to illustrate the importance of adventure tourism for Latin America. The chapter describes the situation of adventure tourism in Ecuador, explores the four different regions of Ecuador and evaluates the advantages of Ecuador's geography for adventure tourism development. The narrative elucidates how indigenous peoples are now active members of the industry and the involvement of the government of Ecuador in adventure tourism. Finally, it reviews the future of adventure tourism in Ecuador.

Adventure Tourism Industry in Ecuador

Adventure tourism is an industry that has been growing in Ecuador in the past 10 years and today a large number of companies work in the adventure tourism field. In Ecuador only some companies can offer adventure tourism services, as those working in adventure tourism must comply with regulations from the Ministry of Tourism (Mintur) and Ministry of Environment of Ecuador. These regulations will be described in more detail later (see Box 13.4), but it is important to note that regulations for adventure tourism have not always existed; they were devised as adventure tourism grew and the government saw the need to implement procedures to control the industry. Ecuador's first Ley de Turismo (Tourism Law) was approved on 27 December 2002, but it did not include specific regulations for adventure tourism (Mintur, 2015). With the growth of the country's adventure tourism it became propitious to introduce protocols for this part of the tourism market and the Reglamento de Operacion Turistica de Aventura (Regulations

for Adventure Tourism Operators) came into force on 11 February 2014 (Mintur, 2016). The first objective was to standardize and provide a structural framework for tourism companies. Secondly, due to the growth of adventure tourism it became necessary to protect the safety of the adventurers; and finally there was a need for specialized guides for different types of adventure tourism. Box 13.1 discusses an accident in the Chimborazo Volcano in Ecuador and highlights the importance of both the Tourism Law and the adventure tourism regulations.

Visitors have the option to purchase tours through travel agencies or tourist operators. The adventure tourism regulations prohibit visitors from buying tours directly from guides and they cannot perform any adventure expeditions by themselves. This is because many tourists have lost their lives in the mountains of the Andes and the Amazon jungle. Most of these accidents are caused by the recklessness of tourists. However, the regulations also have their critics; for example, Jorge Lara, a specialized guide for high mountain expeditions who has over 30 years of experience, believes that the adventure tourism regulations are removing people's freedom to roam.

These regulations apply to Ecuadorian residents and visitors, which means that even residents of Ecuador have to hire guides to enter protected areas where volcanoes and mountains are located. In a personal communication with the author (25 October 2016), Lara said: 'You cannot take away the freedom to Ecuadorian citizens in freely circulating in national parks'. He also believed that foreigners considered as 'pure mountaineers', i.e. experienced mountaineers (who generally have a lot of experience and are aware of the risks), should have the freedom to explore Ecuador without the need to hire the services of a

Box 13.1. Three bodies found in the Chimborazo Volcano.

On Saturday 22 August 2015, the mountain guide Manuel Calapiña descended the Chimborazo Volcano (6267 m (20,561 ft)) with tourists, when in the distance he distinguished some unusual objects at about 5600 m (18,372 ft). On approaching he discovered the remains of three people. Afterwards, he took photos, and told other guides what had happened once he reached the first shelter of the Chimborazo and then proceeded to contact the forensic police.

On Monday 24 August 2015, the corpses were rescued. The problem was that the authorities and the guides could not identify the corpses, since no identification was found on them. And in the previous years there were no reports of people lost in the area of the Chimborazo Volcano. Therefore, no information was available to begin the investigation to try to discover the identities of the corpses.

Colonel Carlos Alulema, who was responsible for the police unit dealing with disappearances and violent deaths, said that the accident could have happened 15, 20 or 25 years ago. 'You see, according to the clothes, that they were not rookies, they had climbing equipment: harness, cold protection equipment, etc.' (El Universo, 2015). Alulema also stated that it seemed strange to him that the authorities had not registered any complaint about the disappearance of these people.

Of course, if the accident had occurred 20–25 years ago, it would be difficult to find documentation of missing persons in the mountains, since in Ecuador there was no regulation in adventure tourism or related to tourism. Some tourists arriving in Ecuador hired a guide, while others did not. In addition, there was no regulation for entry to protected areas. Access to protected areas was free and without any regulation.

On the other hand, the Ecuadorian press speculated that they were two foreigners and one Ecuadorian who died in 1993 because of a landslide. In 1995 *LA Times* (Ward, 1995) reported that an avalanche in Chimborazo had killed ten climbers from three countries in November 1993. The US newspaper said that about two dozen mountain guides spent 10 days searching for the bodies. *LA Times* also said that six were French, three were from Ecuador and one was Swiss.

Another hypothesis that the guides suggested was that they could be three Austrians who disappeared in the 1980s. Other guides said that they could be passengers of an airplane that crashed in the Chimborazo in 1976 with 59 passengers, and that the volcano had thawed the bodies recently, allowing the remains to be found 27 years later.

At the end of the investigations the forensic police were able to determine that the victims were members of an expedition of ten climbers buried in an avalanche in 1993.

If regulations for adventure tourism had been in place then perhaps this tragedy could have been prevented by hiring guides for their expedition who would have known the mountain and the conditions of where and when avalanches were likely to occur. The current regulations require those involved in adventure tourism to enact certain safety procedures in the operation of the tours. The regulations require that travel agencies, tour operators and park rangers work together, and, in the event of an accident, act immediately.

Sources:

El Universo (2015) *Así descubrieron en el Chimborazo los restos de escaladores que se cree fallecieron en 1993*. Available at: https://www.eluniverso.com/noticias/2015/08/24/nota/5084714/asi-descubrieron-chimborazo-restos-escaladores-fallecidos-1993 (accessed 3 February 2018).

El Telégrafo (2015) *Restos de los tres andinistas, hallados en el Chimborazo el fin de semana, fueron entregados a sus familiares*. Available at: http://www.eltelegrafo.com.ec/noticias/regional-centro/1/los-tres-andinistas-hallados-en-el-chimborazo-el-fin-de-semana-habrian-sido-identificados-por-la-ropa (accessed 3 February 2018).

Ward, L. (1995) Ecuador elevates climbing safety after fatal avalanche: Mountaineering: Nation's Andes are an increasingly popular tourist destination, with 10 peaks over 16,000 feet. But basic equipment and guide training is in short supply. Available at: http://articles.latimes.com/1995-02-05/news/mn-28176_1_mountain-guides (accessed 3 February 2018).

guide. These experienced mountaineers are the ones who carry the message through word-of-mouth marketing to their home countries, which then encourages the 'normal' tourist to come and buy adventure products. Lara said, 'It has always been that way, since the beginning of adventure tourism in Ecuador'.

In countries such as Peru the visitors do not need a guide to get into the mountains. In Argentina, visitors have to pay to get into the mountains, but the money is used to provide rescue teams, park controls, etc. However, according to statistics from Ecuador's Ministry of Tourism, mountain adventure tourism remains the most popular for visitors seeking adventure (Fig. 13.1). Therefore, it is thought to be necessary to have rules to protect visitors and nature.

Lara (personal communication, 2016) argued that the adventure tourism regulations are expensive and restrictive, as mountain guides must be certificated to work and renew their certificate every 2 years. This certificate is issued by a mountain school approved by the Ministry of Tourism. The certificate costs US$6000, which is a lot of money for the mountain guide. According to Lara, mountain adventure tourism has decreased in the past 2 years, because the most experienced guides (over 20 years of experience) are above 46 years of age and they do not have the certificate that allows them to work. Neither are they interested in paying US$6000 to be certified as a mountain guide. They prefer to invest that money in tourism-related businesses. He also noted that young people who graduate from mountain schools are not interested in being guides, because they have no vocation for it. They see mountaineering as a sport but not as their profession and they earn more money in other areas of tourism.

It is important to note that adventure tourism guides, in all fields, must have a certificate obtained by an approved school of the Ministry of Tourism and guides do not have the option to choose a school that they can afford (ASEGUIM, 2018).

Another type of tourism that is gaining strength and popularity among visitors is water adventures, such as rafting, kayaking, canopying, diving, surfing, snorkelling and whale watching. This type of adventure tourism is growing fast, not only for visitors arriving in the country, but also for locals (Castillo *et al.*, 2015). Ecuadorians now have more money and are more interested in exploring their own country. This has led many

Fig. 13.1. Climbing the Cotopaxi Volcano (5897 m, 20,561 ft) in Ecuador. In the distance are, to the right, Antisana Volcano (5704 m) and, to the left, Cayambe Volcano (5790 m) (photo: Maximo Ortega, Co-owner, Blue Walkers Adventure Travels).

people to create adventure products for the domestic market. For example, Leonardo Cardoso Maldonado is (2016) the owner of Illiniza Lodge in the Illinizas Ecological Reserve (Fig. 13.2). He is interested in promoting family tourism, and the project Los pies sobre la Tierra (Feet on Earth) is an example, with walks of 2–4 hours where children and parents enjoy nature. 'They learn about the flora and fauna of the reserve, and eat what is produced in the land' (L. Cardoso, personal communication, 29 October 2016).

Adventure tourism is growing very fast in Ecuador, which has become one of the main priorities of the Ministry of Tourism (Mintur) (Box 13.2). The economist Rafael Correa (President of Ecuador, 2007–2017) took an active part in promoting tourism in Ecuador. Mintur and Correa worked together on a project called 'Ecuador, the Royal Tour', where Correa performed the work of a tourist guide and featured in journalist Peter Greenberg's 'The Royal Tour' reports, shown on PBS. Greenberg, travel editor for CBS, was also travel editor for NBC's Today, CNBC and MSNBC from 1995 until 2009 (Greenberg, 2018).

A documentary of the 'Ecuador, the Royal Tour' project was filmed (in English); it has a duration of 55 minutes and can be viewed on YouTube (FPLANETA FPLANET, 2016). However, the first 9 minutes of the documentary have a political context not really connected with tourism.

Previously, adventure tourism mainly took place in the mountains and volcanoes. Currently, aquatic tourism is competing with mountain tourism, due to the market constantly seeking new experiences, and also due to the geography of Ecuador.

The physiognomy of physical features is quite extensive, with the highest point being 6267 m (20,561 ft) and the lowest region being the Amazon basin at 100 m (328 ft) above sea level. The landscape includes rivers, waterfalls, lakes, caves, climate, flora, fauna, etc. which is ideal for aquatic adventure tourism. There are all levels of difficulty for rafting, kayaking, rappelling, canopying, snorkelling and diving. Aquatic tourism has served to accelerate the growth of other types of adventure such as bungee jumping, paragliding and parachuting. For example, Montañita and Canoa are small villages located on

Fig. 13.2. Illiniza Ecological Lodge (photo: Leonardo Cardoso).

the coast of Ecuador that are becoming important for surfers, together with equestrian tourism.

Guides who work in aquatic adventure tourism need a certificate from a school approved by the Ministry of Tourism. Diving is perhaps one of the best organized adventure tourism activities in Ecuador, but not all aquatic tourism guides have a certificate obtained with an approved organization. An illustration of this is in the Amazon jungle; many of the guides are local community members who know the rivers and waterfalls because they grew up in these places, but who have no formal training as adventure tourism guides. Nevertheless, these local guides know the river better than the guides who are trained in larger cities and only practise their skills on weekends.

Expeditions to the Amazon Rainforest are an expanding activity of adventure tourism and these companies are controlled by inhabitants of the Amazon (this is explored in depth in the section 'Indigenous Communities' below). The most popular adventure tourism products in the Amazon Rainforest are kayaking and rafting, but just having the opportunity to walk in the jungle and enjoy its megadiversity (i.e. great biodiversity) is an adventure in itself, which is reflective of the growth of slow tourism.

Comparison of Adventure Tourism in Iceland and Ecuador

Iceland has a scenic landscape which is undoubtedly ideal for adventure tourism (see Chapter 14).

Both Ecuador and Iceland are exotic countries, perfect for adventure; both countries are newcomers to the tourism industry; and both countries have seen adventure tourism become an important source of income. However, Ecuador and Iceland are very different from each other, not only in their geography, climate, culture, economy, etc. but also in the growth of their adventure products. Table 13.1 compares certain aspects that the author considers relevant in adventure tourism.

Unlike Iceland (apart from adventure tourism), Ecuador has a significant market in ethnic tourism, colonial tourism, tourism of ancient civilizations, gastronomic tourism, archaeological tourism, tourism for retirees, etc. For Iceland adventure tourism is the main tourist product, as Iceland offers trips to the mountains, glaciers, rafting, diving, hiking tours, whale watching, Northern Lights, ice climbing, equestrian tourism and much more.

In the author's opinion, the growth of adventure tourism in Iceland has been so fast that the government and the tourism industry has had little time to develop safety policies and operating regulations for adventure tourism. In addition, Iceland has about 330,000 inhabitants, but according to the Iceland Tourist Board in 2015 it received 1,608,442 visitors. As a consequence of this exponential growth (see Chapter 14, Fig. 14.1), Icelanders have a great challenge in handling the growth in tourism, yet there is still no clear policy from the government regarding regulations for adventure tourism (Icelandic Tourist Board, 2017).

Table 13.1. Comparison of adventure tourism in Ecuador and in Iceland.

	Ecuador	Iceland
Adventure tourism	It is becoming the most popular type of tourism	It is the main tourism in Iceland
Regulation for adventure tourism	Yes, by Ministry of Tourism of Ecuador	Yes
Safety policy for adventure tourism	Yes, by Ministry of Tourism of Ecuador	Yes
Professional guides	Most of the guides are professionals, and others are locals who know the area and work as guides	Some of the guides are professionals, and others are locals who know the area and work as guides
Environmental protection regulations.	Yes, by Ministry of Environment of Ecuador	Yes, by Icelandic Tourist Board. VAKINN Quality & Environmental System
Quality certification for adventure tourism	No	No
Quality certification for tourism	Yes, Distintivo 'Q' de Calidad ('Q' for Quality)	Yes, VAKINN

However, issues such as sustainability, safety policies for tours and tourist industry regulations are topics that are currently being researched and discussed in universities such as the University of Iceland. There are many travel agencies that, on their own, have developed safety policies for their adventure products and waste management policies. This suggests that the government will soon establish operating regulations for adventure tourism companies.

The Four Different Regions of Ecuador

In 1998, Conservation International identified 17 'Megadiverse Countries in the World', defined as countries with a high number of species, including a significant percentage of endemic species (at least 5000 endemic plants) and having a marine ecosystem within the country's borders (Revolvy, 2014; World Atlas, 2017). Ecuador is one of these 17 countries but one of the smallest. It is also described as the most diverse country in the world by area. Being such a small country with such a diverse geography makes Ecuador an ideal place for adventure tourism. For example, climbing in the Andes, or rafting in the rivers of the Amazon, or surfing on the Ecuadorian coast, can be done without the need to travel for hours to change the environment. It is very common that travellers take breakfast in the Amazon rainforest, then have lunch in the Andes Mountains, and finally have dinner watching the sunset on the Pacific Ocean, all in the same day.

Geographical location

Ecuador is located in South America (Fig. 13.3). It has a coastline on the Pacific Ocean and borders Colombia in the north and Peru in the south and east.

The total area of Ecuador, including the Galapagos Islands, is 283,561 km^2 (land area 276,841 km^2; water area 6720 km^2). The highest point is the summit of the Chimborazo Volcano at 6267 m (20,561 ft), with the Amazon rainforest at an elevation of 100 m (328 ft) above sea level.

Four different worlds in one country

Ecuador, like some other countries in South America (Peru and Colombia), has territories on the Pacific Coast and in the Andes Mountains and the Amazonas Rainforest. Ecuador also owns the famous Galapagos Islands. Each of these four different regions has its own flora, fauna, climate and distinctive food. Even the physical and cultural characteristics of people vary according to the region and it is important to note that Ecuador is one of the most ethnically diverse countries in South America. The four regions are known as La Sierra (the highlands), La Costa (the coast), La Amazonia and La Region Insular (the island region).

Sierra (highlands)

The capital of Ecuador is Quito, which is located in the Sierra. Like many other towns in the highlands, Quito is surrounded by mountains, volcanoes,

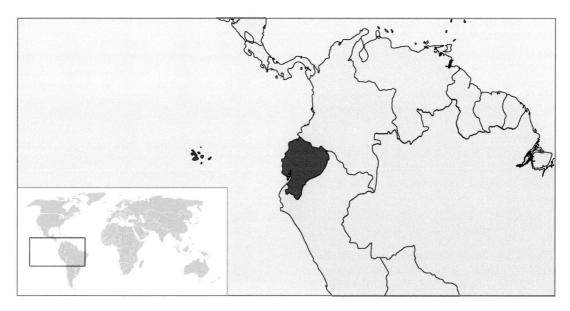

Fig. 13.3. Map of Ecuador.

national parks, ecological reserves, etc. It takes about 1–2 hours to reach the nearest adventure tourism attractions from the capital. In this region there is a cultural legacy of the Inca Empire. The ruins of Ancient Ingapirca, an Inca city, is part of the Inca trail or Inca road system, which passes through Colombia, Ecuador, Peru, Bolivia, Chile and Argentina. The legacy of the Spanish conquest can be seen in almost all cities in the Sierra. Quito and Cuenca have the largest colonial historical centres in Latin America. The cities that are at higher altitudes have a temperature range from 7°C to 25°C (44–77°F) compared with cities that are in the valleys, which are 18–28°C (64–82°F). There are a number of glaciers and volcanoes in the region and temperatures here can reach well below 0°C (32°F).

The Sierra of Ecuador is part of the mountain range of the Andes. The Sierra has seven National Parks, four Ecological Reserves, two National Recreation Areas, one Biological Reserve, one Fauna Production Reserve, one Wildlife Refuge and one Geo-botanical Reserve. The Sierra has 44 volcanoes, including the Cotopaxi Volcano, considered the largest active volcano in the world and 5897 m (19,347 ft) high (see Fig. 13.1), and the Chimborazo Volcano, suggested as the highest point on earth, if measured from the centre of the earth, at 6267 m (20,561 ft) high.

In the Sierra the largest mammal is the spectacled bear, also known as the Andean bear, which is an omnivorous animal: it is more of a vegetarian than any other bear. Other animals live here too, such as llamas, alpacas and vicunas (these last three are closely related camelids), and wild horses, but none of these animals pose a threat to humans. The Sierra landscape of volcanoes, mountains, valleys, lakes and rivers provides a backdrop for many adventure tourism activities.

The Costa (the coast of the Pacific Ocean)

Guayaquil is the largest city in Ecuador and is located in the Costa region. The average temperature of the Ecuadorian coast is 18–32°C (64–89°F). Most of the coast of Ecuador is accessed by a road called La Ruta del Spondylus (Spondylus Route); this route is very important to tourism, because it crosses the coast parallel to the Pacific Ocean. The road takes tourists to different places where visitors can perform activities such as surfing, diving, snorkelling, paragliding, parachuting, trekking, hiking, whale watching, etc. This route also leads to an important legacy for Ecuadorians: there are archaeological sites that show the pre-Inca ruins, i.e. cultures that lived in Ecuador before the Inca conquest, such as Valdivia, Chorrera and Machalilla. As a bonus, tourists have the option to combine adventure tourism with archaeological tourism, and learn from the pre-Inca culture of Ecuador.

The Costa has one National Park, four Ecological Reserves, four National Recreation Areas, two Fauna Production Reserves, eight National Wildlife Refuges and one Marine Reserve. In this region Ecuador has the tallest mangroves in the world. The biodiversity of the Costa is immense. There are 6300 species of plants, of which 1200 are native and cannot be found outside Ecuador. There are 800 bird species, more than 20% of which are native; 142 species of mammals live there (54 native) and 253 types of reptiles and amphibians. The Costa has so much biodiversity that it is easy to find eco-adventure in every corner.

The Amazon Rainforest

The temperature of the tropical Amazon Rainforest is 15–45°C (59–113°F). Ecuadorian Amazon has two National Parks, one Ecological Reserve, four Biological Reserves, one Fauna Production Reserve, one Wildlife Refuge and one Ecological Conservation Area. When you descend from the Andes to the Amazon jungle, you can see an endless green carpet. Below this green carpet, it is a megadiverse world, a natural laboratory with a wide variety of medicinal plants, exotic animals and an extensive network of rivers, the ideal place for visitors seeking adventure in activities such as rafting and kayaking.

The Amazon rainforest is home to thousands of indigenous peoples belonging to 200 different ethnic groups. Among the best known are the Siona, Secoya, Cofan, Shuar, Zaparo, Huaorani and Quichua. The indigenous tribes that inhabit the Ecuadorian jungle are the ancestral guardians of the region's and the world's biological heritage. Having lived there for more than 10,000 years, they know their plants, their animals and their jungle's secrets better than anyone.

As mentioned earlier, rafting and kayaking are very popular activities in the Amazon. But the adventure in the jungle has a plus, since adventure tourism offers visitors the opportunity to get to know indigenous communities, and to take adventure expeditions with native guides to the interior of the Amazon. On these expeditions visitors have the opportunity to camp in the jungle, enter caves, hunt for their own food and observe flora and fauna, and much more. In the Amazon Rainforest, due to its megadiversity, a simple walk can become the adventure of a lifetime.

The Galapagos Islands

The Galapagos Islands are located 973 km (605 miles) from the mainland and consist of 22 islands and 107 islets and rocks. The Galapagos Islands Region is a Global Biodiversity Sanctuary, which is why UNESCO in 1979 declared it a Natural Patrimony for Humanity, also extending the declaration to cover a marine reserve. The Galapagos now has one National Park and one Marine Reserve.

These islands have unique animal and plant species that are not found anywhere else in the world and, partly due to the global status, the animals on Galapagos are not afraid of humans, as they have for some time interacted with visitors. The adventure offered by the Galapagos is soft adventure and more related to ecotourism.

Geography: the Benefits to Ecuadorian Adventure Tourism

For a better idea about the size of Ecuador, its surface area (276,841 km^2) is slightly larger than that of the United Kingdom. This highlights the fact that Ecuador is a relatively small country and for that reason it is easy to visit all regions without travelling long distances.

Because of Ecuador's four physically different regions, each with its own important megadiversity, the physiognomy is ideal for adventure. Firstly, the fact that the country is small helps to make trips more economical, because visitors do not need to travel for days or even weeks to reach the places where adventure activities are located within these different climatic zones and landforms. The rugged geography of Ecuador offers adventure tourism many alternatives; for instance, visitors can choose from a scenic slow adventure walk, to technical rock climbing or glacial climbing in the Andes. In addition there is class I rafting on rivers and lakes, to class V rafting on rapids (torrential rivers) that flow down from the Andes to the Amazon or the Costa of Ecuador. More slow adventures can be had by exploring the flora and fauna of the Amazon Rainforest, with an expedition of several days' camping in the jungle, crossing rivers and descending caves.

Another advantage of having so many climatic zones in a very small country is that travel agencies and tour operators can adapt to sudden changes in weather and offer alternatives without necessarily increasing the cost of their operations. For example, in the author's experience having worked in adventure tourism in Ecuador, many companies based in Quito in the highlands sell adventure tours like surfing, paragliding, rafting and kayaking (7-day tour) as the coast is only 5 hours away by car. In some years, however, the Fenómeno del Niño (El Niño phenomenon) was so strong that they could not sell these tours on the coast of Ecuador. Instead, they offered 4-day rafting and kayak tours in the Amazon Rainforest, 3 hours away by car from Quito, together with 1-day paragliding tours in Ibarra, a highlands city located 2 hours from Quito.

The most successful companies are those that take advantage of the geographical diversity of Ecuador. However, there are companies that specialize in only one type of adventure tourism, and they are the ones that are affected more by climate changes or natural disasters.

Indigenous Communities

In the author's experience, attitudes in general to the native or indigenous (pre-Columbian) peoples of the Americas, whether they are known as Native Americans (USA), First Nations (Canada), aborigines or *indígenas* (Latin America), need to be changed. A common misapprehension is that these peoples have little knowledge of the modern world, and that they have minimal understanding of concepts such as global warming, protection of nature and sustainability. Yet the current evidence (Lahrich, 2016) is that many indigenous peoples understand many of these concepts, more than we imagine. This is the case of some of the indigenous peoples of the Ecuadorian Amazon.

Today many members of the indigenous communities of the Amazon leave their communities and go to big cities in order to study at university (Box 13.3). This is possible since the government of Ecuador offers student scholarships and also student loans, and there are private universities that offer scholarships to students who have poor economic resources. Furthermore, communities in the Amazon also have small businesses in their villages where they obtain money which they use to educate younger members of the community. Therefore, it is not unusual for indigenous communities to have engineers, economists, tour operators, doctors, etc. living in the locale. Some, once they have finished their studies,

no longer return to their communities but stay in the cities. Others return to work for their community, not to change their traditions and way of life but in order for the community to move forward in tandem with the world around them, together with contributing to Ecuador's economic system. Indigenous communities are proud and aware of the importance of their culture and their ancestral knowledge, but are also able to benefit from new economic products such as adventure tourism.

There are also companies controlled by indigenous groups, such as Napo Wildlife Center (Fig. 13.5) supported by the Quichua Anangu Community. They offer tours within the Yasuní National Park (Napo Wildlife Center, 2018).

Most people working at Napo Wildlife Center are young and many adults in the Amazon communities do not have a university education or speak Spanish, but they do work as guides, because they are experts in jungle expeditions and are competent guides leading these jungle adventures.

The Role of Government in Adventure Tourism

In order to protect and safeguard the integrity of adventure travellers in Ecuador, the Ministry of Tourism has developed the Reglamento de Operacion Turistica de Aventura, or Regulations for Adventure Tourism Operators (Mintur, 2014), which govern any adventure tourism operation in the country. The Regulations are summarized in Box 13.4. It is important to emphasize that adventure tourism can include various forms of tourism products and organizations (including travel agencies and tour operators) in adventure travel.

It can be concluded that the law for adventure tourism in Ecuador is designed to take into account the protection of nature, the welfare of visitors, the sustainability of protected areas and quality of service. There are some companies that do not meet all the requirements, and there are still companies that are not complying with all the provisions of the adventure tourism Regulations, even though the law was issued in 2014.

Safety and Sustainability

As noted earlier, regulations were necessary because adventure tourism had grown over the past 10 years in Ecuador. The 2014 Regulations

Box 13.3. Tocari Boya Enqueri, a Huarani Member and Student of Tourism Operations.

The new generation of indigenous peoples are now university students, professionals and entrepreneurs and Sergio Tocari Boya Enqueri is an example of this. He is 27 years old and belongs to the Huarani people of the Amazon jungle of Ecuador. Tocari is a student of Tourism and studies at the best university in Ecuador (Universidad San Francisco de Quito). He has already started to work in tourism, with his own company.

Here are some important features:

1. Rather than 'adventure tourism', Tocari calls his tours 'Ancestral Survival Tourism', which transmits more mystery, emotion and adrenalin – fundamental ingredients for those seeking adventure.

2. Why 'Ancestral Survival Tourism'? Because Tocari's tours seek to offer direct contact with the jungle. The tours do not have a path or some established tourist circuit. The tour consists of making its way through the jungle, in order to teach visitors how to guide and survive in the Amazon using the ancestral knowledge of the Huarani people. For those who have been in the jungle, they will understand that the profusion of trees makes it is very difficult to navigate. Tocari is applying one of the key concepts in tourist products, providing a tangible experience, in this case the direct contact with the jungle, using the ancestral knowledge of the Huarani culture.

3. Tocari opens or creates new paths for each tour; in other words, each tour has a different circuit. This is done for a number of reasons. Firstly, it is to protect nature, reducing repeated damage to plants.

In addition on the journey, there may be small insects or animals that tourists might tread on, and to prevent this happening the leading Huarani guide walks 10 m ahead of the group. Here, clearly Tocari is thinking about the sustainability of the product and protection of nature. Tocari does this not because he has a university education, but because sustainability and protection of nature is an ancestral principle that has been passing from generation to generation. Secondly, the fact that the leading guide goes 10 m ahead is also intended to ensure the safety of the visitors, as there can be large and dangerous animals on the path. Tocari is ensuring the minimization of risk for his clients, which is part of the safety policy of the company.

4. Customers have to take their own tent, bedding and clothes for the jungle trek. The food is included in the tour and consists of eating what the jungle provides; that is, they eat what they hunt. The food is usually fish; tourists are taught which baits to use and how to fish in the Huarani ancestral way. For tourists who are more experienced hunters, they have the opportunity to hunt more difficult animals, such as big rodents or frogs. Hunting for food is part of the unique Ancestral Survival Tourism product.

Figure 13.4 shows Tocari Boya Enqueri (in traditional dress) and his family on his graduation day. Tocari graduated with a BA degree in Tourism Operations and National Guidance, at the San Francisco University of Quito (USFQ).

---

address the issue of safety in adventure tourism, as well as sustainability. Although not all companies are consistent in engaging with the Regulations, a company does need to have a safety and sustainability policy in order to legally establish an agency or operator for adventure tourism. However, having a policy is not the same as implementation and some companies fail to action these policies. On the other hand, there are many companies that do implement safety and sustainability policies and see them as a priority. To ensure some consistency, Mintur has a safety control programme, which verifies the maintenance and correct use of equipment, materials and infrastructure that are used by these adventure tourism companies (Mintur, 2014).

The Future of Adventure Tourism Industry in Ecuador

In the author's opinion, adventure tourism in Ecuador is developing along the right lines and will continue to grow. A number of facts support this assertion.

1. The government, through the Ministry of Tourism, identifies adventure tourism as a profitable business and even the President has been directly involved in promoting the country through adventure tourism.

2. The adventure tourism Regulations provide the industry with competent and effective guidelines to follow, which must improve the image and quality of the adventure activities.

Fig. 13.4. Tocari Boya Enqueri graduation day.

3. The companies and staff running adventure tourism are now qualified professionals who specialize in adventure products and are fully aware of what is required to run successful adventure tourism business.

4. The roads connecting Ecuador are considered as some of the best road systems in Latin America. This is a fundamental factor for the development not only of adventure tourism but of tourism in general.

> According to the Global Competitiveness Report 2015–2016, prepared by the World Economic Forum, Ecuador ranks first … in Latin American countries with the best quality of roads and in 25th place worldwide near Nations such as Sweden.
>
> (Andes, 2016).

However, Ecuador is a developing country and this brings with it many challenges in terms of global competition for adventure tourism.

Fig. 13.5. Ecolodge administered by the Quichua Anangu Community (photo: Napo Wildlife Center, sourced from Wikimedia Commons).

Box 13.4. Regulations for Adventure Tourism.

In order to offer adventure, it is mandatory to have a tourist registration and annual operating licence, under the Tourism Law.

However, if adventure tourism is carried out in a Protected Natural Area and in the province of Galapagos, the legal framework applicable to the special regimes must also be observed and complied with.

Adventure Activities

The Regulations control the different tourist adventure products, which are classified according to the natural environments: land, water and air.

Accepted activities of adventure on **land** are horse riding, canyoning, cycling, climbing, exploration of caves, mountaineering and trekking. With **water**, the acceptable recreational activities are motorized boats (parasailing and water skiing), diving, sea/lake kayaking, river kayaking, kite surfing, rafting, snorkelling, surfing and tubing. In the **air**, the activities are delta-wing flying, canopying and paragliding or hang-gliding.

Requirements

(a) Basics requirements
These are related to the physical space used, operational organization chart, a civil liability policy, a plan of operations for each type of adventure tourism it offers, and a risk assessment.

(b) Commercialization requirements
Companies must comply with requirements to maintain responsible business practices and be accurate in advertising. These include maintaining valid sales vouchers with authorization from the Internal Revenue Service, information of the tourist product of adventure offered, describing the service, detailing the equipment and locations, where the activities are carried out; also description of the people who will participate, and the levels of risk that the activity involves.

If the adventure tourism activity is carried out in a Protected Area of the Ecuadorian State or in the Province of Galapagos, operators or travel agencies must obtain quotas, permissions and corresponding authorizations from the Protected Area Authority.

(c) Service provision
A company must have: (i) appropriate infrastructure (when applicable), equipment, accessories for each type of adventure activity, maintenance and replacement of materials and accessories; (ii) appropriate transportation for adventure tourism operations that comply with the regulation of the National Transit

Agency; and (iii) specialized guides for all tourist adventure types described in the Agreement, except surfing and motorized boats where they must have a specialized instructor.

Guides and Instructors

The guides must have a certificate issued by an institution recognized by the Ministry of Tourism. The guides and instructors must take first aid courses for extreme conditions and cardiopulmonary resuscitation (CPR), and appropriate training courses, including periodic updating.

Tour guides for land and air should also take courses in techniques of rescue, survival and evacuation. Tour guides and instructors of water activities and canyoning must also take courses in open-water rescue techniques (if the adventure product is on the sea or lake system) or for fast-flowing waters. If the adventure is done on a river system, evacuation and survival skills are also required.

The delta-wing guide, in addition to the above, must have a commercial delta-wing tandem pilot licence issued by the competent authority of Ecuador. The paraglider guide, in addition to the above, must have a paragliding pilot's licence (or similar) or commercial paragliding pilot, issued by the competent authority of Ecuador. For diving the dive guide must also have an international dive licence issued by a World Diving Association that qualifies to the level of Dive Master.

If the adventure tourism is carried out within a Protected Area of the Ecuadorian State, the guides must obtain their Nature Guide credentials in the relevant areas.

Settings

The Regulations also establish the parameters that must be fulfilled in each of the tourist adventure activities to be carried out on land, water and air, encompassing the number of tourists, ages, equipment and accessories used, number of guides.

In addition, the Regulations establish emergency response mechanisms in the practice of adventure tourism and the planning of emergency response mechanisms.

Tourist Resorts

The Regulations state that accommodation, food and beverage establishments and community tourist centres may develop adventure tourism, provided that they are carried out within their boundaries,

Continued

Box 13.4. Continued.

where they shall be governed by the Regulations for Adventure Tourism Operators.

The third general provision states that neither the guides, nor the instructors, nor any particular person can market directly to tourists. These adventures should always be marketed through a travel agency or tour operator registered with the Ministry of Tourism.

Periodic controls

Agencies and tourist operators will be subject to periodic checks carried out by the Ministry of Tourism or the decentralized autonomous governments to which authorization has been transferred to evaluate the status and functioning of company infrastructure, equipment and credentials of the guides and instructors (Fig. 13.6).

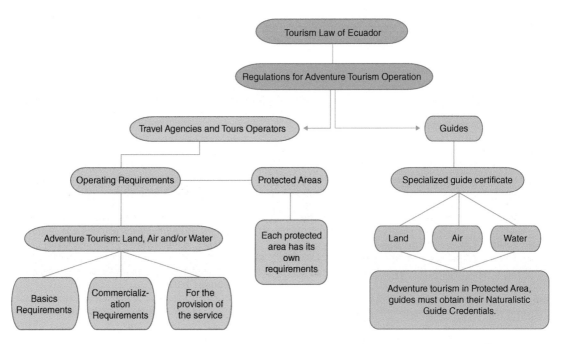

Fig. 13.6. Ecuador Ministry of Tourism's periodic checks on adventure tourism agencies and operators. (Source: Max Ortega)

References

Andes (2016) Ecuador el país con la mejor calidad de vías en América Latina, según el World Economic Forum. Available at: http://www.andes.info.ec/es/noticias/economia/1/46548/ecuador-pais-mejor-calidad-vias-america-latina-segun-world-economic-forum (accessed 20 February 2018).

ASEGUIM (Asociación Ecuatoriana de Guías de Montaña) (2018) Escuela de Guías de Montaña. Available at: https://aseguim.org/que-hacemos/ (accessed 3 February 2018).

Castillo, E., Martínez, F. and Vázquez, E. (2015) El turismo en Ecuador nuevas tendencias en el turismo sostenible y contribución al crecimiento económico. Available at: http://www.usc.es/econo/RGE/Vol24/rge2426.pdf (accessed 9 November 2017).

El Telégrafo (2015) Restos de los tres andinistas, hallados en el Chimborazo el fin de semana, fueron entregados a sus familiares. Available at: http://www.eltelegrafo.com.ec/noticias/regional-centro/1/los-tres-andinistas-hallados-en-el-chimborazo-el-fin-de-semana-habrian-sido-identificados-por-la-ropa (accessed 3 February 2018).

El Universo (2015) Así descubrieron en el Chimborazo los restos de escaladores que se cree fallecieron en 1993. Available at: https://www.eluniverso.com/noticias/2015/08/24/nota/5084714/asi-descubrieron-chimborazo-restos-escaladores-fallecidos-1993 (accessed 3 February 2018).

FPLAMETA FPLANETA (2016) Ecuador: The Royal Tour. Available at: https://www.youtube.com/watch?v=mn7dMzG-T2w (accessed 18 October 2017).

Greenberg, P. (2018) Who is Peter Greenberg? Read his story. Available at: https://petergreenberg.com (accessed 18 October 2017).

Icelandic Tourist Board (2017) Granting licenses and legislation. Available at: https://www.ferdamalastofa.is/en/about-us/icelandic-tourist-board (accessed 1 February 2018).

Lahrich, K. (2016) These indigenous Amazonians are standing up to Ecuador's oil invasion. Available at: https://www.pri.org/stories/2016-02-13/these-indigenous-amazonians-are-standing-ecuador-s-oil-invasion (accessed 20 February 2018).

Ministerio de Turismo (2015) Mintur: Turismo de Aventura, producto priorizado en el Ecuador. Available at: https://www.turismo.gob.ec/mintur-turismo-de-aventura-producto-priorizado-en-el-ecuador/ (accessed 1 February 2018).

Mintur (2014) Mindo consolida su oferta de turismo de aventura. Available at: http://www.turismo.gob.ec/mindo-consolida-su-oferta-de-turismo-de-aventura/ (accessed 20 February 2018).

Mintur (2015) *Ley de Turismo* (Tourism Law). Available at: https://www.turismo.gob.ec/wp-content/uploads/2015/04/LEY-DE-TURISMO.pdf (accessed 15 November 2017).

Mintur (2016) *Reglamento de Operaciones Turísticas de Aventura* (Adventure Tourism Regulations). Available at: http://www.turismo.gob.ec/wp-content/uploads/2016/04/REGLAMENTO-DE-TURISMO-DE-AVENTURA.pdf (accessed 25 January 2018).

Napo Wildlife Center (2018) Napo Wildlife Center Ecolodge – Yasuni National Park Ecuador. Available at: https://www.napowildlifecenter.com (accessed 20 February 2018).

Revolvy (2014) Megadiverse countries. Available at: https://www.revolvy.com/main/index.php?s=Megadiverse%20countries (accessed 20 February 2018).

Ward, L. (1995) Ecuador elevates climbing safety after fatal avalanche. Mountaineering: Nation's Andes are an increasingly popular tourist destination, with 10 peaks over 16,000 feet. But basic equipment and guide training is in short supply. Available at: http://articles.latimes.com/1995-02-05/news/mn-28176_1_mountain-guides (accessed 3 February 2018).

World Atlas (2017) 17 Most Ecologically Diverse Countries On Earth. Available at: https://www.worldatlas.com/articles/ecologically-megadiverse-countries-of-the-world.html (accessed 20 February 2018).

Further reading and additional resources

Agencia Nacional de Tránssito (2018) Licencias Internacionales. Available at: https://www.ant.gob.ec/index.php/licencias/1792-menu-lice#.Wo7I7Gaca9a (accessed 22 February 2018).

Ecuador Turístico (2012) Turismo aventura playa surf en Bahía de Caraquez. Available at: https://www.ecuador-turistico.com/2012/08/turismo-aventura-playa-y-surf-en-bahia-de-caraquez.html (accessed 9 November 2017).

El Telégrafo (2016) El turismo acuático es potencia en la laguna de Yambo. Available at: https://www.eltelegrafo.com.ec/noticias/regional/1/el-turismo-acuatico-se-potencia-en-la-laguna-de-yambo (accessed 9 November 2017).

En El Ojo Films (2014) Ecuador: Todo en un solo lugar. Available at: https://www.youtube.com/watch?v=MAo0MAnn--s. (accessed 20 February 2018).

Ministerio de Turismo (2018) Recomendaciones para viajeros. Available at: http://www.turismo.gob.ec (accessed 22 February 2018).

Viaje Jet (2018) Consejos, documentación y requisitos para viajar a Ecuador. Available at: https://www.viajejet.com/consejos-documentacion-y-requisitos-para-viajar-a-ecuador/#documentacion (accessed 22 February 2018).

14 I Came to Enjoy Iceland and Arrived at Þingvellir ('Þingvellir – where am I again?')

HARALD SCHALLER

Ranger, Thingvellir National Park

Introduction

I studied Industrial Engineering and continued with a degree in Environment and Natural Resources, and Geography. During my studies, I conducted research in Germany, Iceland and Japan; my later focus was on sustainable tourism management and public participation in protected areas. Within my studies I focused on questions regarding the social and environmental aspects of sustainability in tourism. My previous publications concerned ecological sensitivity and hiking trail assessment, as well as conflict management within protected areas, and the perception of nature by tourists and tour guides. Since 2016, I have been working for the Thingvellir (Þingvellir) National Park as a ranger but also had the opportunity to work in the tourism sector in Iceland for the past 5 years. In this time, I was in close contact with tourists and the tourism industry itself. The role of a ranger in Thingvellir entails maintenance work, but a large segment of the job is occupied by interpretative work and the monitoring of visitors' compliance with regulations.

The National Park was established in 1930 to commemorate the importance of the place with regards to the first parliament meeting a thousand years earlier. The initial area of the Park was enlarged in 1997 and it became a UNESCO World Heritage Site in 2004 (Þingvellir National Park, 2004, 2017). Thingvellir is an important place for Icelanders but enjoys much attention from foreign visitors as well. Recent statistics show that about 1.2 million travellers visited the Park in 2016 (Þórhallsdóttir and Olafsson, 2017), compared with a total of 1.8 million travellers coming to Iceland in the same year (Icelandic Tourism Board, 2017), which amounts to about two out of three visitors making a stop in Thingvellir. As a UNESCO World Heritage site, Thingvellir does contain physical remains of the historical parliament gathering, but as it lies within the rift valley of the Middle Atlantic Ridge, geological features are very dominant. Nowadays, many different activities are offered within the borders of the park. Besides hiking, angling, horseback riding, snorkelling and diving are very popular (Thingvellir National Park, 2018a, b, c). Especially the latter two activities are subject to increased regulations, as these are adventure sports that have major impacts on the Park (Thingvellir National Park, 2018d).

Thoughts on Adventure Tourism

Tourism in Iceland has been growing rapidly over the past decade, with yet another record number of foreign visitors coming to Iceland in 2017. At the time of the eruption of Eyjafjallajökull in 2010, about 488,000 foreign citizens travelled to Iceland, and the number increased to about 2,220,000 visitors in 2017. This means that the number of visitors increased annually by about 24% (Fig. 14.1).

Recent statistics show that most of the tourists visiting Iceland name nature as one of the major influencing factors for their decision, and many also mention that they have always wanted to come to Iceland (Icelandic Tourism Board, 2017). Some of the tourist activities in the National Park fall into the definition of adventure tourism (Thingvellir National Park, 2018d). For example, at Thingvellir we have a long tradition of horseback riding and hiking (Fig. 14.2) and more recently diving.

Visitors in the period Jan.-Nov.

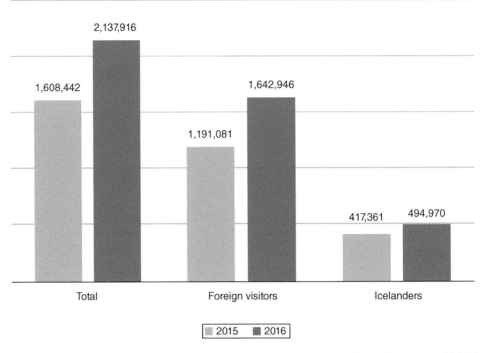

Fig. 14.1. Development of number of foreign visitors to Iceland (airport and seaport) over time – years highlighted for better comparison 2010 and 2017 (Icelandic Tourism Board, 2014; Thingvellir National Park, 2018a).

Fig. 14.2. Early forms of transportation in Iceland were (a) on horse or (b) with cars on barely existing roads.

Nowadays, other forms of activities are offered within the boundaries of the Park. The summer of 2017 saw the first company to offer bike tours through the National Park, and there has been a long tradition of snorkelling and diving within the Silfra fissure. The first mention of diving in Silfra within the documents of the National Park is from 1994 (Sigurjónsdóttir, 2015) and by 2014 some 20,000 divers and snorkellers who participated in this adventure activity were recorded (Þorbjörnsson, 2015); since then it has grown significantly in popularity and had more than doubled by 2017. The popularity of snorkelling and diving in Thingvellir is because of the exceptionally clear water and the geological properties of the rift valley between two tectonic plates. It can be assumed that the number of tourists who purchase

Fig. 14.3. Hiking trail through the moss-covered landscape of the Thingvellir valley.

this activity will increase, especially since cold-water and free diving are growing in fame, due to prominent extreme athletes like Wim Hof.

The different types of marketing around Thingvellir (social media, Icelandic Tourist Board, etc.) and the activities on offer fuel a growing demand for exciting and especially challenging ways to engage with the environment (Giddy and Webb, 2016). This development might be partly due to a growing demand from 'bucket-list' tourists who would like to visit exotic places or take part in adventurous activities to reproduce an experience that they have seen or heard about on the internet. Others see adventure tourism as a means to differentiate themselves from their peers. Another aspect of the attractiveness of adventure tourism is linked to the fact that it appears as something cool, active and challenging. Furthermore, adventure tourism's characteristics of physical and psychological challenges have a resonance with the National Park and can be linked to commodification and economic returns (Rokenes *et al.*, 2015). Operators and tourist agencies see an opportunity to develop adventure tourism in the Park for commercial gain. Most tourists need guides and equipment to participate in these activities (horse riding and diving), which the commercial operator has to organize (Cater and Cloke, 2007). In return the operator then externalizes the pressure on the Park and demands an increase in its service amenities.

Experience in Guiding in Iceland

For many years, I have been guiding for several companies in Iceland, most of which offer soft and hard adventure tourism, including hiking and trekking around Iceland. But within the National Park, the rangers also offer guided tours, to provide visitors with a detailed experience of the history and nature of the park. Guides and rangers alike are the essential role in managing three aspects of tourism: the host community, the natural environment and the customer – the tourist. As such their role is therefore not only to be the mediator and translator, but also a gatekeeper for the tourists to the land and its culture (Howard *et al.*, 2001). They provide the interface between the host destination and the tourists, including safety and entertainment (Cohen, 1985; Ap and Wong, 2001).

Over the past few decades there has been a change in the expectations of the guide's function. Speaking with guides who already worked in the 1970s in Iceland revealed that much of the guiding activity did not change with regards to the service tourists needed. However, the type of visitors was different as well as the transportation. Previously, rather wealthy tourists came to Iceland and they had a better knowledge and understanding of travelling in Iceland. Currently, more people can now afford to visit Iceland and guiding has become more commercialized, but also less time is spent travelling within the country. Even in winter, tourists expect to be able to visit areas that are considered very difficult to reach. The guide is now under immense pressure to provide a quality experience while being overwhelmed by the demands of many more tourists and most also try to ensure minimal environmental damage, caused by the exponential growth of tourist at visitors' hotspots.

Assessment of Tourists

Thingvellir receives a large array of types of visitors. Most of them arrive on their trip to see the Golden Circle (a tour consisting of three main attractions: Thingvellir National Park; Geysir; and the Gullfoss waterfall). Only a few visit Thingvellir for itself and explore the area further. The majority of the visitors concentrate on the area of the visitor centre at Hakið and the valley between the Öxaráfoss waterfall and the Silfra fissure.

What can be noticed is the change in the tourism landscape due to the sheer amount of visitors coming to Iceland, and also in the attitude of visitors. Many of the visitors seek an authentic and individual experience in order to fulfil their wish for the 'true' experience, not realizing that the site itself has become a space for commodification and which is the creation of a 'quasi-experience' (something slightly less than authentic, beautiful, unique, etc.) (Büscher and Fletcher, 2017). As an example, a visit to Thingvellir and snorkelling within Silfra will give the illusion of being able to 'touch the two tectonic plates', while in reality the site is located mainly in the rift valley that extends over several kilometres between the two tectonic plates. However, the visitor is 'experiencing' what is promised by the advertisement, which makes this recreational activity a 'quasi-experience'. Many visitors are not aware of the 'unreality' of the experience. Many tourists simply accept the commodified experience as being real, having done little, if any, research on the tourist attraction before arriving.

Judging from the questions the rangers get from the tourists, it can be said that many have only a fragmented understanding of the history of the place and its environmental setting. Many visitors are not familiar with the history of the place and its meaning for Icelandic culture and most tourists lack a sense of cultural and environmental importance of the location. Many visitors are on a tight time schedule and try to see as many interesting things as possible while staying in Thingvellir. As rangers we are often astonished by the kind of knowledge and expectation the tourists bring with them. Often their information seems to have come merely from internet blogs, advertisements and even popular TV shows. These images and expectations of Iceland can influence the different forms of interactions with nature, as well as the tourist's bodily experience of natural forces. This can be dangerous for visitors and damaging to the environment (as in the case of access to geothermal features or the cold water of Silfra).

The internet and popular media are the main sources of knowledge and inspiration and what most tourists access before arriving in Iceland, as confirmed by talking with other guides. Recent research in this field with guides at the Vatnajökull National Park showed a similar pattern amongst tourists, where the use of social media becomes a major factor in tourism. Visitors come with the desire to have a unique experience of a wild and untouched environment, an image that is perpetuated by domestic and international tourism marketing. Iceland has become a vehicle for an online pilgrimage, in a sense that people travel to an almost spiritual place of beauty and solitude, which is what they desired on their visit, yet the reality is somewhat different (Schaller, 2016).

Impacts on Thingvellir

As one of the most popular travel destinations in Iceland, Thingvellir mirrors the sharp increase in visitors to the country. Therefore, the National Park is faced with a difficult situation. The growth in tourists comes along with a larger strain on the existing infrastructure and the need to impose stricter regulations on access to areas in order to improve safety while preventing environmental degradation. At the time of writing this text, the National Park has not implemented any limitation (physical or economic) on the tourists entering the Park. However, there is a current debate concerning the possible need for limiting access to specific sites within the Park and Iceland in general. The natural environment is suffering from the increased amount of trampling, and recent accidents at Silfra raise the question of stricter rules for tourists and companies alike. It is difficult to say if and to what extend limitation of access is feasible and how effective it might be. However, snorkelling and diving at Silfra appear to be among the first activities that might see some sort of limitation of access (Sigurjónsdóttir, 2015). It is difficult to say what the carrying capacity of these sites are, and future studies would be needed to provide sound evidence on this.

The National Park is financially dependent on government funding but also receives revenues from service charges and generates its own revenue (Þingvallanefnd, 2017). These revenue streams are important to maintain the existing infrastructure, but also to extend it to cope with the increase in visitation. Currently, the Park is building a new visitor centre and parking lot that will enlarge the existing services at Hakið. With its planned completion in July 2018, the Park is able to welcome more visitors and provide tourists with an improved interactive exhibition about the history and nature of Thingvellir. As most visitors concentrate on a small portion of the Park, it will be interesting to see if there are plans to make other areas accessible. One of the major impacts within the Park has been on the existing roads. Since Thingvellir received the status of a UNESCO World Heritage Site in 2004, pressure has been put on improvements to the road system (Jónasson, 2011). The existing main road through Thingvellir can hardly keep up with the increase in use. However, an extension of the road leads to criticism due to the loss of pristine woodland for the road development.

Future for Adventure Tourism in Iceland

It is difficult to say what adventure tourism will look like in the future. It is dependent on an array of factors, dealing with the environmental impacts and capacity of the country, the economic feasibility of trips to Iceland, and the social implications of current and future growth in numbers of visitors. It can be said that the economic aspect of tourism looks very positive and that most of the stakeholders in tourism, as well as the public, appear to be happy about the development (Huijbens and Bjarnadóttir, 2015; Íslandsbanki, 2016; Icelandic Tourism Board, 2017). It is also important to state that tourism finds itself at a crossroads, as the three pillars in tourism (economic prosperity, societal acceptance and environmental resilience) increasingly diverge from each other due to the continuous growth in numbers of visitors and the apparent absence of proactive management in the industry and government alike. This leads to a concern that the development of tourism threatens its very future.

Evaluating the sharp increase of adventure tourists to Silfra, it can be expected that adventure tourism in Iceland will follow the same pattern. However, research on adventure tourism is fragmented, and an improved knowledge about the carrying capacity of adventure sites is essential, suggesting that the future for adventure tourism is difficult to predict. Many guides have expressed their deep concern about how the tourism industry has inherited certain weaknesses that are not adequately being addressed. The sharp increase in visitors has led to some poor management practices emerging within the tourism industry. Many guides notice how the lack of foresight within the industry creates an environment where individuals stop caring (environment and cultural impacts) and focus on their intermediate interest: the tourist. Currently, the 2.2 million tourists, including a significant number of adventure tourists, has led to crowding, environmental degradation and a growing shortage of adequate accommodation.

On a positive note, Iceland is a safe and stable country, which makes it safe for many visitors, like student groups. These aspects are also important if Iceland is to consider attracting high-spending tourists ('affluent adventurers') and building on a tourism sector that continues to contribute to the economy of the country, while providing a high quality of experience and limiting the environmental and cultural impacts (Boston Consulting Group, 2013).

References

Ap, J. and Wong, K.K.F. (2001) Case study on tour guiding: professionalism, issues and problems. *Tourism Management* 22(5), 551–563. doi: 10.1016/S0261-5177(01)00013-9.

Boston Consulting Group (2013) *Northern Sights: The future of tourism in Iceland - A perspective from the Boston Consulting Group*: Boston Consulting Group, Boston, Massachusetts.

Büscher, B. and Fletcher, R. (2017) Destructive creation: capital accumulation and the structural violence of tourism. *Journal of Sustainable Tourism* 25(5), 651–667. doi: 10.1080/09669582.2016.1159214.

Cater, C. and Cloke, P. (2007) Bodies in action. *Anthropology Today* 23(6), 13–16. doi: 10.1111/j.1467-8322.2007.00548.x.

Cohen, E. (1985) The tourist guide: The origins, structure and dynamics of a role. *Annals of Tourism Research* 12(1), 5–29. doi: 10.1016/0160-7383(85)90037-4.

Giddy, J.K. and Webb, N.L. (2016) The influence of the environment on adventure tourism: from motivations to experiences. *Current Issues in Tourism*, 1–15. doi: 10.1080/13683500.2016.1245715.

Howard, J., Smith, B. and Twaithes, J. (2001) Investigating the roles of the indigenous tour guide. *Journal of Tourism Studies* 12(2), 32–39.

Huijbens, E. and Bjarnadóttir, E. J. (2015) *Viðhorf Íslendinga til ferðafólks og ferðaþjónustu [Icelanders' attitude to tourists and tourism]* (RMF-S-01-2015). Rannsóknamiðstöð ferðamála (Icelandic Tourism Research Centre), Akureyri.

Icelandic Tourism Board (2014) Foreign visitors to Iceland 1949–2013. Available at: http://www.ferdamalastofa. is/en/recearch-and-statistics/numbers-of-foreign-visitors (accessed 30 August 2018).

Icelandic Tourism Board (2017) *Tourism in Iceland in Figures*. Available at: http://www.ferdamalastofa.is/ en/research-and-statistics/tourism-in-iceland-in-figures (accessed 30 August 2018).

Íslandsbanki (2016) Skýrsla um íslenska ferðaþjónustu [Report about the Icelandic Tourism Industry]. Available at: https://www.islandsbanki.is/fyrirtaeki/ serthekking/ferdathjonusta/islensk-ferdathjonusta/ (accessed 30 August 2018).

Jónasson, P.M. (2011) The UNESCO World Heritage Conservation. In: Jónasson, P.M. and Hersteinsson, P. (eds) *Thingvallavatn – A Unique World Evolving.* Opna Publishing, Reykjavik, pp. 293–307.

Rokenes, A., Schumann, S. and Rose, J. (2015) The art of guiding in nature-based adventure tourism – how guides can create client value and positive experiences on mountain bike and backcountry ski tours. *Scandinavian Journal of Hospitality and Tourism* 15(suppl.), 62–82. doi: 10.1080/15022250.2015.1061733.

Schaller, H. (2016) Tour guides in nature-based tourism: Perceptions of nature and governance of protected areas, the case of Skaftafell at the Vatnajökull National Park. In: Rancew-Sikora, D. and Skaptadóttir, U.D. (eds) *Mobility to the Edges of Europe: The Case of Iceland and Poland.* Scholar Publishing House, Warsaw, pp. 187–214.

Sigurjónsdóttir, J.K. (2015) *Silfra í þjóðgarðinum á Þingvöllum: Stjórnun takmarkaðrar auðlindar [Silfra in the Thingvellir National Park: Management of limited resources].* (BS), Landbúnaðarháskóli Íslands. Available at: http://hdl.handle.net/1946/22096 (accessed 30 August 2018).

Thingvellir National Park (2004) *Þingvellir National Park Management Plan 2004–2024.* Available at: https://www. thingvellir.is/en/protection-management/management-plan-2004-2024/ (accessed 30 August 2018).

Thingvellir National Park (2017) Stærð og mörk þjóð-garðsins [Size and boundaries of the national park]. Available at: http://thingvellir.is/um-thjodgardinn/staerd-og-moerk-thjodgardsins.aspx (accessed 30 August 2018).

Thingvellir National Park (2018a) Angling. Available at: https://www.thingvellir.is/en/plan-your-visit/angling/ (accessed 30 August 2018).

Thingvellir National Park (2018b) Diving. Available at: http://thingvellir.is/plan-your-visit/diving.aspx (accessed 30 August 2018).

Thingvellir National Park (2018c) Horseback riding. Available at: http://thingvellir.is/plan-your-visit/horseback-riding. aspx (accessed 30 August 2018).

Thingvellir National Park (2018d) Lög og Reglur [Laws and Regulations]. Available at: http://thingvellir.is/ um-thjodgardinn/loeg-og-reglur.aspx (accessed 30 August 2018).

Þingvallanefnd (2017) *Starfsskýrsla Þingvallanefndar 2013–2016 [Staff Report of the Thingvellir Committee 2013–2016].* Available at: Reykjavik: http://thingvellir. is/um-thjodgardinn/starfsskyrslur.aspx (accessed 30 August 2018).

Þorbjörnsson, J.G. (2015) Impacts of SCUBA Divers in the Silfra Groundwater Fissure: Ecological Disturbance and Management. MSc in Aquatic Biology, Hólar University College. Available at: http://hdl.handle.net/ 1946/23777 (accessed 30 August 2018).

Þórhallsdóttir, G. and Ólafsson, R. (2017) *Dreifing ferðamanna um landið - Talningar ferðamanna á áfangastöðum [Tourist distribution across the country - tourist count on destinations].* Available at: Reykjavik: https://www. ferdamalastofa.is/is/tolur-og-utgafur/utgefid-efni/ umfang-og-ahrif/dreifing-ferdamanna-um-landid-talningar-ferdamanna-a-afangastodum (accessed 30 August 2018).

15 Call of the Wild in Wales

Mark Soanes

Director, Call of the Wild

Introduction

I am a Director and Co-founder, together with Geraint Lewis, of Call of the Wild (Adventure Activities) Ltd. We set up Call of the Wild in 1998 as two old school friends from Neath, Wales, who gave up our professional careers and returned to our home-town to pursue our dream of owning and running a training and adventure travel company with a difference. We are committed to ensuring that clients are introduced to the wonderful local environment with a view to enhancing their learning, appreciation and enjoyment of the unique countryside within Neath, Gower and the Brecon Beacons National Park, Wales, all of which are situated 3 hours west of London.

After 20 years of running the company, we did not think that we would have this many people enjoying the fantastic Welsh countryside. It is the countryside combined with spectacular experiences and our hospitable staff that mean that people refer us on to friends, work colleagues and family. They have an unforgettable experience which they tell everyone else about. We are blessed with having some of the best outdoor wilderness locations in the UK (Fig. 15.1).

Our longevity and sustainability are associated with how clients relate to our business ethics and our 'business with a purpose' approach. We do not just measure success based on profit and loss but rather what social impact we have within our community. Trust, belonging and building a vibrant community are just as important to us.

This chapter is about the lessons we have learnt as an adventure travel business: the things we know now and wish we had known back then; and the things you wish you could have asked someone who has been there and got the t-shirt.

Mission statement

Our mission is to create powerful learning and development experiences for our clients and customers.

Vision statement

Our vision is to pursue sustainable business growth in line with client demand whilst adopting socially responsible business practices, respecting ethical values and the interests of all stakeholders and seeking to respect and preserve the natural environment.

We place considerable emphasis on the corporate social responsibilities (CSR) obligations the company has to the community, seeking to invest in the community particularly with respect to charitable activities and environmental stewardship.

Why Will You Get Out of Bed Each Morning?

When you get into a car to go on a long journey you do not just head off without first planning the trip using a map or by setting the satnav to guide you to your desired destination. The satnav will let you know what route you are going to take, estimate how long it will take you to get there and highlight traffic problems on the way.

Why don't we do the same in business? Do you know where you want to get to, by when and how you are going to get there? Do you have your strategy in place with your Vision, Mission and Values clearly defined?

One of the biggest mistakes that new start-ups make is not giving proper consideration towards their vision and strategy for achieving it. Yes, we have all had to prepare the obligatory business plan for lenders or to secure other funding sources, often paying lip service to the difficult question: where do you see the business in 5 years? In reality these documents are often written to meet the eligibility criteria of the specific funding source and are not aligned to the actual motivation or drivers of the person setting up the business enterprise.

Fig. 15.1. Call Of The Wild logo. Source: Mark Soanes.

Individuals look through a lens and take a blink-ered short-term view just to secure the funding. They do not also balance this with the more important long-term perspective and ask themselves the fundamental questions:

- Why am I doing this?
- What am I looking to achieve?
- What is going to inspire me to get out of bed each morning even during the difficult times?
- What will success look like?

In the outdoor sector what you often find is that those looking to establish their own businesses are technically competent at their chosen activity, such as climbing or caving, but they do not have any business experience. They see other companies appearing to be busy and earning money, think it looks easy and decide to set up on their own. There is little more substance to the decision other than 'I can earn more doing this on my own'.

With little thought or analysis going into their decision, there is no strategy or vision as to how they are going to build their operation so that it becomes a sustainable proposition. The result is:

- a short-lived, ill-conceived business which stops trading within 2–3 years; or
- a grand idea that contracts into a hobby business barely making ends meet.

Basic questions are not considered. Against this background the result is almost inevitable. This is especially pertinent to the tourism sector and the outdoor adventure business in particular. In the UK, given our climate, in our personal experience, the outdoor adventure market is seasonal.

In 2015 almost four in every six holiday visits were during the middle quarters of the year (31% April to June, 32% July to September) whilst around one in six (16%) were in the first 3 months of the year and one in five (21%) in the last 3 months (Visit Britain, 2016). That is, most visits will be generated during the best weather months of May to September. There may also be an upturn in April which coincides with public and school holidays but this can be dependent on the weather.

Little thought can be given to this factor when starting out. We struggled to contend with the fact that the large majority of our income was generated in basically 6 months of the year. If, as we did, you plan at the outset to build a sustainable business employing staff on permanent 12-month contracts, how do you manage your finances to enable this to happen? Although there are many factors that influence this, one of the main ones is having that understanding at the outset about why you are doing this and having the 'road map' in place to achieve it.

We have seen many others who have not adopted this approach and struggle to build their business for this reason. The outcome has been that they have almost become a 'hobby business' operating for part of the year or just on their days off from their main job.

What is a hobby?

A hobby is a pastime or leisure activity conducted in your spare time for recreation or pleasure. The benefits of being a hobby include the following (Australian Government DIIS, 2018):

- Personal enjoyment and satisfaction.
- You can gift or sell your work for the cost of materials.
- You can do it in your own time or when people contact you.
- You don't have the reporting obligations of a business

Such operations struggle to generate enough income to make a sustainable 12-months-of-the-year business. They can make enough to make it worth running the operation for 6 months but not without supplementing that income with other work during the remainder of the year. For some this may be satisfactory and is all they set out to achieve – 6 months in the UK and then working in other countries in the outdoor adventure sector for the other 6 months.

What we have learnt is that to build a sustainable business you need the following.

1. A Vision. What will success look like to you at a particular point in the future? What will make you get out of bed in the morning?
2. Mission. Bitesize steps moving you towards the vision. These can be annual or aligned to your financial year.
3. Strategy. Your plan of action or 'road map' as described above to achieve your mission.
4. Values. Often overlooked but very important, to spell out how, as a business, you will operate and what you expect of your employees and those working for you. Issues such as trust, taking responsibility, being supportive and so on will all need to be spelt out and actioned if you are to achieve your desired outcomes.
5. Monitor and review.

Of 300 'global' corporations interviewed, 74% admitted that they had not achieved the strategy they set out to deliver (Ernst and Young, 2014). That is why it is important to keep revisiting your vision, mission and strategy on a regular basis to ensure that you are still achieving your objectives, and that circumstances have not changed which mean that your vision has to be amended.

The Lone Ranger

When we started our business we thought we knew best in many respects. We had a business background and thought we could go it alone without seeking advice or looking to trade associations and other business support organizations for help and advice.

Many years on and having first-hand experience of representing the outdoor sector on many trade association boards and committees, we can now reflect on our initial approach and firmly state that to have ignored such valuable support networks was a mistake.

From the outside looking in we were often critical and scornful of some of the decisions being made in our so-called best interest. As many of these organizations were also principally led by public sector officials, we were dismissive of their commercial awareness and their adherence to their politcal agendas and limitations imposed on them by their public sector employers.

However, we came to realize that these organizations, even though sometimes we did not agree with some of their actions, were seeking to act in the best interests of the sector. Therefore we took the view that it would be better to be on the inside influencing decisions rather than being on the outside being negative and critical of what was happening, without shaping things for the better by using our own experience.

This was partly down to a lack of confidence at the start, given we were a start-up so what did we know which would be worthwhile contributing in that arena, which would carry any authority or weight? We were wrong. That is the very reason for many of these trade organizations existing – to represent the views and thoughts of all their members, big or small.

In the first instance we tentatively joined a few tourism trade associations. The two principal ones were Tourism Swansea Bay and the Brecon Beacons Tourism Association. Tourism Swansea Bay is the trade association representing tourism and leisure businesses, not just locally but on a regional and national level, as the independent voice of the tourism and leisure operators in the Swansea, Mumbles, Gower, Neath and Port Talbot area of South Wales, west of Cardiff. The Association, which has over 300 members, provides business support, training and networking opportunities for all our members, enabling them to be more effective in their business,

therefore giving the visitor/tourist to Swansea Bay a better experience.

The Brecon Beacons trade association, Brecon Beacons Tourism, was established in 2006 by a team of local tourism businesses who wanted to support each other and network with the various tourism support agencies. They aimed to see the area developed as a high-quality destination, where grassroots needs would be served and represented at a strategic level.

Several years later, around 250 local tourism businesses of all types and sizes have joined Brecon Beacons Tourism as members. It is situated in the Brecon Beacons National Park, covering 519 square miles, approximately 30 miles north of Cardiff and running from Llandovery in the west to the market town of Abergavenny in the east near the England/Wales border. Together they have raised the profile of the Brecon Beacons as a great place to visit and have provided valuable information on many tourism-related matters for their member businesses, as well as networking opportunities.

When we first became members of these organizations we did not fully understand how helpful they could be. In the first instance after joining we began to receive their newsletters and became better informed about the sector and what was happening within it. Then we started to attend their membership meetings and find out in more detail what was going on in the tourism sector. We started to network with other businesses and understood that many of the issues we faced were common to all. We could then know what solutions others had used successfully to address such problems. In addition the meetings had:

- presentations from relevant speakers;
- factsheets;
- consultations on possible policy or plans which might impact on the sector;
- latest policy updates;
- relevant regulation/legislation;
- funding opportunities;
- competitions;
- member success stories and examples of good practice; and
- training opportunities to upskill in areas such as social media, e-marketing, and so on.

Networking was also important for building up contacts and relationships to help build our business, whether it be support services, suppliers or referrals for new customers. This was particularly true for accommodation providers such as hoteliers looking to provide multiple reasons for people to visit and to lengthen their stay.

We found this approach so beneficial that we became committee members of a number of representative bodies. We have also been involved as founders of a new adventure activities trade association and gone on to represent the sector at regional and national level.

The Race to the Bottom: Price Strategy

We have found that, as we have become an established adventure activity provider, then others look to us for ideas and start to benchmark against what we do. This extends to how we price our services. We have seen countless examples of new operators copying various aspects of our business operations. One of the most blatant was actually copying word for word the web pages relating to a specific service offer of ours and then just uploading that same content to their own new website.

That also extends to lifting and copying photographs from our website. We have even had marketing emails sent to us from competitor organizations where they have actually copied content from our website and incorporated it into their newsletter which we were then sent!

This can be viewed as a form of flattery in that others think that we are doing things professionally and very well. You can often find instances such as this by doing simple searches online and the reaction when you do catch someone is often varied. Some will try to deny it until shown the evidence, whilst others will own up when first confronted. It would be nice to think that they could be more original in their thinking without having to plagarize what others have done. No originality or creativity.

However, what is more worrying is when new start-ups or operators are clearly basing their pricing strategy on ours. The implications of this can be wide ranging and distort the market for the many over a long period of time before things settle to an equilibrium again. In the interim many lose money and some go out of business. Why is this?

There are many theories out there on pricing and cost structures. One just has to search online. However, the basic rule of thumb we use is to first understand our costs. What does it actually cost to deliver a specific service? Once you have established this baseline, you are ready to go and research the market. This is the time to look at what others are doing, as there is probably a good reason for it. The main one is this: the sustainable figure that can be charged which is acceptable to the customer, whilst also making enough money for you to make a living. So once you know your costs and have researched your market, then you are in a strong position to come up with your pricing.

In our experience this does not happen in many cases with new operators entering the market. What seems to happen is that they do not work out their costs but just look at what others are charging and then simply undercut those others by a significant amount to ensure that they attract the business.

What they then find over a period of time is that their pricing is not sustainable to make them enough money and they cease trading. However, whilst they have been trading they have distorted the market in terms of pricing, hence the reference to the famous race to the bottom. Some well established operators will react to this undercutting and look to discount their rates if they see a loss in the numbers of customers. This then creates problems and could threaten their very existence.

You can predict what happens when new operators arrive. We get phone calls from customers asking how much a specific service is and when we tell them, they respond by explaining that the new operator is charging far less. Our response is that we know the value of our service and they are, for instance, guaranteed a safe and memorable experience (we do turn up, unlike some of these newer operators who struggle to provide that guaranteed quality service due to cutting corners as they are financially under pressure).

Cash is King: the Importance of Cash Flow

This issue is one of the most important factors in determing the success or failure of a business. We cannot overstate how important it is to get this aspect of running a business correct. This point is also closely linked to the previous section on pricing strategy.

The saying 'Turnover is vanity, profit is sanity and cash is reality' holds true to this day. If you are running a business you may have an impressive amount of money coming in but if your profit margin is low and/or running costs are high it will affect how much you make and determine the viability of the business.

A large number of businessess are unsuccessful through a failure to prepare detailed cash flow forecasts and manage cash flow efficiently. There are three aspects to this: (i) selling enough (turnover); (ii) selling at the correct profit margin (costs and pricing); and (iii) getting paid (cash flow).

This means that you may be selling your services and making a sufficient profit margin but until you actually have the money in your hand the volume of sales and profit margin means nothing.

As described with our pricing strategy section, you might be selling a significant volume of products or services and as a result turnover is good. However, if you have got your pricing strategy wrong and not accounted for certain costs, your profit margin will be low. Therefore you will be a busy fool working for nothing.

Cash is king. Unless you can ensure that your customers pay you, in full and on time, you have to question if they are the type of customer you want to work with. It does take up a huge amount in time, effort and resources to hound late-paying customers. Without that money being paid for the work you have done, how are you going to cover your costs? You may have staff salaries and suppliers to pay. A business is not financially sustainable without money coming in from customers. Even if you are profitable, you will not survive if the cash does not come in.

Environmental Good Practice

In our business we have to have access to adventure activity venues to enable our activities to take place. By the very nature of the business, these venues are in remote wilderness locations and as a result are environmentally sensitive, containing much of value in terms of their flora and fauna. By their very nature they attract visitors to come and visit so that they can experience these special qualities, which in itself puts pressure on them. With activity venues this is exacerbated, as you have not only casual visitors but also organized groups, with activity providers all using the same venues.

Historically, to gain access to these venues has been a case of having goodwill verbal agreements with landowners. Provided that you were not a nuisance to anyone, then you could use the sites. Over the years and certainly more recently this has changed. Awareness of the impact that such activities and overuse can have on these sensitive pristine environments has risen. There has been increasing pressure on so-called 'honeypot' sites where many people, in organized groups and organizations, go to undertake and enjoy the outdoor activities

available. This could be anything from a casual walk to a waterfall or an organized canyoning session where you jump off a waterfall (Figs 15.2 and 15.3).

As mentioned above, a new collaborative way of working has to be adopted to ensure that continued access is maintained to activity venues in sensitive locations such as within national parks. With this in mind we became co-founders of the South Wales Outdoor Activity Providers Group (SWOAPG), a body representing all outdoor adventure providers in South Wales. This was formed due to the threat from a landowner to remove access to one of the more popular activity venues in the region. This threat was born from a perceived overuse of the venue by activity providers and was the catalyst for all providers to come together and join forces to put forward one voice representing all providers.

The outcome was that access was maintained by entering into an agreement with the landowner on behalf of all adventure activity providers. This included a code of conduct relating to the sensitive use of the site and showing consideration for all users.

This template has now been used on maintaining access to a large number of similar venues. The lesson here is that all providers need to become members of and support their representative bodies. If one does not exist, then create one.

Risk Management

Reference has been made above to costs. One of the largest costs is likely to be insurance cover. If you can demonstrate that you have robust risk management procedures and operating procedures in place, this could help to reduce insurance costs. Also, if you do not have such risk mangement in place this could result in having recurring accidents with customers. Not only will this lead to negative feedback and publicity, which will inevitably impact on sales, but also it will lead to claims for compensation for negligence.

With the growth in social media and people now using this as a reference point before booking, the impact on a business could be enormous, especially if there are recurring reviews referring to accidents. In addition, with people becoming more risk averse and the growth of a claims culture, you have to have the necessary risk management procedures in place.

The options are to employ the services of an external supplier who will be an expert in this field to draw up the procedures for you, or employ your own expert. You can also undertake your own

Fig. 15.2. Neath Valley Water Falls. Source: Mark Soanes.

Fig. 15.3. Gorge Jumping Neath Valley. Source: Mark Soanes.

training to ensure that you can manage this process in the future. You should also remember that this process does not stop when the procedures have been agreed and implemented.

With risk management the situation is dynamic and always changing. Close monitoring is required at all times. For instance, you need to have a robust reporting system in place and an open culture to encourage staff to disclose incidents. Organizational culture is of the utmost importance in this respect.

There cannot be an internal fear of failure and a reluctance to admit mistakes due to the organizational response. Small failures are the early warning signs that are vital to prevent incidents escalating into major accidents. As Eleanor Roosevelt put it, 'Learn from the mistakes of others. You can't live long enough to make them all yourself.'

Conclusion

We hope there is something for you to take from the lessons we have learnt since setting up our company. These are personal views and obviously circumstances will differ, but we think many of the problems we have encountered along our journey are common to others and certain lessons can be learnt. Good luck! And here is our quick toolbox guide:

1. Vision: know where you're going and how you're going to get there.
2. Work with others: join relevant trade bodies and associations to help.
3. Know your costs: you can thereby price accordingly.
4. Always know your cash flow position: this is the difference between success and failure.
5. Respect the environment and the environment will respect you: venue access is becoming increasingly difficult.
6. Manage your risk: have robust systems and procedures in place.

References

Australian Government DIIS (2018) Plan and start a business or hobby. Department of Industry, Innovation, and Science, Canberra, Australia. Available at: https://www.business.gov.au/planning/new-businesses/a-business-or-a-hobby (accessed 30 August 2018).

Ernst and Young (2014) Top 10 Risks and Opportunities Report. Available at: https://www.ey.com/Publication/vwLUAssets/The_top_10_risks_and_opportunities_for_global_organizations/$FILE/Business%20Challenge%20main%20report-%20SCORED.pdf (accessed 30 August 2018).

Visit Britain (2016) Inbound Tourist Performance, 2016 Snapshot. Available at: https://www.visitbritain.org/2016-snapshot (accessed 30 August 2018).

16 Thoughts on the Adventure Sports Industry

Jo Dennison

Head of the Surf Academy, Snowdonia's WaveGarden

Introduction

It is a really exciting time to be involved in the adventure sports industry and it is becoming more popular; over the past decade adventure sports have been accepted as Olympic Sports such as slopestyle snowboarding, BMXing, and Big Air skiing, to name just a few. These lifestyle sports continue to grow: in Tokyo 2020, surfing will appear in the Olympic Games for the first time. Adventure sports are now becoming mainstream; the hippie surfing from the 1980s has transformed into a professional sport and can become a career path. The Olympics will help the surfing industry to grow even more and see more artificial training centres and sponsorship deals creating more opportunities in the adventure industry. Not only is surfing growing as a competitive sport; the technology for training and recreating waves is also developing. In 2015 the first commercial wave garden in the world was opened in North Wales (Fig. 16.3). However, the traditional wave pool drop technology has been around much longer. With lots of land-locked countries like Germany, Belgium and inner cities with no access to waves, engineers and scientist have been developing wave pool technology and wave pools will be found more frequently in many countries in the coming years.

The World Surfing League (WSL) will add KSwaveco (Kelly Slater wave pool) as one of the event stops on the 2018 tour, further fuelling the popularity of wave pool and artificial surfing, and will help to develop a new division of surfing.

Surf Snowdonia has now (2018) been running for what will be its fourth season. This is one industry that is going to expand very quickly over the next decade or two. North Wales specifically has become the adventure capital of the UK, known to many as the 'Heart of Adventure'. There is also the world's fastest zip wire, as well as hiking, climbing centres, mountain bike trails and whitewater rafting. The area as a whole has been marketed by Visit Wales for its adventure sports and activities and is bigger than ever. Surf Snowdonia alone had 170,000 visitors in 2017, 12% from overseas (20,000 international visitors).

Why I Wanted to Have a Career in Adventure

I was driven by sport from a very young age. I started swimming when I was 4 years old and turned competitive a few years later, competing in the West Wales elite squad. I also competed for my county in athletics, cross-country, netball and hockey. I became a pool lifeguard at 16 and began my career in the sport and leisure industry. I wanted a career that would take me a little further than just lifeguarding so that I could influence others and share my passion for sport.

I went to university to study for an HND in Water Sports and Adventure Activity Management at Swansea. Throughout the course I tried a wide variety of activities in the industry, but surfing just clicked for me. The adventure, looking at the weather charts, choosing locations, and then the activity itself – something I became addicted to. The adrenalin of riding a wave makes you want to go faster, try different spots and a diverse range of waves. Within my degree I also completed my beach lifeguard course and International Surfing Association level 1 Surf Instructor. When I left university I was ready for a career in the adventure industry.

Positives and Negatives for Females Working in Adventure

The surfing/adventure industry is male dominated, which at times has played to my advantage. I spent

8 years as a surf instructor across the world in places like France, Spain, Portugal, Morocco, Australia and the UK. Most surf schools I applied to accepted my application with comments such as, 'I need a female surf instructor that can surf on the team.'

On the flip side, the surfing industry is very competitive. You really have to prove yourself as a surfer to get any recognition and it may be even harder sometimes to move up the ladder to supervisor or management roles. I had originally applied for water operations manager at Surf Snowdonia, but they gave the role to a male candidate and I had to work really hard to prove my ability before I got the job.

My Career Path

I graduated from university in 2007 with a BA Hons in Sport and Recreation Management (converting my HND to a BA on a 1-year conversion course). I started competing in surfing competitions and surf coaching during the last year of my degree. I left university as British University Women's Surf Champion and 2 × Welsh Champion. I thought I would start a

career in the surfing industry and see how far I could go (Fig. 16.1). I picked up a product and equipment sponsor, Billabong, and continued to compete on the British Professional surf tour. I gained a few more surf titles in the UK, including British Women's Champion. I continued as a surf coach as it was a really good way to travel, live by good surf breaks for training and have connections in the surfing industry.

Once I had gained the British title I started to compete in Europe and moved to the South of France for better training conditions and to be closer to the major surf brands and the surfing capital of Europe (Hossegor). I competed in the World Qualifying Series (WQS), ISA World and European Surf Games. I represented both Wales and the British National Surf Team on a number of occasions. I worked in surf schools, camps and academies, sharing my passion for surfing and expanding my experience in the surf industry. My biggest achievement during this time was going to Panama with the British junior squad as one of the coaches. My best result was 4th place in ISA European

Fig. 16.1. Tour Surf Snowdonia event winner Jo Dennison.

Championships. Without gaining a proper sponsorship deal as an athlete and being self-funded, I had to stop competing.

I focused on furthering my career in the surf industry and after a visit to the WaveGarden test facility in Spain I applied for a position at Surf Snowdonia WaveGarden. Ten of us were invited for an interview and I was the only female in the room. I was offered 'Head of the Surf Academy', which was not the actual position I had applied for but I happily accepted it. I had to carry out 'Normal Operating Procedures' and 'Emergency Action' plans, to ensure safe running of lessons and surfing on the lagoon. I also designed the surfing products and surf scheme in the academy along with a schedule, online booking system, staff rotas, media interviews and conference speaking (Fig. 16.2) and appearances on national TV shows like *Blue Peter*, *The One Show* and *CBeebies*. I also featured as an ambassador for Visit Wales in its 'EPIC' campaign.

During 2015 I carried out the recruitment process to end up with a team of 15 Surf Instructors. After the first season I stepped up to 'Water Operation Manager' and this is still my current job role. I am responsible for all the water activities at Surf Snowdonia – the lifeguard and water safety management as well as programming and scheduling products, recruitment, training and health and safety. I am a trainer assessor for Surf Life Saving Great Britain (SLSGB) to train all the staff in-house. This will be the fourth year I have been with Surf Snowdonia. With probably the biggest surf school in the UK, during summer we run four lessons every hour for 10 hours, which is up to 40 lessons a day, and 280 lessons a week. My team now consists of around 20 Surf Instructors and 30 lifeguards during peak season.

Recommendations for New Recruits: What to Do and Not Do

For new recruits in the adventure sports industry, I would recommend that they specialize in something. There are lots of qualifications and courses that allow you to become a novice in lots of activities. It is a rare trait that you are an expert at one thing, but this is the activity that will make you stand out from the crowd and put you in position for that higher role. For me this was surfing; I competed at an international level and had some sponsorship and also surf coached everything from beginners to British junior squad at the World Surfing Games in Panama. It is easy to see that I am very passionate about it. Along with my degree

Fig 16.2. Conference Surf Park Summit at Surf Snowdonia.

Fig 16.3. Surf Snowdonia.

I have gained a lot of experience in the industry; I am positive that all my experience added up and helped me get the position I have today.

The Future for Adventure: Females and Equality of Opportunities

I would say that there is still a long way to go in the adventure industry for equality. The media has a big part to play in the perceptions that people have of females. Take surfing, for example: there is still a 'model versus athlete' debate.

Big brands are using their marketing budgets on female models, more so than backing a talented athlete to compete, because the images that they would rather post are of those of a model. Here are a few quotes from professional females who have suffered the effects (ABC, 2015): Rebecca Woods states, 'Sponsors were ignoring surf talent in favour of model looks,' and Brooke Mason says, 'Girls that kick arse should be getting paid rather than girls that show their arse.'

A Roxy advert was published in the media to advertise a surf event in Biarritz and they ended up pulling the advert because of its negative feedback. In this instance, it was even a 6 × World Champion and they still did not have any footage of her shredding the waves (Daily Life, 2013).

I would like to see a display of athleticism, skill and sport to inspire younger generations of females rather than a focus on a female's body for marketing purposes. The influencers have more power than ever with social media accounts. If we continue to portray females as sex symbols rather than athletes, then that is the example that we have set for the next generation. Surfing females are gifted and creative athletes; they could positively influence other females' lives if we use all the marketing to focus on athleticism rather than sexism.

The dominance of males in the industry can be illustrated by a recent professional event (2017) held at Surf Snowdonia. This event is held annually, attended by wave pool-related organizations such as investors, owners and companies that sell wave pool products. When I did a presentation on water operations there must have been around 40 men in the room but only two females: myself and our onsite photographer. It was an honour to be the only female speaker at the event but also an eye opener for myself on the gender bias in the industry. It needs to change.

References

ABC (2015) Female surfers call for end to sexist culture in sport. Australian Broadcasting Corporation, Sydney, Australia. Available at: http://www.abc.net.au/news/2016-04-15/female-surfers-call-for-end-to-sexist-culture-in-sport/7329932.

Daily Life (2013) We never see her face, we never see her surf. Fairfax Media, Pyrmont, New South Wales. Available at: http://www.dailylife.com.au/news-and-views/dl-opinion/we-never-see-her-face-we-never-see-her-surf-20130708-2plvf.html.

17 Being an Outdoor Instructor: James's Experience

JAMES MARTIN

Instructor, Call of the Wild, Wales

Introduction

Adventure tourism is about experiencing something new, providing exciting opportunities to explore the unknown. Adventures are relative to the individual. For me, adventure tourism is exciting when I discover a new place. This does not have to be the top of a mountain or an E6 climbing route. It could be a lake in the middle of the Brecon Beacons, a new cave to explore, or seeing a river in full spate. Some adventure tourists may think that an adventure is sleeping in a tent for the first time; for others it may be climbing to the top of Pen Y Fan or crawling into the depths of Porth Yr Ogof. My experience of adventure tourism as an industry, in South Wales, is people looking for a buzz such as jumping off a waterfall or going down an abseil or zip wire, but at the same time they want to be reassured that they are doing it with safe and knowledgeable individuals. The latter are the Outdoor Instructors.

Inspirations

In all honesty my inspiration came from people around me rather than a famous individual. My Scout Leader gave me a lot of support and helped me to find a volunteer role as an assistant in a local scout boating centre. As things progressed I looked for inspiration from the people I worked with; the head instructor of the boating centre trained some of the Olympic kayaking teams. I looked up to the instructors I worked with, who were good at their jobs, provided a fun experience, and had a wealth of knowledge that they were willing to share with anyone who would listen. For example, Call of the Wild (COTW) Chief Instructor Dave Thomas was a Marine for 25 years. His mountaineering experience is fantastic and he always has the answer to my questions. I am inspired by those who have

been successful in setting up adventure tourism attractions, such as Sean Taylor, owner of Zip World in North Wales, and those who wanted to protect the natural environment such as John Muir, who inspired the formation of the first national park.

Why I Decided to Become an Outdoor Instructor

As a child, I was heavily involved in scouting and every weekend was spent going camping, building dens and taking part in outdoor activities. As I got older I started to think about what I would do when I left school. I had to consider the skills I had, academically or otherwise. My reading and writing skills were not my strongest attribute, so I wanted to do something using the skills I had learnt in scouting. I also wanted to choose a profession where I could make a difference to another person or group of people by providing a good experience.

How I Became an Outdoor Instructor

On a summer camp with scouts I enquired about how to become an instructor and spoke to a volunteer who was also a maths teacher. He suggested that I should continue with my education and get some sort of management qualification so that I had something extra to bring to the table and something to fall back on.

I listened to this advice and applied for the HND in Water Sports and Adventure Activities Management course at Swansea Metropolitan University, where I was accepted and commenced the 3-year course. It was during the first year that I met Dave Thomas. Call of the Wild was a service provider to Swansea Metropolitan University and offered adventure activities every Friday for students on the Water Sports course. This was exactly what I wanted from the course: practical experience and management theory so that I could go on to be an instructor and run my own centre.

In the second year of the course, the course tutor had provided a budget for National Governing Body (NGB) Qualification courses. During the summer, as part of the course, I spent 6 months at PGL (the adventure holiday company based in Ross-on-Wye, Herefordshire) gaining experience in kayaking and completing my level-two kayak training. I wanted to acquire this qualification before I finished the course, so the university supported me to travel to Southampton to complete the course.

Dave Thomas was able to provide the Single Pitch Award (SPA), which would be a useful quali-fications for me to gain if I wanted to work in the adventure industry. After this I bought a rack of climbing gear and completed my consolidation period (time frame given to you by SPA to build up your log book and climbing experience) and with other members of the course we made a commit-ment to go climbing every Sunday to improve our practical skills and experience (Fig. 17.1).

At the end of my second year it was mandatory to find another work placement. In the months leading up to this we were to contact a number of

Fig. 17.1. James Martin abseiling with Call of the Wild. (Photo: James Martin)

work placements providers, perfect our CVs and organize our placement.

Call of the Wild was the first company that I approached. I sent a letter of application and had a conversation with Dave, who invited me for an interview. After quite a nerve-wracking interview with directors Geraint Lewis and Mark Soanes as well as Dave, it was agreed that I could come and take part in a placement scheme.

This is where I would start to be a real instructor. I was excited and the activities I would be doing were real adventure activities on rocks, rivers and caves. Most of the adventure activities I had done up until then, on my work experience, had been on flat water or on climbing towers.

In my first year, on placement with Call of the Wild, I was just finding my feet, everything was new, I was learning every day and when I got home I was exhausted. The most exciting part of my new role was canyoning – jumping off waterfalls! Wow! This was great and I would often head back to the river after work with my partner in crime, Rebecca Davies, who had started the same placement as I had. Together we worked all day then went off in the evening to find our own adventures.

I was really lucky to be teamed up with Rebecca as she was keen to develop and helped me through my first and second year as an outdoor instructor. We became close friends and she was best 'man' at my wedding.

Call of the Wild allowed me to develop at a fast pace. I was quickly allowed to lead groups in kay-aking, gorge walking and canyoning. I soon found myself as course director, taking charge of an entire school's visit, and had begun to write pro-grammes for school groups. I was working with stag groups, school groups and corporate groups. I had been on a trip to the Pyrenees. I was then also allowed to stay on part-time to complete my HND over the winter months. I felt that I was in a great place.

Success!

Call of the Wild offered me a full-time position work-ing alongside Dave. I would head up the school groups, book staff, help Dave with the licensing work and continue working as I was before. Fantastic! What a result! This was exactly what I wanted.

Canyoning was my favourite part of the job: it was exciting and the buzz of excitement from the clients was great.

Fig. 17.2. Canyoning with Call of the Wild (photo: James Martin).

At this point I was already a member of the British Canoe Association and I became a member of the British Mountaineering Council and British Caving Association soon after this. I applied for log books and began to log instructing hours and personal experience for Climbing and Caving (Fig.17.2).

We also went on a number of trips, both training and with clients; the Pyrenees was one (as mentioned above) and another that stands out was staff training in the Mendips. We had four days to log as many caving trips as possible. It was such a good experience, with like-minded people all there to encourage each other and support. Dave Thomas, Dave Hanham, Rebecca Davies and Lee Thomas were some of those on the trip. Most days off were spent climbing on the Gower.

Disaster!

At the end of my third year with Call of the Wild, on a training exercise in the Mellte Gorge I slipped. I had fallen 20 ft on to a slab of rock. The result was a broken elbow and forearm and severely bruised hip. I was air lifted to hospital, where I was operated on and patched up. I was told by a consultant that I should consider a new career as I would not be able to continue as an instructor.

I thought long and hard about what that consultant had said. I was also visited by family members, friends and my colleagues, all giving support and generally saying that I would be fine. One particularly important visit to me at the time was from Mark Soanes. He said that Call of the Wild would continue to support me on full pay and he hoped I would make a full recovery.

I wanted to get back to work and did what I could during the winter months. By the time the summer season had started again I was back on track and working with school groups on climbing sessions and walking activities.

My Thoughts and Feelings

As time has gone on, my career has developed with Call of the Wild. I have been employed for 12 years now and have been supported throughout my time by the company. I have worked with a hundred or more different instructors, and an estimated 12,000 individuals, which has been and continues to be a fantastic opportunity and experience. On a personal note, I feel that the flexibility and support of the company has allowed me to continue my career, as well as given me the flexibility to be with my children.

My career has also developed and I am now a qualified instructor. I currently hold Single Pitch Climbing Award , Level 2 Kayaking and Canoeing

Coach, Walking Group Leader Award, Gorge Walking and Canyoning Leader and Local Cave Leader Level 1, but I am still learning. A good instructor will always have room to grow and learn as there will always be a situation or an opportunity that you have not come across before.

Advice to Future Instructors

Since I started in the industry I have seen an increase in the number of groups, companies and organizations using the outdoor environment to provide adventure tourism. The venues we use have become increasingly busy, leading to issues such as environmental impact, parking, etc. becoming more of a problem. On a positive note, it is obvious that the industry is becoming more and more popular.

If you are looking to become an outdoor instructor, the best way in my opinion is to become a trainee instructor and work hard to gain qualifications. All outdoor centres require instructors to have NGB qualifications. As an assistant instructor, you gain experience working with groups and log the hours needed for the qualifications. One bit of advice I would give is to ask questions, use the instructors around you as a walking Google. Make an action plan and review it and ultimately work hard every day.

The Future of Adventure Tourism

Adventure tourism is continuously expanding; more and more people are going to the national parks to gain new experiences. There is an increasing need from society for adrenalin experiences and how to get the next fix, so the idea of jumping off a waterfall or walking on the highest peaks or scaling the nearest mountain is becoming ever more appealing to people.

18 My Path to Adventure

PETER ABELL

Head Coach, Kingsurf Surf School, Cornwall

Introduction

Classroom environments were not the best form of learning for me and my desire was always to be outside engaged in the outdoors, especially the sea. This I found far more rewarding, yet I knew I had to get some qualifications to pursue a career in adventure tourism. I still managed to pass all my GCSEs, allowing me to study a National Diploma in Outdoor Recreation Management. This then gave me the opportunity to pursue a work placement at an outdoor activity centre in Newquay, Cornwall (Fig. 18.1). Some of the work was not the most stimulating, but part of the job, after lots of painting and cleaning, gave me the chance to do my beach lifeguard award and run bodyboard lessons for children. Once I had obtained my national diploma I applied for the Higher National Diploma (HND) in Water Sports Activity Management at a Welsh university, which I topped up to a degree in Leisure and Tourism Management. During my time in Wales I was taught everything I needed to know about running a business in this industry: writing risk assessments, how to manage risk, how to manage people, industry trends, profit and loss and writing a business plan, were just a few of the things that I learnt along the way. This was all useful information for my launch into the adventure industry.

For one of our assignments we had to go through a simulation of starting our own business, developing our ideas with all the financial calculations for the assignment. The project I chose to start was a surf school and I realized that this idea had potential to make a profit and would allow me to do something that I loved; I was very keen to try it out in real life. The HND in Water Sports provided each individual student with financial support, managed by the tutor and myself. I used the monies towards obtaining a National Governing Body (NGB) qualification. I chose to become a qualified surfing coach and began teaching surfing on the Gower Coast and in Cornwall. Just before I left university I had to complete the dreaded dissertation and decided to do a case study on surf tourism and how it was rapidly developing in Portugal and similarly in Cornwall. This all inspired me to work in the surfing industry.

Just 3 days before my dissertation hand-in date I received a phone call from Kingsurf Surf School in Cornwall, where I had been working the previous summer (Fig. 18.2). They asked me if I was interested in taking on the business. They wanted to sell the surf shop, bungalow and café that the surf school was run from and were wondering whether I fancied buying the surf school equipment, name and website from them. I could also offer lessons from the same location opposite the beach entrance here in Mawgan Porth. Talk about timing! Just when you are stressing about entering the real world of work and still are not too sure what you are going to do to survive, you get the opportunity to slip into an existing, well established surf school! This is where I have to hold my hand up and wholeheartedly thank my father. I did not have any money and the bank was not keen to lend me any either. My father took out a bank loan and was able to advise me on many business decisions too. I paid him back over the course of the next 3 years and we are now entering our 11th year of trading, having had year-on-year growth.

The surf industry is still growing and we are now finding ourselves busy all year round. We have invested heavily in good-quality kit to keep people warm and are continuously restocking surf boards and keeping up with the latest developments, both online and here at the base. With surfing due to become an Olympic sport and the emergence of artificial wave gardens, it appears that surfing is going from strength to strength.

My staff are superb and help with the administration and other aspects of the business. I genuinely

Fig. 18.1. On the Cornish wave. (Photo: Pete Abell)

Fig. 18.2. Kingsurf instructors. (Photo: Pete Abell)

still love teaching and get in the water every day to help out with lessons. It is February half-term right now and I have just got back from a surf safari with customers I have known for years. This demonstrates the all-round nature of the surf industry in the UK.

What Got Me into Surfing

During family holidays to Cornwall at the age of 5, I became obsessed with standing in the sea seeking waves that would allow me to surf on my belly all the way back to the shore. Every wave felt different and I just had to keep going back for a better one! I always looked up to the older guys out back who were standing up on surf boards and carving up the waves and dreamed about joining them when I grew up. I would often spend up to 4 hours at a time in the sea bodyboarding. The obsession for riding waves has not left me one bit and I go out pretty much every day if I can, just for fun. I am so obsessed with riding waves that I have found myself surfing the River Severn Tidal Bore every full moon. It is not always a big wave but you need to read the wave's energy well in order to stay on it and it is always a different experience, which makes it interesting. Last year I proposed to my wife whilst we were surfing the Severn Bore and it went viral!

Difficulties

I have faced many difficulties whilst working in the outdoor adventure tourism industry – one being the British weather! Since 2003, the months of July and August have had many inoperable days due to fog, high winds, dangerous surf and sometimes pollution caused by sewage overflow due to heavy rain. Bad weather also puts people off and I would go as far as to say: if we had an epic run of good sunny weather with great waves we could see up to a 30% rise in profits. Then came 2018, the best season we have had so far, with a great run of weather from early May to late August bringing tourism to an all-time high in Cornwall. The British beaches are as good as any in the world when we have the weather to complement them.

Cornwall County Council has recently decided to charge us a licence fee of £3000 for using the wet sand (just for walking across it). This was not in my business plan and has placed me on an uneven playing field, compared with other competitors who are exempt from the licence fee.

The prices of boards and wetsuits have also increased by at least 20% in the past 6 years, making our start-up costs more expensive each year.

Positives

We have seen seasons become much longer. Ten years ago we would open from June until October; now we are open all year round. This may be due to the growth in the popularity of surfing and also the quality of wetsuits. A new market for winter surfing has recently opened up and we are finding many more people arriving with winter wetsuits, willing to pay a premium to have a more bespoke, advanced surf experience. These customers are mainly people who live far from the beach and want to improve via an intense surf camp experience. Cornwall is seeing a growth in tourism with people saying that stay-cations are as popular as ever. There are many theories as to why this is the case. One is the weakening pound against the euro so you get less for your money if you travel to Europe for a holiday. Furthermore, in 2017 there were also travel problems and long queues at the Channel Tunnel and ferry ports. Additionally, long-term weather forecasts for British summers always seem to be good, encouraging more people to stay at home. Other reasons might include the addition of new airport destinations in the UK and greater health consciousness by the general public and recognition that outdoor activities are a great way to keep fit and healthy. Indeed, adventure sports in general seem to be becoming more and more popular. The winter and summer Olympics are including so many more adventure sports in their list.

Advice to Students

When I first began the business of owning and running a surf school, social media had only just been invented, Trip Advisor was only for hotels, websites were basic, and people did not expect a reply from an email for at least 3 days. I had an advantage in that having come straight from university, I was fresh and knowledgeable about the latest developments in tourism marketing and the potential of the internet. I recognized that Trip Advisor was becoming the future of how people research what to do on holiday and I could also see how important social media was becoming as a platform for advertising your business. I realized that this would allow the creation of a database of customers who want to hear about Kingsurf's latest activities. Having a quick-loading and simple website with good-quality pictures and a professionally filmed promotional video to watch were not as important 10 years ago as they are today. I am basically saying that you must keep abreast of what is happening and changing. The outdoor industry is highly competitive and very technologically savvy, so it is imperative to look good online in every aspect.

I have always tried to think of new ways to gain people's attention, encouraging them to surf with us. One idea I had was to make a video with *Made in Chelsea* star Andy Jordan, with us leaving our London office in suits with our wetsuits under our arms, running through the City to the airport and flying on to Newquay. But the best advice is to always remember to treat every customer who walks in the door with fantastic hospitality and professionalism, which I think is the main reason we are still operating in this increasingly competitive industry and because we live and love what we do and people spread our passion to others. Word of mouth has been key and 50% of our business is returning customers.

Sustainability Issues

As a business we rely on the environment and as surfers it is an area of great concern. We do our best to be as sustainable as we can; our boards are handmade in Cornwall and repaired instead of replaced; our wetsuits are recycled into dog collars and beer coolers by a local lady or donated to local children; we only use electricity to charge our laptops and mobile phones; and we clean the beach of rubbish on a regular basis, as we are supporters of Surfers Against Sewage.

I am very concerned with the ever-growing amount of plastic pollution we are seeing on our beaches. It is our generation that has to stand up to this and lead more environmentally green lives, as we are aware of how bad the situation actually is. From a business perspective, we do not want our customers surfing in polluted water and can envisage a situation where people will no longer spend time at the beach if it is covered in plastic waste.

Just Do It!

Finally, I have no regrets going into adventure tourism and it has provided me with a business and surfing lifestyle that I can live to the full, while also encouraging others to participate in a sport that makes life worth living!

Index

Note: bold page numbers indicate figures; italic page numbers indicate tables; adventure tourism is abbreviated to AT in subentries.

CABI – who we are and what we do

This book is published by **CABI**, an international not-for-profit organisation that improves people's lives worldwide by providing information and applying scientific expertise to solve problems in agriculture and the environment.

CABI is also a global publisher producing key scientific publications, including world renowned databases, as well as compendia, books, ebooks and full text electronic resources. We publish content in a wide range of subject areas including: agriculture and crop science / animal and veterinary sciences / ecology and conservation / environmental science / horticulture and plant sciences / human health, food science and nutrition / international development / leisure and tourism.

The profits from CABI's publishing activities enable us to work with farming communities around the world, supporting them as they battle with poor soil, invasive species and pests and diseases, to improve their livelihoods and help provide food for an ever growing population.

CABI is an international intergovernmental organisation, and we gratefully acknowledge the core financial support from our member countries (and lead agencies) including:

Ministry of Agriculture
People's Republic of China

Australian Government
Australian Centre for
International Agricultural Research

Agriculture and
Agri-Food Canada

Ministry of Foreign Affairs of the
Netherlands

Schweizerische Eidgenossenschaft
Confédération suisse
Confederazione Svizzera
Confederaziun svizra

Swiss Agency for Development
and Cooperation SDC

Discover more

To read more about CABI's work, please visit: **www.cabi.org**

Browse our books at: **www.cabi.org/bookshop**,
or explore our online products at: **www.cabi.org/publishing-products**

Interested in writing for CABI? Find our author guidelines here:
www.cabi.org/publishing-products/information-for-authors/